Better Homes and Gardens

EASY EVERYDAY

LOW

Carb

COOKBOOK

Better Homes and Gardens® Books
Des Moines, Iowa

2003

Better Homes and Gardens® Books
An imprint of Meredith® Books

Easy Everyday Low Carb Meal Plans
Editor: Kristi M. Thomas
Contributing Editors: Janet Figg, Spectrum Communication Services, Inc., Joyce Trollope, Mary Williams
Contributing Writer: Alice Lesch Kelly
Design Director: Barbara J. Gordon
Copy Chief: Terri Fredrickson
Copy and Production Editor: Victoria Forlini
Editorial Operations Manager: Karen Schirm
Managers, Book Production: Pam Kvitne, Marjorie J. Schenkelberg, Rick von Holdt
Contributing Copy Editor: Karen Fraley
Contributing Proofreaders: Emmy Clausing, Gretchen Kauffman, Susan Kling
Indexer: May Hasso, Boston Informatics
Electronic Production Coordinator: Paula Forest
Editorial and Design Assistants: Karen McFadden, Mary Lee Gavin
Test Kitchen Director: Lynn Blanchard
Test Kitchen Home Economists: Marilyn Cornelius; Juliana Hale, Laura Harms, R.D.;
    Jennifer Kalinowski, R.D.; Maryellyn Krantz; Jill Moberly; Dianna Nolin; Colleen Weeden;
    Lori Wilson; Charles Worthington

Meredith® Books
Editor in Chief: Linda Raglan Cunningham
Design Director: Matt Strelecki
Executive Editor, Food and Crafts: Jennifer Dorland Darling

Publisher: James D. Blume
Executive Director, Marketing: Jeffrey Myers
Executive Director, New Business Development: Todd M. Davis
Executive Director, Sales: Ken Zagor
Director, Operations: George A. Susral
Director, Production: Douglas M. Johnston
Business Director: Jim Leonard

Vice President and General Manager: Douglas J. Guendel

Better Homes and Gardens® **Magazine**
Editor in Chief: Karol DeWulf Nickell
Deputy Editor, Food and Entertaining: Nancy Hopkins

Meredith Publishing Group
President, Publishing Group: Stephen M. Lacy
Vice President-Publishing Director: Bob Mate

Meredith Corporation
Chairman and Chief Executive Officer: William T. Kerr

In Memoriam: E. T. Meredith III (1933-2003)

Our seal assures you that every recipe in *Easy Everyday Low Carb Meal Plans* has been tested in the Better Homes and Gardens® Test Kitchen. This means that each recipe is practical and reliable, and meets our high standards of taste appeal. We guarantee your satisfaction with this book for as long as you own it.

All of us at Better Homes and Gardens® Books are dedicated to providing you with the information and ideas you need to create delicious foods. We welcome your comments and suggestions. Write to us at: Better Homes and Gardens Books, Cookbook Editorial Department, 1716 Locust St., Des Moines, IA 50309-3023.

If you would like to purchase any of our cooking, crafts, gardening, home improvement, or home decorating and design books, check wherever quality books are sold. Or visit us at: bhgbooks.com

Low Carb Basics 4

Meal Planning 14

Appetizers, Snacks & Beverages 45

Salads & Salad Dressings 69

Eggs 93

Meat 113

Chicken & Turkey 147

Fish & Seafood 181

Side Dishes 207

Desserts & Sweets 225

Index 248

Low Carb Basics

Knowledge about health benefits of various foods has exploded during the past few decades. As scientists have worked to ferret out specific compounds in foods that fight disease, they have also sought to determine what combination of carbohydrate, protein, and fat is most beneficial. Not long ago, it was believed that the optimal diet was low in fat and protein and fairly high in carbohydrates. However, researchers have concluded that some of the healthiest cultures in the world owe their robust well-being in part to the considerable amounts of fish oils and monounsaturated fats that they consume. Today, many scientists agree that curbing carbohydrates and eating moderate amounts of lean protein and heart-healthy fat is the best way to fight disease and maintain ideal body weight.

Reducing carbohydrates in your diet isn't hard, but doing it healthfully requires some thought. Of course, you can cut down on carbohydrates by choosing an enormous steak for dinner instead of a bowl of pasta, but that won't help your cholesterol level or your weight. The secret is to replace starchy carbohydrate-rich meals with nutritious, delicious, low-carb dishes that will benefit both your health and your waistline. Those are just the kind of foods you'll find in this book. With these luscious, easy-to-prepare recipes, you'll reduce the carbohydrates in your diet while enjoying delectable meals that are packed with flavor and nutrients.

Why Choose a Low-Carbohydrate Diet?

Many Americans are adopting low-carbohydrate diets. People are tired of surviving on tasteless low-fat foods such as watery salad dressings and rubbery cheeses. They are thrilled with the idea of being able to eat more of the foods that have been discouraged in low-fat eating plans, such as meats and cheeses.

Stories abound of people who swear by low-carbohydrate diets as an effective way to lose weight. Not only do they drop pounds, but they are able to do so while eating foods they love. Because they enjoy their food, they are better able to stick to their diets. What's more, many people report (and studies support this) that low-carbohydrate diets leave them feeling less hungry than high-carbohydrate, low-fat diets.

Before you start reducing the carbohydrates in your meals, it's important to understand how to do it in a healthful way to lose weight and decrease your risk of disease. Read on and find out why eating fewer carbohydrates may make sense for you.

Building Blocks

Food is made up of three macronutrients: protein, fats, and carbohydrates.

Carbohydrates provide immediate energy. There are three types of carbohydrates: complex carbohydrates, simple carbohydrates (sugars), and fiber. Complex carbohydrates include foods such as whole grain breads and cereals, fruits, vegetables, and legumes. Simple carbohydrates include white breads, table sugar, and soft drinks such as cola or sweetened iced tea. Foods that are rich in fiber include fruits, vegetables, whole grains, and legumes.

Fats offer a concentrated source of energy, but they have other jobs as well. Fats transport fat-soluble vitamins through the blood, help maintain healthy skin, assist in maintaining cell structure, help manufacture hormones, and insulate body tissues. The fats in food are made of different types of fatty acids: saturated, polyunsaturated, monounsaturated, and trans fatty acids.

Protein supplies amino acids, the building blocks that erect, repair, and maintain your body tissues. It transports vitamins and minerals in the blood and helps build muscle. Protein also can provide energy when your body's supply of carbohydrates and fats is low.

Food also contains vitamins, minerals, water, and other nutrients such as phytochemicals. A healthful diet includes all of these elements of good nutrition. However, too much of one and not enough of the others can throw your body out of balance, foster weight gain, and boost your risk of disease.

Glucose and Insulin

Many people eat too many carbohydrates, particularly simple carbohydrates and sugars—mostly "white" foods such as sugar, white bread, bagels, pasta, rice cakes, pretzels, potatoes, cake, popcorn, cookies, and muffins, as well as sugary soft drinks. Although these foods taste good, they trigger a chemical reaction in the body that can, over time, cause damage. Here's how: When you eat a high-carbohydrate food, your body's level of blood sugar, or glucose, rises. In response, the pancreas releases a hormone called insulin, which has the job of ushering glucose into the body's cells, where it is either used immediately for energy or stored for future use. Insulin's function is to move glucose out of the blood and into muscle and fat cells as quickly as possible. If it lingers too long in the blood, glucose can harm blood vessels and other tissues.

Highly processed, high-sugar foods—for example, sugarcoated cereals—trigger a large, rapid dump of glucose into the blood. Minimally processed foods that are low in carbohydrates—scrambled eggs, for example—cause a slower, smaller release of glucose into the blood. The more high-carbohydrate foods you eat, the more glucose is released in the blood and the more insulin your pancreas secretes. A low-carbohydrate food, on the other hand, results in less glucose and, therefore, less insulin release in the bloodstream.

Large amounts of glucose and insulin in the blood can cause trouble for your cardiovascular system. Excessive amounts of insulin can raise blood pressure and triglyceride levels in the blood and can reduce HDL, also known as the "good" cholesterol. High blood pressure, high triglycerides, and low HDL all boost the risk of heart disease.

Over time, repeated surges in blood glucose and insulin can lead the body to become insulin-resistant, which means that the body must release more and more insulin in order to clear glucose from the blood. The American Diabetes Association (ADA) calls this insulin-resistant condition "pre-diabetes." Someone with pre-diabetes has blood glucose levels that are higher than they should be, but not yet high enough to be considered diabetes. Pre-diabetics have a 50 percent increased risk of heart disease or stroke compared to people with normal glucose levels.

People with pre-diabetes are at a very high risk of developing full-blown diabetes, a serious disease that can lead to heart disease, eye problems, circulatory problems, kidney disease, and death. More than 17 million Americans have diabetes, the sixth leading cause of death in the United States, and according to the ADA, an additional 16 million have pre-diabetes.

Carbohydrates and Weight Loss

Diets that are low in carbohydrates appear to foster weight loss. As several major studies have shown, people tend to get hungry sooner after a high-carbohydrate meal than they do after a low-carbohydrate meal. The reason for this relates, once again, to glucose and insulin. To illustrate, say you are hungry for a quick snack and you munch on a handful of pretzels, which are a starchy, high-carbohydrate food. Glucose floods into the bloodstream quickly, and the pancreas swiftly churns out insulin to escort the glucose out of the blood into the cells. The body burns the energy-producing glucose that it needs at that moment and stores the rest as fat. Once the glucose is either burned

or stored, your blood sugar drops quickly—often to below-normal levels—triggering the surge of another kind of hormone that stimulates hunger and cravings for more high-starch foods.

In other words, when you eat a high-starch snack, you feel satisfied for a while. Before long, however, you're very likely to be walloped with sudden hunger pangs that trigger cravings and send you searching for another high-starch snack that will restore blood sugar levels. Chances are, you'll be so hungry that you'll choose another high-carbohydrate snack or meal that will set the cycle in motion again.

Now, say you reach for a handful of low-carb, high-protein, high-monounsaturated-fat peanuts instead of those pretzels. After you eat the peanuts, glucose is released slowly into the blood, rather than quickly, which gives your body a steady source of energy and no glucose spikes. Your body responds by releasing insulin at a steady rate and in reasonable amounts. Your hunger returns gradually, not suddenly, and because it comes on slowly, you're more likely to satisfy it with a smart, healthful meal or snack, rather than a binge.

Not all carbohydrates are alike, however. Starchy foods such as white bread, sugar-coated cereals, and sugury sweets trigger a sudden dump of glucose into the bloodstream. Such foods are said to have a high glycemic index, or GI. (A food's glycemic index is determined by how much glucose it releases into the blood.) Complex carbohydrates such as those found in some fruits and vegetables and whole grains trigger a slower, less intense glucose response and are described as low-GI foods. (See Glycemic Index vs. Glycemic Load, below.)

High-GI foods have been found to be less satiating than low-GI foods. Studies at the Obesity Program at Children's Hospital in Boston, among other research centers, have found that several hours after eating high-GI meals, study subjects ate as much as 81 percent more than they did after low-GI meals with the same number of calories.

Some researchers believe that a low-carbohydrate diet promotes fat burning. This is a controversial theory, and so far, there is limited research to support it. However, there is some evidence to suggest that high insulin levels promote the storage of fat and restrain the release of fatty acids from fat cells. In other words, when you eat foods that are rich in carbohydrates, the body is more anxious to store those calories as fat (and keep them stored!) than to burn them as fuel. On the other hand, when you eat a low-carbohydrate meal, the body is more apt to burn those calories as fuel than to store them in the form of body fat.

There is also some research that supports the theory that a low-carbohydrate diet boosts the metabolism, giving you more energy and enabling your body to burn more calories throughout the day, even when you're at rest. More study is needed to prove this, but anecdotal evidence from people who have adopted low-carbohydrate diets seems to back it up. Many people who cut down on carbohydrates report feeling more energetic.

Glycemic Index vs. Glycemic Load

The glycemic index (GI) is a score assigned to foods based on how high the food raises blood sugar levels compared to how high table sugar raises blood sugar levels (table sugar raises blood sugar more than any other food). Carbohydrate-containing foods that break down slowly release glucose into the bloodstream slowly and, therefore, blood sugar levels don't rise quickly. These foods are assigned a low GI. Conversely, carbohydrate-containing foods that break down quickly cause a high increase in blood sugar levels and are assigned a high GI.

Many popular books recommend avoiding foods that have a high glycemic index. These recommendations have been challenged by some experts because a carrot, for example, has about the same GI score as table sugar. This translates into eating six or seven servings of carrots to match the blood glucose effect of one-fourth cup of sugar.

Many think the glycemic load (GL) scoring may be a better measure of a food's effect on blood sugar. This score is determined by multiplying the grams of carbohydrate in a serving of food by the food's glycemic index. A GL score takes into account how much carbohydrate is in a serving of food, rather than just how high a standard amount of carbohydrate in a food raises blood sugar levels. Carrots, for example, have a glycemic index of 131. When using the GL score, carrots drop to a GL of 10, which is more appropriate for carrots, say proponents of GL scoring. This score gives a more accurate picture of the effect foods have on blood sugar, whereas the GI score unnecessarily vilifies healthful foods.

Alternate Choices

In a world where carbohydrate-rich foods so often take center stage, you may wonder what will fill your plate in a low-carbohydrate diet. Believe it or not, scientists recommend replacing some of the carbohydrates in your diet with heart-healthy fats. This may sound shocking, considering that we have been told for so long that a healthful diet is a low-fat diet and that all fats should be reduced. Recent research shows that monounsaturated fat—the fat that is found in foods such as nuts, olive oil, fatty fish, and avocados—is actually good for you.

In a landmark study conducted at Pennsylvania State University several years ago, researchers found that diets high in monounsaturated fats are superior to low-fat diets for heart health. Diets high in "good" fat actually improve risk factors for heart disease such as total cholesterol, LDL cholesterol, HDL cholesterol, and triglycerides. A diet rich in monounsaturated fats reduced the risk of heart disease by 21 percent, the study found, while the low-fat diet reduced it only 12 percent.

Monounsaturated fat can be an effective partner in a weight loss program, according to recent studies. For example, researchers at the Harvard School of Public Health and Brigham and Women's Hospital in Boston found that people in their study found it easier to stick to a moderate-fat, reduced-calorie diet than to a low-fat, reduced calorie diet. In that study, all subjects consumed between 1,200 and 1,500 calories per day. Half ate a moderate-fat diet (35 percent of calories from fat) and half ate a low-fat diet (20 percent of calories from fat). The moderate-fat group substituted high-saturated fat foods, like butter, with healthier monounsaturated fat foods such as peanut butter. They tossed almonds on their salads instead of croutons and poured small amounts of full-fat dressings on their salads instead of non-fat dressings. Both groups lost an average of 11 pounds. However, those in the low-fat group gained back most of their weight quickly, but the moderate-fat group maintained their weight loss for at least 2½ years.

It's important to remember, however, that although low-carbohydrate diets allow more meat, you should continue to limit saturated fat-rich foods such as marbled red meat; full-fat dairy products; fatty cuts of pork, chicken, and other meats; along with tropical oils such as palm and coconut. Eating too much saturated fat raises your blood cholesterol level, which increases your risk of clogged arteries, coronary artery disease, and heart attack. Because saturated fat is associated with higher risks of heart disease, certain cancers, and stroke, it should contribute no more than 7 to 10 percent of daily calories. If you consume 1,800 calories a day, for example, no more than 180 calories—and ideally, less than that—should come from saturated fat.

You should also limit your intake of trans fats, the fatty acids that are created when unsaturated fats undergo the chemical process of hydrogenation. Hydrogenated fats have replaced animal fats in many manufactured foods because they contribute flavor and texture to foods such as cakes, cookies, crackers, donuts, and chips and extend foods' shelf lives too. Foods fried in partially hydrogenated fats, such as fast-food French fries, taste pleasingly crispy and are nicely browned. Margarines can also be very high in trans fats, although lately, many margarine manufacturers have reformulated their recipes to rely less on hydrogenated fats. If you use margarine, choose a brand with no trans fats.

The problem with trans fats is that they raise the LDL, or bad cholesterol, in the blood nearly as much as saturated fat. High blood levels of LDL are a major contributor to heart disease, which kills more than 710,000 people in the United States each year. Trans fats may reduce levels of HDL, or good cholesterol, in the blood as well.

A number of studies bear this out. For example, the Nurse's Health Study, a long-term look at the health habits of about 80,000 nurses, found that those with the highest intake of trans fat were 27 percent more likely to develop heart disease than those with the lowest intake. Unfortunately, trans fats are not currently listed on food labels, so you have to read ingredient lists to root them out. Look for the words "partially hydrogenated vegetable oil" or "vegetable shortening," which indicate the food contains trans fat.

What about Protein?

Cutting down on carbohydrates doesn't mean you can go wild on protein. Very high-protein diets force the kidneys to work overtime trying to get rid of the excess waste products of protein and fat, called ketones. A buildup of ketones in the blood (called ketosis) can cause the body to produce high levels of uric acid, which is a risk factor for gout (a painful swelling of

the joints) and kidney stones. Ketosis can be especially risky for people with diabetes because it can speed the progression of diabetic kidney disease.

That said, however, there is some research that suggests a diet that is higher in protein and lower in carbohydrates than what is currently recommended by the U.S. Department of Agriculture (USDA) Food Guide Pyramid may help people lose weight and keep it off. For example, at the University of Illinois at Urbana-Champaign, researchers put two groups of overweight women on a 1,700-calorie-a-day eating plan for 10 weeks. The control group ate according to the USDA pyramid—55 percent of their calories came from carbohydrates, 15 percent from protein (a total of 68 grams per day), and 30 percent from fat. The experimental group ate a moderate-protein diet consisting of 40 percent of calories from carbohydrates, 30 percent from protein (125 grams a day), and 30 percent from fat.

The average weight loss in both groups was the same—16 pounds. However, the higher-protein group lost more fat than muscle—seven times more. The higher-protein group lost 12.3 pounds of fat compared with the lower-protein group, which lost 10.4 pounds of fat. (Both groups did the same amount of physical activity.)

The University of Illinois researchers believe that eating more high-quality protein increases the body's stores of leucine, an amino acid that helps people maintain muscle mass and reduce body fat during weight loss. Although the body does make many amino acids, it is not able to produce leucine, which is found primarily in beef, dairy products, poultry, fish, and eggs.

Subjects in the higher-protein group also had higher levels of thyroid hormones in their blood, which suggests a higher rate of metabolism. Additionally, their blood levels of heart-harming triglycerides were down, and their HDL ("good") cholesterol had risen slightly.

The women in the study ate more than just protein, however: Their daily diet included, in addition to 9 to 10 ounces of lean beef and other meats, three daily servings of low-fat dairy foods, five servings of vegetables, two fruits, and four servings of grains, pasta, and rice.

Following a Low-Carbohydrate Diet

Whether you choose to limit the carbohydrates a little or a lot, this book can help. In the following pages, you'll find a month of menus for daily carbohydrate intakes of 45, 60, 80, and 100 grams. All menus include recipes from this book. You'll discover 195 tasty recipes for appetizers, snacks, salads, egg and cheese dishes, main dishes, side dishes, and desserts that are low in carbohydrates. Using the meal plans and recipes, you'll be able to put together a delicious diet that will be just right for you.

How Do I Begin?

Switching to a low-carbohydrate diet requires more than just swapping meat for pasta, and eggs for your morning bagel. The following tips, suggestions, and advice will help ease the transition from a high- to low-carbohydrate diet.

- **Make every carbohydrate count.** When you eat carbohydrates, reach for complex carbohydrates such as wholegrain breads and pasta, legumes, non-starchy fruits, and vegetables.
- **Pick produce that triggers lower glucose response.** Fruits and vegetables with the lowest glycemic index include apples, apricots, asparagus, broccoli, Brussels sprouts, cauliflower, celery, cherries, cucumber, grapefruit, green beans, lettuce, mushrooms, onions, plums, spinach, strawberries, sweet peppers, tomatoes, and zucchini. Moderate-GI produce includes cantaloupe, grapes, oranges, orange juice, peaches, peas, pineapple, yams, and watermelon. High-GI fruits and vegetables include bananas, beets, carrots, corn, potatoes, and raisins.
- **Read labels.** Food labels are required to show how many grams of carbohydrates are in each serving. By reading labels carefully, you can track how many carbohydrate grams are in all the foods you eat.
- **Skip the soft drinks.** Soda, sports drinks, sweetened juices, and other soft drinks are chockful of low-quality carbohydrates. For example, a can of ginger ale contains 36 grams of carbohydrates, and a serving of sweetened iced tea made from a mix has 19 grams of carbohydrates. What's more, sweetened drinks don't fill you up, according to a study at Purdue University. The study found that people who ate 450 calories per day of jellybeans adjusted their dietary intake during the rest of the day to compensate for the calories from the jellybeans, and their daily caloric intake stayed stable. But when they drank 450 calories' worth of soda each day, their daily caloric

intake soared by 17 percent. When you're thirsty, choose diet sodas, sugar-free iced tea, or seltzer water with a splash of lemon instead.

- **Think ahead when dining out.** You can eat in restaurants when you're on a low-carbohydrate diet, but you'll succeed best if you choose wisely. First, pick a restaurant whose menu doesn't revolve around bread or pasta—a seafood restaurant is an excellent choice. Second, plan your day's diet around the restaurant meal. If you've got your heart set on a hunk of French bread at dinner, go light on carbohydrates at breakfast and lunch. Third, when you place your order, don't be afraid to ask the waitress to leave off the bun or breading. You're paying for the meal, after all, and it should be served the way you like it.

- **Stock your kitchen with low-carbohydrate foods and snacks.** Fill the pantry and fridge with non-starchy fruits and vegetables, fresh fish and shellfish, lean meats and poultry, dairy products, and low-carbohydrate snack bars.

- **Go nuts about nuts**. A variety of studies have shown that peanuts and other nuts, which are rich in monounsaturated fats, help contribute to weight loss and heart health. What's more, they are rich in magnesium, folate, fiber, copper, vitamin E, and arginine, all of which play an important role in the prevention of heart disease. Smear peanut butter on a sliced apple, sprinkle chopped almonds on a salad or in yogurt, or reach for a handful of nuts instead of a bag of potato chips.

- **Have an oil change**. Select heart-healthy monounsaturated oils such as peanut, olive, and canola oil for cooking and salad dressings.

- **Watch your condiments.** Carbohydrates hide in condiments such as relish and ketchup, which each have 4 grams of carbohydrates per tablespoon, and barbecue sauce, with about 8 grams of carbohydrates per tablespoon.

- **Choose lean meats.** If you're switching from a low-fat to a low-carbohydrate diet, you might think you now have license to eat lots of fatty meats. Forget it. Fatty meats are high in saturated fat, which is bad for your heart. Select lean beef, pork, or poultry. Remove any skin and trim visible fat.

- **Fill up on fish**. Seafood is high in protein and contains omega-3 fatty acids, which are polyunsaturated fatty acids that protect against heart attack and are vital to the proper function of brain and nerve cells. Omega-3 fatty acids are particularly abundant in higher-fat, cold-water fish such as mackerel, albacore tuna, salmon, sardines, and lake trout. All seafood, including shellfish and crustaceans such as oysters and shrimp, contain omega-3 fatty acids.

- **Get out and move.** Exercise is a crucial part of any diet. It speeds up metabolism, burns calories, strengthens and tones muscles, increases flexibility, boosts mood, improves circulation, and so much more. Aim for at least 30 minutes of moderate exercise such as walking, biking, or swimming at least five days a week, and more if you can fit it in. Make exercise more enjoyable by working out with friends, giving yourself nonfood rewards when you reach your goals, and trying new sports. Combining moderate exercise with a healthful, low-carbohydrate eating plan will help you lose weight and stay healthy.

Carb Counts of
Fresh Fruits & Vegetables

Fresh Fruit	Serving	Calories	Carb (g)
Apple, with skin	1 medium (5 oz.)	81	21
Apricots	4 (1 oz. each)	68	16
Banana	1 small (6 inch)	93	24
Blueberries	¾ cup	61	15
Cantaloupe	1 cup, cubes	56	13
Cherries, sweet	13	62	15
Cranberries	1 cup	47	12
Figs, large	1 (2½ inch)	48	12
Grapefruit	½ large	51	13
Grapes, seedless	17	60	15
Honeydew melon	1 cup, cubes	59	16
Kiwifruit	1 large (4 oz.)	56	14
Mango	½ cup, sliced	54	14
Nectarine	1 (2½ inch)	67	16
Orange	1 (5 oz.)	62	15
Papaya	1 cup, cubes	55	14
Peach	1 large (6 oz.)	67	17
Pear	½ of a large	62	16
Pineapple	¾ cup	57	14
Plums	2 (2 inch)	73	17
Raspberries	1 cup	60	14
Strawberries, whole	1½ cups	65	15
Tangerines, medium	2 (3 inch)	74	19
Watermelon	1¼ cups, cubes	62	14

Fresh Vegetables (nonstarchy)	Serving	Calories	Carb (g)
Asparagus, cooked	½ cup	22	4
Asparagus, cooked	8 spears	29	5
Beans, snap green, cooked	½ cup	22	5
Bean sprouts, raw	1 cup	31	6
Beets, cooked	½ cup	37	8
Broccoli, raw	1 cup	25	5
Broccoli, cooked	½ cup	22	4
Brussels sprouts, cooked	½ cup	30	7

Fresh Vegetables (nonstarchy)	Serving	Calories	Carb (g)
Cabbage, cooked	½ cup	17	3
Cabbage, raw	1 cup	18	4
Carrot, raw,	1 medium (2 oz.)	26	6
Carrot, cooked	½ cup	35	8
Cauliflower, raw	1 cup	25	5
Cauliflower, cooked	½ cup	14	3
Celery, raw	1 cup	19	4
Cucumber, raw	1 cup	14	3
Eggplant, cooked	½ cup	13	3
Greens, cooked			
Collard	½ cup	17	4
Kale	½ cup	21	4
Mustard	½ cup	10	2
Turnip	½ cup	14	3
Lettuce, iceberg	1 cup	7	1
Mushrooms, raw, whole	1 cup	24	4
Mushrooms, cooked	¾ cup	32	6
Okra, cooked	½ cup	25	6
Pea pods, raw	1 cup	61	11
Pea pods, cooked	½ cup	34	6
Romaine	1 cup	8	2
Spinach, raw	1 cup	7	1
Spinach, cooked	½ cup	20	4
Squash, summer, raw	1 cup	25	5
Squash, summer, cooked	½ cup	18	4
Tomato, raw, chopped	1 cup	38	8
Tomato, raw, whole, sliced	1 (2½ inch)	26	6
Turnips, cooked	1 cup cubes	33	8
Zucchini, raw	1 cup	17	4
Zucchini, cooked	1 cup	29	7

Fresh vegetables (starchy)	Serving	Calories	Carb (g)
Corn, sweet, yellow, cooked	½ cup	88	21
Peas, green cooked	½ cup	67	13
Potato, white, baked	3 oz.	93	22
Potato, white, boiled	½ cup	68	16
Squash, winter	1 cup	82	22
Potato, sweet, baked	½ of a medium (4 oz.)	59	14

Source: USDA Nutrient Database for Standard Reference

Meal Planning

The following pages (15 through 44) feature 30 days of menus using recipes from this book. Choose from four levels of carbohydrates: 45, 60, 80, or 100 grams, whichever suits your needs. The menus with lower grams of carbohydrate are ideal for giving you a jump-start on weight loss. As you get closer to your goal, you should gradually increase your carbohydrate intake. If you begin to gain weight, simply drop to the level below your current intake. Eventually, you'll be able to manage your weight and your carbohydrate intake easily.

Using Nutrition Labels

Obviously, you won't be making all of your meals from recipes. What about food you buy off the supermarket shelf? Food labels can really help. They are accurate, up-to-date, and contain all the information you need to make appropriate choices. Take a look at these two lines of the label:

- **Total carbohydrate grams.** There's no need to pay attention to or count grams of sugars or other information under Total Carbohydrate. These are already included in Total Carbohydrate.
- **Serving size.** Make sure the serving size you'll eat is equal to the amount on the Nutrition Facts label. If it's more or less, adjust the amount of total carbohydrates you've eaten accordingly.

Foods Without Nutrition Labels

Most fresh produce, meat, poultry, and fish do not include a Nutrition Facts label. Meat, poultry, and fish do not contain significant amounts of carbohydrate unless they are breaded or stuffed. (See pages 12 and 13 for carbohydrate values of fresh produce.) You can also find food values for thousands of foods on USDA's web site nal.usda.gov/fnic/foodcomp/index.html.

Portion Control

The opportunities to overeat are constant whether it's a buy-one-get-one-free offer, super-sizing a fast-food meal, eating at an all-you-can-eat buffet, or temptations to overindulge at the family dinner table. Controlling portion sizes is an important part of counting carbs. Concentrate on eating reasonable portions. Downsize or double-check the accuracy of your portions with these portion-control tools and tips:

- **Use a food scale.** After weighing foods for awhile, you'll be able to determine an appropriate serving size based on weight.
- **Train your eyes.** Determine accurate measurements by regularly using measuring cups and spoons to get used to visually estimating amounts.
- **Measure with your hands.** Your hands can provide a quick visual guide to portions:
  Tip of the thumb (to first knuckle) = 1 tsp.
  Whole thumb = 1 Tbsp.
  Palm of your hand or the size of a deck of playing cards = 3 ounces. (This is the portion size of cooked meat [protein] most people need at a meal.)
  Tight fist = ½ cup
  Loose fist or open handful = 1 cup
  Note: These guidelines hold true for most women's hands. Check the size of your hand's measurements with measuring cups, spoons, and a scale.

DAY 1

Breakfast—45 g Carb

Cheddar omelet (2 eggs,
1 tablespoon butter and
½ cup shredded cheddar
cheese)
⅓ cup fresh blueberries
Hot tea

For 60 g Carb add
1 slice whole wheat toast
1 teaspoon butter

For 80 g Carb
No additions

For 100 g Carb
No additions

Lunch—45 g Carb

1 (3 to 4 ounces) broiled
hamburger patty with
1 ounce melted provolone
cheese, 1 teaspoon catsup,
and ½ teaspoon mustard
Vegetables Primavera
(p. 221)
Sugar-free lemonade

For 60 g Carb
No additions

For 80 g Carb add
½ medium papaya, sliced

For 100 g Carb
No additions

Dinner—45 g Carb

Braised Chicken with Beans
and Squash (p. 156)
¾ cup watermelon cubes
Sparkling water

For 60 g Carb
No additions

For 80 g Carb
No additions

For 100 g Carb add
1 breadstick
½ cup watermelon cubes

Snack—45 g Carb

Greek Salad Bites (p. 49)

For 60 g Carb
No additions

For 80 g Carb add
¾ ounce dry roasted almonds

For 100 g Carb add
¾ ounce dry roasted almonds

DAY 2

Breakfast—45 g Carb

8 ounces plain yogurt
1 cup sliced fresh
 strawberries
3 slices turkey bacon
Hot coffee

For 60 g Carb
No additions

For 80 g Carb
½ English muffin, toasted
1 teaspoon butter

For 100 g Carb
½ English muffin, toasted
1 teaspoon butter

Lunch—45 g Carb

3 ounces thinly sliced ham
Big Green Salad with Two-
 Pepper Dressing (p. 83)
Iced tea

For 60 g Carb
No additions

For 80 g Carb add
½ cup milk

For 100 g Carb add
½ cup milk

Dinner—45 g Carb

Fiery Southwestern Seafood
 Skewers (p. 205)
2 fresh apricots, halved
Sparkling water

For 60 g Carb add
⅓ cup hot cooked brown rice

For 80 g Carb
No additions

For 100 g Carb
No additions

Snack—45 g Carb

Fennel and Onion Dip
 (p. 58)

For 60 g Carb
No additions

For 80 g Carb
No additions

For 100 g Carb
No additions

DAY 3

Breakfast—45 g Carb

Spinach and Cheese Omelet (p. 98)
1 cup fresh raspberries
Hot tea

For 60 g Carb add
½ plain bagel, toasted
1 tablespoon cream cheese

For 80 g Carb
No additions

For 100 g Carb
No additions

Lunch—45 g Carb

½ turkey sandwich (1 slice whole wheat bread, 2 ounces thinly sliced turkey, 1 ounce sliced Gruyère cheese, 1 thin slice tomato, 1 lettuce leaf, ½ teaspoon mustard)
Hit-the-Spot Lemon Water (p. 68)

For 60 g Carb
No additions

For 80 g Carb add
½ turkey sandwich (same as above)
½ medium carrot, cut into sticks

For 100 g Carb
No additions

Dinner—45 g Carb

Mustard-Glazed Halibut Steaks (p. 192)
Pan-Fried Baby Bok Choy (p. 211)
Sparkling water

For 60 g Carb
No additions

For 80 g Carb
No additions

For 100 g Carb
No additions

Snack—45 g Carb

Fresh Fruit Dip (p. 59)

For 60 g Carb
No additions

For 80 g Carb
No additions

For 100 g Carb add
1 ounce pretzel sticks

DAY 4

Breakfast—45 g Carb

1 scrambled egg
2 ounces ham
1 small tangerine
Hot coffee

For 60 g Carb add
1 slice raisin bread (without icing), toasted
1 teaspoon butter

For 80 g Carb add
1 slice raisin bread (without icing), toasted
1 teaspoon butter

For 100 g Carb
No additions

Lunch—45 g Carb

Tuna-Vegetable Salad (p. 201)
3 shredded whole wheat crackers
Sugar-free lemonade

For 60 g Carb
No additions

For 80 g Carb add
3 shredded whole wheat crackers

For 100 g Carb
No additions

Dinner—45 g Carb

Asian Beef and Noodle Bowl (p. 128)
1 small fresh plum, sliced
Sparkling water with a lemon wedge

For 60 g Carb
No additions

For 80 g Carb
No additions

For 100 g Carb
No additions

Snack—45 g Carb

Yogurt-Herb Dip (p. 55)

For 60 g Carb
No additions

For 80 g Carb
No additions

For 100 g Carb add
3 cups popped popcorn

DAY 5

Breakfast—45 g Carb

½ toasted cheese sandwich (1 slice whole wheat bread; 2 ounces sliced cheddar cheese, provolone cheese, Monterey Jack cheese, or combination; 1 teaspoon butter)
Hot tea

For 60 g Carb add
1 small orange

For 80 g Carb
No additions

For 100 g Carb
No additions

Lunch—45 g Carb

3 ounces cooked, peeled, chilled shrimp
Stand-Up Tomato Salad (p. 72)
Sparkling water

For 60 g Carb
No additions

For 80 g Carb add
1 (1-ounce) rye dinner roll
1 teaspoon butter

For 100 g Carb
No additions

Dinner—45 g Carb

Turkey Enchiladas (p. 179)
½ cup cantaloupe cubes
Iced tea

For 60 g Carb
No additions

For 80 g Carb
⅓ cup cantaloupe cubes

For 100 g Carb
No additions

Snack—45 g Carb

½ cup milk

For 60 g Carb
No additions

For 80 g Carb
No additions

For 100 g Carb add
1 small muffin
½ cup milk

DAY 6

Breakfast—45 g Carb

1 hard-cooked egg
1 fresh peach, sliced, or
½ cup canned peach slices
   in light syrup
Hot tea

For 60 g Carb
No additions

For 80 g Carb add
1 (2-inch) cube corn bread
1 teaspoon butter

For 100 g Carb
No additions

Lunch—45 g Carb

3 ounces thinly sliced roast
   beef
Greek Salad Bites (p. 49)
Sugar-free lemonade

For 60 g Carb
No additions

For 80 g Carb add
½ cup milk

For 100 g Carb
No additions

Dinner—45 g Carb

Turkey Steaks with Sweet
   Pepper-Citrus Salsa
   (p. 170)
Roasted Summer Cherry
   Tomatoes (p. 217)
Hot tea

For 60 g Carb
No additions

For 80 g Carb
No additions

For 100 g Carb add
Baked Coffee Custards
   (p. 239)
½ medium carrot, cut into
   sticks

Snack—45 g Carb

Stuffed Celery Bites (p. 52)
1 ounce provolone cheese
   cubes

For 60 g Carb add
1 small apple

For 80 g Carb
No additions

For 100 g Carb
No additions

DAY 7

Breakfast—45 g Carb

8 ounces plain yogurt
¼ cup cubed mango pieces
2-ounce sausage patty
Hot coffee

For 60 g Carb add
½ cup cubed mango pieces

For 80 g Carb
No additions

For 100 g Carb
No additions

Lunch—45 g Carb

3- to 4-ounce grilled turkey
  burger with 1 teaspoon
  mustard
Asian Pea Pod Salad (p. 81)
Iced tea

For 60 g Carb
No additions

For 80 g Carb
1 cup milk

For 100 g Carb
No additions

Dinner—45 g Carb

Spicy Seafood Stew (p. 203)
1 cheese breadstick
Sparkling water with lemon
  wedge

For 60 g Carb
No additions

For 80 g Carb add
1 cheese breadstick

For 100 g Carb add
Berry Cheesecake Dessert
  (p. 229)

Snack—45 g Carb

Proscuitto-Arugula Roll-Ups
  (p. 50)

For 60 g Carb
No additions

For 80 g Carb
No additions

For 100 g Carb
No additions

Breakfast—45 g Carb

1 scrambled egg
1 ounce Canadian-style
   bacon
⅓ cup fresh blackberries
Hot tea

For 60 g Carb add
1¼ cups milk

For 80 g Carb add
½ English muffin, toasted
1 teaspoon butter

For 100 g Carb add
¼ cup fresh blackberries

Lunch—45 g Carb

2 ounces thinly sliced turkey
   salami
Vegetable Pasta Salad
   (p. 92)
Orange spritzer (¼ cup
   orange juice and 8 ounces
   sparkling water)

For 60 g Carb
No additions

For 80 g Carb
No additions

For 100 g Carb
No additions

Dinner—45 g Carb

Thai-Spiced Scallops
   (p. 204)
⅓ cup hot cooked brown rice
Iced tea

For 60 g Carb
No additions

For 80 g Carb
No additions

For 100 g Carb add
⅓ cup hot cooked brown rice

Snack—45 g Carb

Cheese-Stuffed Pecans
   (p. 61)

For 60 g Carb
No additions

For 80 g Carb
⅓ cup honeydew melon
   cubes

For 100 g Carb
No additions

DAY 9

Breakfast—45 g Carb

½ cup cooked oatmeal
¼ cup milk
2 ounces ham
Hot coffee

For 60 g Carb
No additions

For 80 g Carb
No additions

For 100 g Carb add
½ cup cooked oatmeal
⅓ cup milk

Lunch—45 g Carb

Grilled 3-ounce chicken
  breast half
Lemony Caesar Salad
  (p. 88)
Sparkling water

For 60 g Carb add
1 slice French bread
1 teaspoon butter

For 80 g Carb
No additions

For 100 g Carb
No additions

Dinner—45 g Carb

Steak with Roasted Garlic
  and Herbs (p. 117)
Seared Vegetable Medley
  (p. 220)
Hot green tea

For 60 g Carb
No additions

For 80 g Carb add
Baked Rice Pudding (p. 241)

For 100 g Carb
No additions

Snack—45 g Carb

Deviled Eggs with Spicy
  Crab (p. 48)

For 60 g Carb
No additions

For 80 g Carb
No additions

For 100 g Carb
No additions

DAY 10

Breakfast—45 g Carb

1 scrambled egg
2 slices bacon
½ grapefruit
Hot tea

For 60 g Carb
No additions

For 80 g Carb
No additions

For 100 g Carb add
1 slice seven-grain bread,
  toasted
1 teaspoon butter

Lunch—45 g Carb

3 ounces sliced roasted
  turkey breast
Tomato and Sweet Pepper
  Salad (p. 71)
Sugar-free fruit-flavored
  beverage

For 60 g Carb add
1¼ cup
ps milk

For 80 g Carb
No additions

For 100 g Carb
No additions

Dinner—45 g Carb

Basil Halibut Steaks (p. 184)
Skillet-Roasted Potato Salad
  (p. 90)
Iced tea

For 60 g Carb
No additions

For 80 g Carb add
1¼ cups sliced fresh
  strawberries
½ cup steamed broccoli

For 100 g Carb add
½ cup steamed broccoli

Snack—45 g Carb

Hot Artichoke Dip (p. 57)

For 60 g Carb
No additions

For 80 g Carb
No additions

For 100 g Carb
No additions

DAY 11

Breakfast—45 g Carb

8 ounces plain yogurt
1 fresh apricot, sliced
1 tablespoon granola
Hot tea

For 60 g Carb add
1 fresh apricot, sliced

For 80 g Carb
No additions

For 100 g Carb
No additions

Lunch—45 g Carb

1 (3-ounce) grilled pork
   loin chop
Lemony Caesar Salad (p. 88)
Iced tea

For 60 g Carb
No additions

For 80 g Carb add
½ cup fruit cocktail in light
   syrup

For 100 g Carb add
Chocolate Shortbread
   (p. 237)

Dinner—45 g Carb

Turkey Mushroom Marsala
   (p. 171)
½ cup steamed asparagus
½ baked potato (3 ounces)
1 teaspoon butter
Sparkling water

For 60 g Carb add
½ cup steamed asparagus

For 80 g Carb
No additions

For 100 g Carb
No additions

Snack—45 g Carb

Sugar-free lemonade

For 60 g Carb add
1 (2½-inch square) graham
   cracker

For 80 g Carb add
1 (2½-inch square) graham
   cracker

For 100 g Carb
No additions

DAY 12

Breakfast—45 g Carb

1 poached egg
½ English muffin, toasted
1 teaspoon butter
Hot tea

For 60 g Carb
No additions

For 80 g Carb add
½ English muffin, toasted
1 teaspoon butter
1 tablespoon fruit spread

For 100 g Carb
No additions

Lunch—45 g Carb

Gingered Pork and Cabbage
  Soup (p. 142)
Hot coffee

For 60 g Carb add
1½ cups raw vegetable sticks
  (cucumber, celery, carrot,
  or zucchini)
3 tablespoons sour cream dip

For 80 g Carb
No additions

For 100 g Carb add
⅔ cup canned peach slices in
  light syrup

Dinner—45 g Carb

Herbed Beef Tenderloin
  (p. 124)
½ cup steamed green beans
⅓ cup mandarin orange
  sections
Sparkling water with lime
  wedge

For 60 g Carb add
½ cup steamed green beans

For 80 g Carb
No additions

For 100 g Carb
No additions

Snack—45 g Carb

½ ounce dry roasted
  macadamia nuts

For 60 g Carb
No additions

For 80 g Carb
No additions

For 100 g Carb
No additions

DAY 13

Breakfast—45 g Carb

Weekend Scramble (p. 94)
⅓ cup blueberries
Hot tea

For 60 g Carb add
1 slice whole wheat bread,
  toasted
1 teaspoon butter

For 80 g Carb
No additions

For 100 g Carb add
⅓ cup blueberries

Lunch—45 g Carb

3 ounces broiled fish with
  melted butter and one
  lemon wedge
Asparagus with Warm
  Vinaigrette (p. 208)
Iced tea

For 60 g Carb
No additions

For 80 g Carb add
1 cup milk
⅓ cup chopped fresh
  pineapple

For 100 g Carb
No additions

iDinner—45 g Carb

Skillet Veal Scaloppine with
  Marsala (p. 132)
⅓ cup hot cooked couscous
Small spinach salad (1 cup
  torn spinach; 2 tablespoons
  chopped tomatoes;
  1 tablespoon slivered
  almonds, toasted; and
  2 tablespoons blue-cheese
  salad dressing)
Hot coffee

For 60 g Carb
No additions

For 80 g Carb
No additions

For 100 g Carb
No additions

Snack—45 g Carb

2 cheddar cheese mini
  popcorn cakes
Iced tea

For 60 g Carb
No additions

For 80 g Carb
No additions

For 100 g Carb add
Cranberry spritzer (¼ cup
  cranberry juice cocktail
  and 1 cup sparkling water)

DAY 14

Breakfast—45 g Carb

½ cup cooked oatmeal
¼ cup milk
2 ounces turkey ham
Hot tea

For 60 g Carb
No additions

For 80 g Carb add
1 small nectarine

For 100 g Carb
No additions

Lunch—45 g Carb

Chef's salad (1½ cups torn mixed greens, ¼ cup chopped tomato, 1 chopped hard-cooked egg, 2 ounces chopped chicken breast, 1 ounce shredded cheddar cheese, ¼ cup sliced cucumber, and 2 tablespoons bacon and tomato salad dressing)

For 60 g Carb add
1¼ cups milk

For 80 g Carb add
¼ ounce pretzel sticks

For 100 g Carb add
¼ ounce pretzel sticks

Dinner—45 g Carb

Roasted Italian Chicken (p. 148)
Lemon-Braised Baby Broccoli (p. 212)
½ cup watermelon cubes
Hot coffee

For 60 g Carb
No additions

For 80 g Carb
No additions

For 100 g Carb add
Walnut Cream Roll (p. 226)

Snack—45 g Carb

Artichoke-Feta Tortilla Wraps (p. 46)

For 60 g Carb
No additions

For 80 g Carb
No additions

For 100 g Carb
No additions

DAY 15

Breakfast—45 g Carb

8 ounces plain yogurt
1 (2½-inch square) graham cracker
¼ cup red raspberries
Hot coffee

For 60 g Carb
No additions

For 80 g Carb add
½ cup red raspberries

For 100 g Carb add
1 (2½-inch square) graham cracker

Lunch—45 g Carb

1 (3-ounce) grilled chicken breast half
Spring Asparagus Slaw (p. 79)
Iced tea

For 60 g Carb add
1 (1-ounce) wheat bran dinner roll
1 teaspoon butter

For 80 g Carb
No additions

For 100 g Carb
No additions

Dinner—45 g Carb

Broiled Fish Steaks with Tarragon Cheese Sauce (p. 190)
Lemony Mixed Vegetables (p. 219)
Sparkling water

For 60 g Carb
No additions

For 80 g Carb add
1 cup milk

For 100 g Carb add
Mocha Cream Puffs (p. 240)

Snack—45 g Carb

1 fresh plum

For 60 g Carb
No additions

For 80 g Carb
No additions

For 100 g Carb
No additions

DAY 16

Breakfast—45 g Carb

1 fried egg
1 slice whole wheat bread, toasted
1 teaspoon butter
1 teaspoon fruit spread
Hot coffee

For 60 g Carb
No additions

For 80 g Carb
No additions

For 100 g Carb add
1 cup milk
1 slice whole wheat bread, toasted
1 teaspoon butter

Lunch—45 g Carb

2 ounces cheddar cheese cubes
2 slices sesame melba toast
¾ cup honeydew melon cubes
Iced tea

For 60 g Carb
No additions

For 80 g Carb add
1 slice sesame melba toast

For 100 g Carb
No additions

Dinner—45 g Carb

Easy Citrus Salmon Steaks (p. 188)
Steamed broccoli
1 teaspoon butter
Sparkling water

For 60 g Carb add
½ cup cubed mango

For 80 g Carb add
½ baked potato (3 ounces)
1 teaspoon butter
2 tablespoons sour cream dip

For 100 g Carb
No additions

Snack—45 g Carb

Tortellini, Olive, and Cheese Kabobs (p. 51)

For 60 g Carb
No additions

For 80 g Carb
No additions

For 100 g Carb
No additions

DAY 17

Breakfast—45 g Carb

Southwestern Breakfast Bake (p. 102)
Hot coffee

For 60 g Carb
No additions

For 80 g Carb add
½ cup orange juice

For 100 g Carb
¼ cup orange juice

Lunch—45 g Carb

3 ounces thinly sliced smoked turkey breast
Asparagus Finger Salad (p. 77)
Sparkling water

For 60 g Carb
No additions

For 80 g Carb
No additions

For 100 g Carb
No additions

Dinner—45 g Carb

Lemony Flank Steak (p. 119)
½ cup steamed broccoli tossed with ¼ cup hot cooked rice, 1 tablespoon grated Parmesan cheese, and 1 teaspoon melted butter
Iced tea

For 60 g Carb add
1 cup cubed papaya

For 80 g Carb
No additions

For 100 g Carb
No additions

Snack—45 g Carb

Yogurt-Herb Dip (p. 55)

For 60 g Carb
No additions

For 80 g Carb add
¼ ounce mini pretzel twists

For 100 g Carb add
½ ounce mini pretzel twists

DAY 18

Breakfast—45 g Carb

1 scrambled egg
2 ounces Canadian-style
   bacon
½ plain bagel (1 ounce),
   toasted
1 tablespoon cream cheese
Hot tea

For 60 g Carb add
1 small orange

For 80 g Carb
No additions

For 100 g Carb
No additions

Lunch—45 g Carb

Salmon-topped tossed salad
(1½ cup torn mixed
greens; ¼ cup chopped
tomato; ½ medium carrot,
sliced; ¼ cup sliced fresh
mushrooms; 1 tablespoon
sliced green onion;
2 ounces cooked salmon,
skin and bones removed;
and 2 tablespoons red wine
vinaigrette)

For 60 g Carb
No additions

For 80 g Carb add
1 cup milk
3 saltine-type crackers

For 100 g Carb
No additions

Dinner—45 g Carb

Filet Mignon with Portobello
   Sauce (p. 114)
¾ cup steamed green beans
⅓ cup blueberries
Sparkling water

For 60 g Carb
No additions

For 80 g Carb
No additions

For 100 g Carb add
½ cup blueberries

Snack—45 g Carb

Really Hot Iced Coffee
   (p. 65)
1 ounce cubed Gruyère
   cheese

For 60 g Carb
No additions

For 80 g Carb
No additions

For 100 g Carb
Fresh Fruit Dip (p. 59)

DAY 19

Breakfast—45 g Carb

½ English muffin, toasted
1 teaspoon butter
2 ounces ham
Hot tea

For 60 g Carb add
½ cup pineapple juice

For 80 g Carb
No additions

For 100 g Carb
No additions

Lunch—45 g Carb

1 (3 ounce) grilled hamburger patty with
1 teaspoon catsup and
½ teaspoon mustard
Cantaloupe and Tomato Salad (p. 84)
Sparkling water

For 60 g Carb
No additions

For 80 g Carb
No additions

For 100 g Carb
⅔ cup milk

Dinner—45 g Carb

Lemon-Herb Swordfish Steaks, (p. 189)
⅓ cup hot cooked rice pilaf
½ cup steamed mixed broccoli, cauliflower, and carrots
Iced tea

For 60 g Carb
No additions

For 80 g Carb add
½ cup steamed mixed broccoli, cauliflower, and carrots

For 100 g Carb add
Strawberry Gelato (p. 246)

Snack—45 g Carb

Sugar-free lemonade
1 ounce cubed cheddar cheese

For 60 g Carb
No additions

For 80 g Carb add
5 vanilla wafers

For 100 g Carb
No additions

Breakfast—45 g Carb

Broccoli Omelet Provençale
(p. 99)
Hot tea

For 60 g Carb
No additions

For 80 g Carb add
1 small banana

For 100 g Carb
No additions

Lunch—45 g Carb

Mexican-Style Turkey Soup
(p. 180)
1 ounce cubed cheddar
cheese
Hot tea

For 60 g Carb add
1 cup milk
3 to 4 tortilla chips

For 80 g Carb
No additions

For 100 g Carb
No additions

Dinner—45 g Carb

Smoked Pepper Halibut
(p. 196)
½ cup steamed broccoli,
green beans, pearl onions,
and red peppers
½ cup blackberries
Sparkling water

For 60 g Carb
No additions

For 80 g Carb add
½ cup steamed broccoli,
green beans, pearl onions,
and red peppers

For 100 g Carb add
¼ cup blackberries
1 (1-ounce) whole wheat
dinner roll
1 teaspoon butter

Snack—45 g Carb

Thai Spinach Dip (p. 56)

For 60 g Carb
No additions

For 80 g Carb
No additions

For 100 g Carb
No additions

DAY 21

Breakfast—45 g Carb

1 slice frozen French toast, cooked
1 (2-ounce) sausage patty
2 tablespoons sugar-free pancake syrup
1 teaspoon butter
Hot tea

For 60 g Carb
No additions

For 80 g Carb
No additions

For 100 g Carb add
1 slice frozen French toast, cooked
2 tablespoons sugar-free pancake syrup
1 teaspoon butter

Lunch—45 g Carb

Mustard-Glazed Halibut Steaks (p. 192)
½ cup steamed green beans
Iced tea

For 60 g Carb add
¾ cup mandarin orange sections

For 80 g Carb add
⅓ cup hot cooked rice pilaf

For 100 g Carb
No additions

Dinner—45 g Carb

Grilled Pork Chops with Mushroom Stuffing (p. 133)
½ cup steamed asparagus
⅓ cup chopped fresh pineapple
Sparkling water

For 60 g Carb
No additions

For 80 g Carb add
½ cup steamed asparagus

For 100 g Carb
No additions

Snack—45 g Carb

1 cup raw vegetable sticks (celery, carrot, and cucumber)
2 tablespoons sour cream dip
1 ounce cubed Swiss cheese

For 60 g Carb
No additions

For 80 g Carb
No additions

For 100 g Carb add
½ cup raw vegetable sticks (celery, carrot, and cucumber)
1 tablespoon sour cream dip

DAY 22

Breakfast—45 g Carb

Spinach Cheese Puff (p. 101)
Hot coffee

For 60 g Carb add
½ cup orange juice

For 80 g Carb
No additions

For 100 g Carb add
½ English muffin, toasted
1 teaspoon butter

Lunch—45 g Carb

Tossed salad with tuna
(1½ cups torn mixed
greens; ¼ cup chopped
tomato; 1 tablespoon
sliced green onion;
2 ounces canned tuna,
drained; ¼ cup shredded
mozzarella cheese;
2 tablespoons Italian
vinaigrette salad dressing)
2 saltine-type crackers
Sparkling water

For 60 g Carb
No additions

For 80 g Carb add
6 saltine-type crackers

For 100 g Carb
No additions

Dinner—45 g Carb

Beef-Vegetable Ragout
(p. 127)
⅓ cup red raspberries
Hot coffee

For 60 g Carb
No additions

For 80 g Carb add
⅓ cup red raspberries

For 100 g Carb
No additions

Snack—45 g Carb

1 ounce cubed salami
Sugar-free lemonade

For 60 g Carb
No additions

For 80 g Carb
No additions

For 100 g Carb add
1 cup raw vegetable sticks
(celery, carrot, zucchini,
and/or cucumber)

Breakfast—45 g Carb

1 scrambled eggs with
2 tablespoons shredded
cheddar cheese
1 slice whole wheat bread,
toasted
1 teaspoon butter
Hot coffee

For 60 g Carb
No additions

For 80 g Carb
No additions

For 100 g Carb add
1 slice whole wheat bread,
toasted
1 teaspoon butter

Lunch—45 g Carb

French Beef Stew (p. 126)
⅓ cup grapefruit sections
Hot tea

For 60 g Carb add
1 cup milk

For 80 g Carb add
1 (1-ounce) whole wheat
dinner roll
1 teaspoon butter

For 100 g Carb
No additions

Dinner—45 g Carb

Beer-Brined Turkey (p. 166)
½ cup cooked julienne cut
carrots tossed with
½ teaspoon melted butter
and 1 teaspoon snipped
fresh parsley
Sparkling water

For 60 g Carb
No additions

For 80 g Carb add
½ cup cooked julienne cut
carrots tossed with
½ teaspoon melted butter
and 1 teaspoon snipped
fresh parsley

For 100 g Carb add
½ cup ice cream

Snack—45 g Carb

½ cup sliced fresh
strawberries

For 60 g Carb add
¼ cup sliced fresh
strawberries

For 80 g Carb
No additions

For 100 g Carb
No additions

DAY 24

Breakfast—45 g Carb

8 ounces plain yogurt
¼ cup red raspberries
1 tablespoon granola
Hot tea

For 60 g Carb add
¼ cup red raspberries

For 80 g Carb add
1 tablespoon granola

For 100 g Carb add
¼ cup red raspberries

Lunch—45g Carb

3 ounces sliced roast beef
Asian Pea Pod Salad (p. 81)
Iced tea

For 60 g Carb
No additions

For 80 g Carb add
Easy Ice Cream Sandwiches
(p. 247)

For 100 g Carb add
make roast beef into
sandwich: Add 2 slices
whole wheat bread,
lettuce, 1 slice tomato, and
1 teaspoon mustard

Dinner—45 g Carb

Roasted Tarragon Chicken
(p. 150)
½ cup steamed broccoli
tossed with ½ teaspoon
butter and ¼ teaspoon
finely shredded lemon peel
½ cup milk

For 60 g Carb add
½ cup steamed broccoli
tossed with ½ teaspoon
melted butter
½ cup milk

For 80 g Carb
No additions

For 100 g Carb
No additions

Snack—45 g Carb

Spiced Popcorn (p. 62)
Sugar-free lemonade

For 60 g Carb
No additions

For 80 g Carb
No additions

For 100 g Carb
No additions

DAY 25

Breakfast—45 g Carb

Baked Brie Strata (p. 108)
Hot tea

For 60 g Carb add
1 small orange

For 80 g Carb
No additions

For 100 g Carb
No additions

Lunch—45 g Carb

½ cup vegetable beef soup
Small tossed salad (1 cup torn mixed greens;
2 tablespoons chopped tomato; 1 tablespoon sliced green onion,
1 ounce shredded provolone cheese, and
2 tablespoons Caesar vinaigrette salad dressing)

For 60 g Carb
No additions

For 80 g Carb add
1 cup milk
1 tangerine

For 100 g Carb
No additions

Dinner—45 g Carb

Turkey Tender Steaks & Sweet Pepper-Citrus Salsa (p. 170)
1½ cups stir-fried zucchini, carrots and cauliflower
Sparkling water

For 60 g Carb
No additions

For 80 g Carb
No additions

For 100 g Carb add
Strawberry-Topped Cheesecake (p. 228)

Snack—45 g Carb

Sugar-free lemonade
1 ounce Swiss cheese cubes

For 60 g Carb
No additions

For 80 g Carb
No additions

For 100 g Carb
No additions

DAY 26

Breakfast—45 g Carb

1 frozen plain waffle, toasted
1 teaspoon butter
2 tablespoons sugar-free
   pancake syrup
2 ounces Canadian-style
   bacon
Hot tea

For 60 g Carb add
2 small tangerines

For 80 g Carb
No additions

For 100 g Carb
No additions

Lunch—45 g Carb

3 ounces sliced roasted
   turkey breast
Spinach-Mushroom Sauté
   (p. 216)
Iced tea

For 60 g Carb
No additions

For 80 g Carb add
1 cup milk

For 100 g Carb
No additions

Dinner—45 g Carb

Grilled Veal Chops with
   Pesto-Stuffed Mushrooms
   (p. 131)
⅓ cup rice pilaf
Hot coffee

For 60 g Carb
No additions

For 80 g Carb add
½ medium tomato, sliced

For 100 g Carb add
¼ cup rice pilaf

Snack—45 g Carb

⅓ cup cantaloupe cubes
½ ounce thinly sliced turkey
   salami

For 60 g Carb
No additions

For 80 g Carb add
⅓ cup cantaloupe cubes

For 100 g Carb add
Herbed Soy Nuts and Seeds
   (p. 60)
Sparkling water

DAY 27

Breakfast—45g Carb

1 poached egg
1 slice wholewheat bread, toasted
1 teaspoon butter
Hot tea

For 60 g Carb
No additions

For 80 g Carb add
1 slice whole wheat bread, toasted
1 teaspoon butter
1 cup milk

For 100 g Carb
No additions

Lunch—45 g Carb

3 ounces thinly sliced roast beef
Orange-Beet Salad (p. 89)
Iced tea

For 60 g Carb add
1 cup milk

For 80 g Carb
No additions

For 100 g Carb
No additions

Dinner—45 g Carb

Vegetable-Stuffed Chicken (p. 152)
½ cup cooked brussels sprouts
½ cup chopped mango
Sparkling water

For 60 g Carb
No additions

For 80 g Carb
No additions

For 100 g Carb add
⅓ cup hot cooked brown rice

Snack—45 g Carb

Summertime Quencher (p. 63)

For 60 g Carb add
½ ounce dry roasted almonds

For 80 g Carb
No additions

For 100 g Carb add
½ ounce dry roasted almonds

DAY 28

Breakfast—45 g Carb

Farmer's Breakfast (p. 95)
½ cup milk

For 60 g Carb
No additions

For 80 g Carb add
½ cup milk

For 100 g Carb add
½ whole wheat bagel
(1 ounce), toasted
1 teaspoon butter

Lunch—45 g Carb

3 ounces sliced roast pork
Jicama-Berry Salad (p. 75)
Iced tea

For 60 g Carb
No additions

For 80 g Carb add
1 slice French bread
(1 ounce)
1 teaspoon butter

For 100 g Carb
No additions

Dinner—45 g Carb

Grilled Tuna with Peanut
Sauce (p. 193)
½ cup steamed pea pods
Hot tea

For 60 g Carb add
1 fresh peach, sliced

For 80 g Carb
No additions

For 100 g Carb add
½ cup steamed pea pods

Snack—45 g Carb

Really Hot Iced Coffee
(p. 65)

For 60 g Carb
No additions

For 80 g Carb
No additions

For 100 g Carb
No additions

Breakfast—45 g Carb

Smoked Chicken-Egg Bake
(p. 104)
Hot tea

For 60 g Carb
No additions

For 80 g Carb add
1 cup milk

For 100 g Carb
No additions

Lunch—45 g Carb

3 ounces grilled turkey
tenderloin
Mesclun with Oranges and
Olives (p. 76)
Iced tea

For 60 g Carb add
⅓ cup hot cooked rice pilaf

For 80 g Carb
No additions

For 100 g Carb add
⅓ cup hot cooked rice pilaf

Dinner—45 g Carb

Italian Steak Sandwiches
(p. 122)
⅓ cup chopped fresh
pineapple
Sparkling water

For 60 g Carb
No additions

For 80 g Carb
No additions

For 100 g Carb add
Small tossed salad (1 cup
torn mixed greens,
2 tablespoons chopped
tomato, 1 tablespoon
sliced green onions,
1 ounce shredded
mozzarella cheese, and
2 tablespoons Italian
vinaigrette)

Snack—45 g Carb

Stuffed Celery Bites (p. 52)

For 60 g Carb
No additions

For 80 g Carb
4 animal crackers

For 100 g Carb
No additions

DAY 30

Breakfast—45 g Carb

1 scrambled egg
1 (2-ounce) sausage patty
1 slice whole wheat bread, toasted
1 teaspoon butter
Hot coffee

For 60 g Carb
No additions

For 80 g Carb add
1 cup milk

For 100 g Carb
No additions

Lunch—45 g Carb

Grilled Mustard-Glazed Pork (p. 139)
½ cup wilted spinach
Sugar-free lemonade

For 60 g Carb add
1 small nectarine, sliced

For 80 g Carb
No additions

For 100 g Carb add
⅓ cup hot cooked rice pilaf

Dinner—45 g Carb

Fish Fillets with Roasted Red Pepper Sauce (p. 183)
½ medium ear corn on the cob with 1 teaspoon butter
Iced tea

For 60 g Carb
No additions

For 80 g Carb
No additions

For 100 g Carb add
½ medium ear corn on the cob with 1 teaspoon butter

Snack—45 g Carb

Herbed Soy Nuts and Seeds (p. 60)
Sparkling water

For 60 g Carb
No additions

For 80 g Carb add
½ small apple, cut into wedges

For 100 g Carb
No additions

Appetizers, Snacks, & Beverages

Artichoke-Feta Tortilla Wraps	46
Cheese-Stuffed Pecans	61
Chili Chicken Appeteasers	47
Deviled Eggs with Spicy Crab	48
Fennel and Onion Dip	58
Fresh Fruit Dip	59
Fruit Juice Cooler	64
Greek Salad Bites	49
Herbed Soy Nuts and Seeds	60
Hit-the-Spot Lemon Water	68
Hot Artichoke Dip	57
Make-Believe Champagne	67
Peppy Tomato Sipper	66
Prosciutto-Arugula Roll-Ups	50
Really Hot Iced Coffee	65
Roasted Carrot Stick Snack	54
Soy-Glazed Squash	53
Spiced Popcorn	62
Stuffed Celery Bites	52
Summertime Quencher	63
Thai Spinach Dip	56
Tortellini, Olive, and Cheese Kabobs	51
Yogurt-Herb Dip	55

Artichoke-Feta Tortilla Wraps

Three cheeses, roasted peppers, and artichokes mingle in these tortilla-wrapped treats. They're a perfect appetizer for a casual gathering of friends.

1 Coat a 3-quart rectangular baking dish with cooking spray; set aside. For filling, in a large bowl stir together the artichoke hearts, cream cheese, green onions, Parmesan cheese, feta cheese, and pesto.

2 Place about ¼ cup filling on each tortilla. Top with sweet pepper strips; roll up. Arrange tortilla rolls in the prepared baking dish. If desired, lightly coat tortilla rolls with additional cooking spray. Bake, uncovered, in a 350° oven about 15 minutes or until heated through.

3 Cut each tortilla roll into thirds and arrange on a serving platter. Serve with Yogurt-Chive Sauce.

Yogurt-Chive Sauce: In a small bowl stir together one 8-ounce carton plain fat-free yogurt and 1 tablespoon snipped fresh chives.

Nutrition Facts per appetizer: 58 cal., 2 g total fat (1 g sat. fat), 5 mg chol., 198 mg sodium, 7 g carbo., 4 g fiber, 3 g pro.

Prep: 15 minutes
Bake: 15 minutes
Oven: 350°F
Makes: 24 appetizers

Nonstick cooking spray
1   14-ounce can artichoke hearts, drained and finely chopped
½   of an 8-ounce tub (about ½ cup) reduced-fat cream cheese
3   green onions, thinly sliced
⅓   cup grated Parmesan or Romano cheese
¼   cup crumbled feta cheese (1 ounce)
3   tablespoons reduced-fat pesto
8   8-inch whole wheat flour tortillas
1   7-ounce jar roasted red sweet peppers, drained and cut into strips
1   recipe Yogurt-Chive Sauce

Chile Chicken Appeteasers

Thai garlic-chili sauce is found in the supermarket in the Asian foods section or in specialty food shops.

1 Cut the nectarines into quarters and remove the pits. Carefully scoop out some of the fruit, leaving a ¼-inch border inside the peel. Chop the scooped-out portion of nectarines.

2 In a medium bowl combine the chopped nectarine, shredded chicken, garlic-chile sauce, and cilantro. Spoon about 1 rounded teaspoon of chicken mixture onto each nectarine wedge.

Nutrition Facts per appetizer: 26 cal., 1 g total fat (0 g sat. fat), 4 mg chol., 12 mg sodium, 4 g carbo., 0 g fiber, 2 g pro.

Start to Finish: 15 minutes
Makes: 16 appetizers

- 4 medium nectarines or peaches
- ½ cup shredded cooked chicken
- 2 teaspoons Thai garlic-chile sauce or chile sauce
- 2 teaspoons snipped fresh cilantro

Deviled Eggs with Spicy Crab

Crab and chutney on top of the deviled egg mixture make these appetizers doubly delightful.

1 Halve the hard-cooked eggs lengthwise and remove yolks. Set whites aside. In a quart-size, self-sealing plastic bag place egg yolks, the ¼ cup mayonnaise, the green onion, mustard, ⅛ teaspoon of the salt, and ⅛ teaspoon of the cayenne pepper. Seal bag. Gently squeeze the bag to combine ingredients. Snip one corner of the bag and pipe mixture into egg white halves.

2 Cut up any large pieces of chutney. In a bowl combine the chutney, the 3 tablespoons mayonnaise, curry powder, remaining ⅛ teaspoon salt, and remaining ⅛ teaspoon cayenne pepper. Gently fold in crabmeat. Top each deviled egg with a spoonful of the crab mixture. Cover and chill for 1 to 2 hours.

Nutrition Facts per appetizer: 91 cal., 8 g total fat (1 g sat. fat), 113 mg chol., 119 mg sodium, 1 g carbo., 0 g fiber, 4 g pro.

Prep: 15 minutes
Chill: 1 to 2 hours
Makes: 16 appetizers

- 8 hard-cooked eggs
- ¼ cup mayonnaise or salad dressing
- 1 tablespoon finely chopped green onion
- 1 to 2 teaspoons flavored mustard, such as Dijon-style mustard or horseradish mustard
- ¼ teaspoon salt
- ¼ teaspoon cayenne pepper
- 1 to 2 tablespoons mango chutney
- 3 tablespoons mayonnaise or salad dressing
- ½ teaspoon curry powder
- ½ cup cooked crabmeat (about 2¾ ounces)

Greek Salad Bites

For ultimate impact, serve these cucumber stacks as soon as you've assembled them.

1 In a small bowl stir together feta cheese, sour cream, parsley, dried tomatoes, garlic, and pepper. Cover; chill for 2 to 24 hours.

2 Using a sharp knife, trim the ends from cucumbers; discard ends. Bias-slice the cucumbers into ¼-inch slices. Spoon 1½ teaspoons cheese mixture onto each cucumber slice. Arrange cucumber slices on a serving platter.

3 In a small bowl combine basil and olives. Spoon some of the mixture over each cucumber slice. Serve immediately.

Nutrition Facts per appetizer: 22 cal., 2 g total fat (1 g sat. fat), 5 mg chol., 57 mg sodium, 1 g carbo., 0 g fiber, 1 g pro.

Prep: 15 minutes
Chill: 2 to 24 hours
Makes: 30 appetizers

1 cup crumbled feta cheese (4 ounces)
½ cup dairy sour cream
¼ cup snipped fresh parsley
2 tablespoons oil-packed dried tomatoes, drained and finely chopped
2 cloves garlic, minced
½ teaspoon cracked black pepper
1½ medium cucumbers
¼ cup finely shredded fresh basil
¼ cup chopped pitted kalamata olives

0 g
carb

Prosciutto-Arugula Roll-Ups

The prosciutto must be sliced thin enough to roll up easily but not so thin that it tears or shreds when separating the slices. Ask your butcher to cut 8 slices that measure 9×3 inches and are about 1/16 inch thick.

1 Stir together semi-soft cheese, goat cheese, and pine nuts. Spread about 2 tablespoons cheese mixture over each prosciutto slice. Top each with arugula leaves.

2 Roll up each slice from a short side. Cut into 1/2-inch slices. Serve immediately or cover and chill up to 6 hours.

Nutrition Facts per appetizer: 33 cal., 3 g total fat (1 g sat. fat), 4 mg chol., 55 mg sodium, 0 g carbo., 0 g fiber, 2 g pro.

Start to Finish: 30 minutes
Makes: about 48 appetizers

- 1 5-ounce container semi-soft cheese with garlic and herb
- 2 ounces soft goat cheese (chèvre)
- 1/3 cup pine nuts, toasted, or chopped almonds, toasted
- 4 ounces thinly sliced prosciutto (8 slices)
- 1½ cups arugula or spinach leaves, stems removed (about 2½ ounces)

Tortellini, Olive, and Cheese Kabobs

Oil-and-vinegar dressing and purchased pesto make a marinade that's simple but full of Mediterranean flavor.

1 For marinade, in a small bowl combine salad dressing and pesto; set aside.

2 Cook tortellini according to package directions. Drain, rinse with cool water, and drain again.

3 Cut each cheese into thirty ½- to ¾-inch cubes. Thread the tortellini, cheese cubes, olives, and pickled peppers on 6-inch picks or skewers. Place skewers in a 13×9×2-inch baking dish. Brush with about half of the marinade. Cover and chill for 3 to 4 hours, brushing with remaining marinade after 2 hours.

Nutrition Facts per appetizer: 74 cal., 5 g total fat (2 g sat. fat), 10 mg chol., 291 mg sodium, 5 g carbo., 1 g fiber, 3 g pro.

Prep: 45 minutes
Chill: 3 to 4 hours
Makes: 30 appetizers

- ¾ cup bottled oil-and-vinegar salad dressing
- 3 tablespoons purchased pesto
- 2 cups frozen cheese-filled tortellini (about 9½ ounces)
- 4 ounces cheddar cheese
- 4 ounces Monterey Jack cheese with jalapeño peppers
- 30 assorted pitted olives (such as ripe, pimiento-stuffed, onion-stuffed, marinated green, or kalamata olives)
- 30 red or green pickled chile peppers

Stuffed Celery Bites

For easiest preparation, spread the cream cheese mixture in the celery first, then slice.

1 Lightly coat a skillet with cooking spray. Add pine nuts and garlic. Cook over medium heat for 3 to 5 minutes or until nuts are golden brown, stirring frequently. Set aside.

2 Remove tops and wide base from celery. Using a vegetable peeler, remove two thin strips from the rounded side of the celery, creating a flat surface.

3 In a small bowl combine the cream cheese and shredded Italian cheese. Spread or spoon cheese mixture into celery. Cut each filled stalk of celery into 2-inch pieces. Sprinkle half the pieces with the pine nut mixture and half with the sunflower seeds. If desired, stuff celery up to 4 hours before serving; cover, chill, cut, and add nuts and seeds just before serving. If desired, garnish with celery leaves.

Nutrition Facts per serving: 132 cal., 13 g total fat (7 g sat. fat), 31 mg chol., 152 mg sodium, 3 g carbo., 1 g fiber, 4 g pro.

Start to Finish: 30 minutes
Makes: 8 servings

    Nonstick cooking spray
 2 tablespoons pine nuts
 1 clove garlic, minced
 8 stalks celery
 1 8-ounce tub cream cheese with
      dried tomato or cream cheese
 ¼ cup shredded Italian cheese blend
      (1 ounce)
 2 tablespoons dry-roasted shelled
      sunflower seeds
    Celery leaves (optional)

Soy-Glazed Squash

The tan rind of the long bell-shape butternut squash is easy to remove with a vegetable peeler.

1 Place squash in a lightly greased 13×9×2-inch baking pan. In a small bowl combine orange peel, orange juice, scallions, soy sauce, brown sugar, and chile oil. Drizzle over squash, tossing to coat.

2 Roast, uncovered, in a 425° oven for 20 to 25 minutes or until squash is tender, stirring twice. Stir cubes again before serving. Place a toothpick in each squash cube. Serve warm.

Nutrition Facts per appetizer: 10 cal., 0 g total fat (0 g sat. fat), 0 mg chol., 58 mg sodium, 2 g carbo., 0 g fiber, 0 g pro.

Prep: 25 minutes
Roast: 20 minutes
Oven: 425°F
Makes: about 48 appetizers

1½   pounds butternut squash, peeled, seeded, and cut into ¾-inch cubes
1   teaspoon finely shredded orange peel
½   cup orange juice
2   scallions or green onions, finely chopped
3   tablespoons soy sauce
1   tablespoon brown sugar
2   teaspoons chile oil

Roasted Carrot Stick Snack

You can cut the prep time to almost nothing if you use purchased carrot sticks. These french-fry mimics are loaded with a whopping amount of vitamin A.

1 Peel carrots. Cut carrots into strips about 3 inches long and ½ inch wide. In a large bowl combine olive oil and snipped dill. Add carrots; toss to coat.

2 In a 15×10×1-inch baking pan spread carrots in a single layer. Roast, uncovered, in a 475° oven about 10 minutes or until carrots are just tender, stirring once. Sprinkle with coarse salt.

Prep: 20 minutes
Roast: 10 minutes
Oven: 475°F
Makes: 6 servings

6 medium carrots (1 pound)
2 to 3 teaspoons olive oil
2 tablespoons snipped fresh dill or basil
   Coarse sea salt or salt

Nutrition Facts per serving: 46 cal., 2 g total fat (0 g sat. fat), 0 mg chol., 27 mg sodium, 8 g carbo., 2 g fiber, 1 g pro.

Yogurt-Herb Dip

Cottage cheese and yogurt pair with fresh herbs for a tasty vegetable dip.

1 In a small bowl stir together the cottage cheese, yogurt, dill, chives, parsley, garlic, salt, and pepper. Cover and chill for 1 to 24 hours. Serve with vegetable dippers.

Nutrition Facts per 1 tablespoon dip with 3 celery sticks: 15 cal., 1 g total fat (0 g sat. fat), 2 mg chol., 106 mg sodium, 1 g carbo., 0 g fiber, 1 g pro.

Prep: 10 minutes
Chill: 1 to 24 hours
Makes: about 1¼ cups dip

¾ cup large-curd cottage cheese
½ cup plain yogurt
1 tablespoon snipped fresh dill
1 tablespoon snipped fresh chives
1 tablespoon snipped fresh parsley
1 large clove garlic, minced
½ teaspoon salt
⅛ teaspoon black pepper
  Vegetable dippers (such as
    celery sticks, cauliflower florets,
    and/or broccoli florets)

Thai Spinach Dip

This stir-together treat delivers big peanut flavor with a hint of heat. The dip takes just minutes to prepare.

1 In a medium bowl combine spinach, sour cream, and yogurt. Stir in mint, peanuts, peanut butter, honey, soy sauce, and crushed red pepper. Cover and chill for 2 to 24 hours. Serve with vegetable dippers.

Nutrition Facts per 1 tablespoon dip with 3 baby carrots: 44 cal., 3 g total fat (1 g sat. fat), 3 mg chol., 61 mg sodium, 4 g carbo., 1 g fiber, 1 g pro.

Prep: 15 minutes
Chill: 2 to 24 hours
Makes: about 2½ cups dip

1   cup chopped fresh spinach
1   8-ounce carton dairy sour cream
1   8-ounce carton plain fat-free yogurt
¼   cup snipped fresh mint
¼   cup finely chopped peanuts
¼   cup peanut butter
1   tablespoon honey
1   tablespoon soy sauce
1   to 2 teaspoons crushed red pepper
    Vegetable dippers (such as peeled
        baby carrots, zucchini slices,
        and/or cucumber sticks)

Hot Artichoke Dip

A combination of leeks, roasted red sweet peppers, and artichokes adds an interesting flavor twist to this hot dip.

1 In a skillet cook leek in hot butter until tender. Remove from heat. Stir in artichoke hearts, the 1 cup Parmesan cheese, sweet peppers, mayonnaise, and black pepper. Transfer mixture to an 8-inch quiche dish or 9-inch pie plate, spreading evenly. Sprinkle with the 2 tablespoons Parmesan cheese and the parsley.

2 Bake, uncovered, in a 350° oven about 20 minutes or until heated through. Serve with assorted dippers.

Nutrition Facts per 1 tablespoon dip with 3 celery sticks: 42 cal., 4 g total fat (1 g sat. fat), 4 mg chol., 88 mg sodium, 1 g carbo., 1 g fiber, 1 g pro.

Prep: 15 minutes
Bake: 20 minutes
Oven: 350°F
Makes: about 3½ cups dip

1 medium leek, quartered lengthwise and thinly sliced, or ⅓ cup sliced green onions
2 teaspoons butter or margarine
1 14-ounce can artichoke hearts, drained and coarsely chopped
1 cup grated Parmesan cheese
1 7-ounce jar roasted red sweet peppers, drained and chopped
1 cup mayonnaise or salad dressing
⅛ teaspoon black pepper
2 tablespoons grated Parmesan cheese
1 tablespoon snipped fresh parsley
Assorted vegetable dippers, flatbreads, and/or crackers

3 g
carb

Fennel and Onion Dip

Sliced green and red onion power up purchased French onion dip; fennel lends a slight anise-like flavor.

1 Wash fennel. Trim off feathery leaves. If desired, chop enough of the leaves to equal 2 tablespoons; set aside. Trim fennel bulb. Chop enough of the bulb to make 1 cup. Cut remaining bulb into strips to use for dippers.

2 In a medium bowl combine chopped fennel, onion dip, red onion, and green onion. Serve immediately or cover and chill in the refrigerator up to 24 hours. (If chilling dip, wrap and chill fennel leaves, if using.) To serve, spoon dip into serving bowl. If desired, sprinkle top with fennel leaves and snipped lemon thyme. Serve with vegetable dippers.

Nutrition Facts per 1 tablespoon dip with 3 fennel strips: 31 cal., 2 g total fat (1 g sat. fat), 0 mg chol., 105 mg sodium, 3 g carbo., 1 g fiber, 1 g pro.

Start to Finish: 15 minutes
Makes: about 2¼ cups dip

- 1 medium fennel bulb
- 1 16-ounce container dairy sour cream French onion dip
- 2 tablespoons finely chopped red onion
- 2 tablespoons thinly sliced green onion
  Snipped fresh lemon thyme and/or snipped fresh chives (optional)
  Vegetable dippers (such as strips of fennel, baby carrots, halved or sliced radishes, sliced cucumbers, and/or sliced zucchini)

Fresh Fruit Dip

**Just three ingredients make up the super-easy dip.
Select fresh fruits that are in season for the dippers.**

1 In a small bowl stir together yogurt, applesauce, and cinnamon. To serve, spear fruit with decorative toothpicks and dip into yogurt mixture.

Nutrition Facts per 1 tablespoon dip with 3 pineapple chunks: 23 cal., 0 g total fat (0 g sat. fat), 1 mg chol., 8 mg sodium, 5 g carbo., 0 g fiber, 1 g pro.

**Start to Finish: 15 minutes
Makes: about 1¼ cups dip**

1   8-ounce carton vanilla low-fat yogurt
¼   cup unsweetened applesauce
⅛   teaspoon ground cinnamon, nutmeg,
      or ginger
    Fresh fruit dippers (such as pineapple
      chunks, strawberries, apple slices,
      and/or peach slices)

Herbed Soy Nuts and Seeds

This addictive party mix is a tasty way to incorporate soy in your diet.

1 In a medium bowl stir together oil, chili powder, basil, oregano, and garlic powder. Add soy nuts and pumpkin seeds; toss to coat. Spread the mixture in a 13×9×2-inch baking pan.

2 Bake, uncovered, in a 350° oven for 15 to 20 minutes or until soy nuts are toasted, stirring after 10 minutes. Stir in dried vegetables.

Nutrition Facts per serving: 126 cal., 8 g total fat (2 g sat. fat), 0 mg chol., 48 mg sodium, 8 g carbo., 2 g fiber, 7 g pro.

*Note: If using unsalted roasted soy nuts, add ⅛ teaspoon salt to the chili powder mixture.

Prep: 10 minutes
Bake: 15 minutes
Oven: 350°F
Makes: 10 servings

- 1 tablespoon olive oil or cooking oil
- 1 teaspoon chili powder
- 1 teaspoon dried basil, crushed
- ½ teaspoon dried oregano, crushed
- ¼ teaspoon garlic powder
- 1½ cups salted roasted soy nuts*
- ½ cup raw pumpkin seeds
- ½ cup dried vegetables (such as carrots, corn, and/or peas)

Cheese-Stuffed Pecans

To pipe the Gouda mixture onto these company-pleasing pecan nibbles, spoon the mixture into a self-sealing plastic bag and snip off a corner.

1 In a medium mixing bowl allow shredded cheese to stand at room temperature for 30 minutes. Add sour cream. Beat with an electric mixer until mixture is creamy. Using a scant teaspoon for each, pipe or mound cheese mixture onto the flat side of half of the pecans. Top with remaining pecans, flat side down. Cover and chill for 30 minutes.

Nutrition Facts per serving: 102 cal., 10 g total fat (3 g sat. fat), 14 mg chol., 94 mg sodium, 1 g carbo., 1 g fiber, 4 g pro.

Prep: 20 minutes
Stand: 30 minutes
Chill: 30 minutes
Makes: 10 servings

1 cup finely shredded Gouda cheese
   (4 ounces)
3 tablespoons dairy sour cream
40 large pecan halves

6 g
carb

Spiced Popcorn

Popcorn is a crunchy low-cal snack that's especially tasty when seasoned with some spicy ingredients.

1 In a small bowl stir together the cumin, chili powder, salt, cayenne pepper, and ground cinnamon.

2 Spread popped popcorn in an even layer in a large shallow baking pan. Lightly coat popcorn with cooking spray. Sprinkle the cumin mixture evenly over popcorn; toss to coat.

Nutrition Facts per serving: 31 cal., 0 g total fat (0 g sat. fat), 0 mg chol., 50 mg sodium, 6 g carbo., 1 g fiber, 1 g pro.

Indian Spiced Popcorn: Prepare Spiced Popcorn as directed, except substitute ½ teaspoon curry powder, ½ teaspoon garam masala, ¼ teaspoon ground turmeric, and ¼ teaspoon black pepper for the cumin, chili powder, cayenne pepper, and cinnamon.

Nutrition Facts per 1-cup serving: 31 cal., 0 g total fat (0 g sat. fat), 0 mg chol., 49 mg sodium, 6 g carbo., 1 g fiber, 1 g pro.

Start to Finish: 10 minutes
Makes: 12 servings

- ½ teaspoon ground cumin
- ½ teaspoon chili powder
- ¼ to ½ teaspoon salt
  Dash cayenne pepper
  Dash ground cinnamon
- 12 cups popped popcorn
  Nonstick cooking spray

Summertime Quencher

Stir gently to prevent the fruit from breaking apart in this white Sangria-like drink.

1 Cut lemon and orange in half crosswise. Cut 1 lemon half and 1 orange half into ¼-inch slices. Squeeze the juice from remaining halves.

2 Place lemon and orange juices in a 2-quart pitcher. Stir in wine, carbonated water, lemon and orange slices, kiwifruit, blackberries, cherries, and strawberries. Serve over ice.

Nutrition Facts per serving: 25 cal., 0 g total fat (0 g sat. fat), 0 mg chol., 13 mg sodium, 4 g carbo., 0 g fiber, 0 g pro.

Start to Finish: 15 minutes
Makes: 8 servings

- 1 lemon
- 1 orange
- 1 750-ml bottle white Zinfandel wine or
     3¼ cups apple juice, chilled
- 2 cups carbonated water, chilled
- 1 unpeeled kiwifriut, sliced
- ¼ cup fresh blackberries, raspberries,
     or other berries
- 8 dark sweet cherries, pitted
- 8 fresh strawberries
     Ice cubes

Fruit Juice Cooler

Sit back, sip, and enjoy this four-fruit beverage on a sweltering afternoon.

1 In a pitcher stir together the peach nectar, orange juice, grapefruit juice, and lemon juice. Slowly stir in the sparkling water. Serve over ice. If desired, garnish with star fruit slices.

Nutrition Facts per serving: 71 cal., 0 g total fat (0 g sat. fat), 0 mg chol., 8 mg sodium, 18 g carbo., 1 g fiber, 1 g pro.

Start to Finish: 10 minutes
Makes: 4 (about 8-ounce) servings

1½ cups peach nectar, chilled
½ cup orange juice, chilled
¼ cup grapefruit juice, chilled
1 tablespoon lemon juice
1½ cups sparkling mineral water, chilled
   Ice cubes
   Star fruit slices (optional)

Really Hot Iced Coffee

A little bit of red pepper, cinnamon, and cardamom in this iced coffee brew is enough to wake up your taste buds.

1 Measure ground coffee into filter-lined coffeemaker basket. Add the cinnamon, pepper, and cardamom. Prepare the coffee according to coffeemaker instructions. Chill for at least 1 hour. Pour into an ice-filled pitcher. To serve, pour into tall, ice-filled glasses and, if desired, sweeten with sugar substitute, top with whipped cream, and sprinkle with nutmeg.

Nutrition Facts per serving: 5 cal., 0 g total fat (0 g sat. fat), 0 mg chol., 5 mg sodium, 1 g carbo., 0 g fiber, 0 g pro.

Prep: 15 minutes
Chill: 1 hour
Makes: 10 servings

⅓ cup ground coffee
2 inches stick cinnamon
¼ to ½ teaspoon crushed red pepper
6 pods cardamom, crushed,
     or ¼ teaspoon ground cardamom
   Ice cubes
   Sugar substitute (optional)
½ cup whipped cream (optional)
½ teaspoon ground nutmeg (optional)

12 g
carb

Peppy Tomato Sipper

Tomato juice never tasted so good, thanks to the citrus juice and horseradish additions. Shake in enough hot pepper sauce to suit your taste.

1 In a small pitcher stir together tomato juice, lime juice, Worcestershire sauce, horseradish, and hot pepper sauce. Serve over ice.

Nutrition Facts per serving: 48 cal., 0 g total fat (0 g sat. fat), 0 mg chol., 911 mg sodium, 12 g carbo., 4 g fiber, 2 g pro.

Start to Finish: 10 minutes
Makes: 2 servings

2 cups tomato juice or vegetable juice
2 tablespoons lime juice or lemon juice
1 teaspoon Worcestershire sauce
½ teaspoon prepared horseradish
Few drops bottled hot pepper sauce
Ice cubes

Make-Believe Champagne

When you're having a celebration, have this nonalcoholic version on hand for toasting.

1 In a large pitcher combine the carbonated water, ginger ale, and white grape juice. Pour over ice cubes in chilled champagne glasses or wine glasses.

Nutrition Facts per serving: 37 cal., 0 g total fat (0 g sat. fat), 0 mg chol., 14 mg sodium, 9 g carbo., 0 g fiber, 0 g pro.

Start to Finish: 10 minutes
Makes: about 20 servings

1 1-liter bottle carbonated water, chilled
1 1-liter bottle ginger ale, chilled
1 24-ounce bottle unsweetened
     white grape juice, chilled
   Ice cubes

4 g
carb

Hit-the-Spot Lemon Water

You'll be amazed at the refreshing flavors that emerge when you soak lemons and fresh herbs in water for an hour or so. No sugar. Just pure, thirst-quenching goodness.

1 Place lemon slices in a large pitcher. Carefully rub the 1½ cups mint leaves between the palms of your hands to slightly bruise the leaves. Add to the pitcher with lemon. Pour in water. Cover and chill for 1 to 8 hours.

2 Strain lemon-water mixture. Discard herbs. Divide lemon slices and additional fresh mint equally among 6 to 8 tall glasses or pint-sized canning jars. For each serving, add 1 cup of ice cubes; fill with the lemon-water mixture.

Prep: 15 minutes
Chill: 1 to 8 hours
Makes: 6 to 8 servings

- 4 lemons, sliced
- 1½ cups firmly packed fresh mint
    or basil leaves
- 6 to 8 cups bottled water or tap water
    Fresh mint or basil sprigs
- 6 to 8 cups ice cubes

Nutrition Facts per serving: 11 cal., 0 g total fat (0 g sat. fat), 0 mg chol., 8 mg sodium, 4 g carbo., 1 g fiber, 0 g pro.

Salads & Salad Dressings

Artichoke and Orange Salad	70
Arugula and Pea Salad	73
Asian Pea Pod Salad	81
Asparagus and Carrots with Asian Vinaigrette	74
Asparagus Finger Salad	77
Big Green Salad with Two-Pepper Dressing	83
Black Bean Salad	87
Butternut Squash Salad	80
Cantaloupe and Tomato Salad	84
Confetti Summer Salad	85
Cranberry-Walnut Cabbage Slaw	78
Italian Bean and Artichoke Salad	86
Jicama-Berry Salad	75
Lemony Caesar Salad	88
Mesclun with Oranges and Olives	76
Orange-Beet Salad	89
Skillet-Roasted Potato Salad	90
Sparkling Kumquat Salad	82
Spring Asparagus Slaw	79
Stacked Tomato Salad	72
Summer Rice Salad	91
Tomato and Sweet Pepper Salad	71
Vegetable Pasta Salad	92

15 g carb

Artichoke and Orange Salad

To ensure that artichokes keep their bright green color, add them to a bowl of water and lemon juice as you trim and clean them.

1 In a medium bowl combine the 1 cup water and lemon juice; set aside. Wash artichokes and trim stems. Peel and snap back leaves at the base until you reach the leaves that have yellow at the bottom. Cut off the top one-third of the leaves. Cut each artichoke into quarters lengthwise. Place artichoke quarters in the bowl with lemon and water; let stand for 10 minutes.

2 In a large saucepan bring 2 inches water to boiling; add artichokes. Reduce heat. Simmer, covered, about 10 minutes or until artichokes are tender. Drain well.

3 Meanwhile, finely shred enough orange peel to measure 1 teaspoon. Juice 1 orange (you should have ⅓ cup juice). In a large bowl combine the orange peel, orange juice, olive oil, balsamic vinegar, salt, and pepper. Add artichokes, onion, and olives; stir to coat. Let stand for 10 minutes.

4 Meanwhile, peel remaining 2 oranges. Slice crosswise into ¼-inch slices. Add to artichoke mixture. Gently toss mixture. Arrange artichokes, onion slices, olives, and orange slices on salad plates.

Start to Finish: 35 minutes
Makes: 6 side-dish servings

- 1 cup water
- 1 tablespoon lemon juice
- 8 to 10 baby artichokes
- 3 oranges
- 3 tablespoons olive oil
- 2 tablespoons balsamic vinegar
- ¼ teaspoon salt
- ¼ teaspoon black pepper
- 1 small red onion, thinly sliced
- ¾ cup pitted kalamata olives or other black olives

Nutrition Facts per serving: 142 cal., 9 g total fat (1 g sat. fat), 0 mg chol., 321 mg sodium, 15 g carbo., 4 g fiber, 2 g pro.

Tomato and Sweet Pepper Salad

When the summer tomatoes and peppers are at their best, try this salad to serve with barbecued meat or poultry hot off the grill.

1 For dressing, in a screw-top jar combine oil, vinegar, chives, basil, sugar, mustard, and black pepper. Cover; shake well. Chill.

2 In a skillet cook sweet pepper rings, covered, in a small amount of boiling water for 1 to 2 minutes or just until crisp-tender; drain and cool. Chill, if desired.

3 To serve, arrange the tomato wedges and sweet pepper rings on a spinach-lined platter. Sprinkle with crumbled cheese. Shake dressing to mix; drizzle over salad.

Nutrition Facts per serving: 204 cal., 13 g total fat (5 g sat. fat), 16 mg chol., 323 mg sodium, 16 g carbo., 3 g fiber, 7 g pro.

Start to Finish: 30 minutes
Makes: 4 to 6 side-dish servings

- 2 tablespoons olive oil
- 2 tablespoons white wine vinegar or balsamic vinegar
- 1 tablespoon snipped fresh chives or sliced green onion
- 2 teaspoons snipped fresh basil
- 1 teaspoon sugar
- ½ teaspoon Dijon-style mustard
- ⅛ teaspoon black pepper
- 3 large yellow sweet peppers, thinly sliced into rings (about 3 cups)
- 3 large tomatoes (1 pound), cut into wedges
  Fresh spinach leaves
- ⅔ cup crumbled Gorgonzola or blue cheese (3 ounces)

5 g
carb

Stacked Tomato Salad

If you prefer, you can substitute already cooked shrimp instead of peeling and deveining your own fresh shrimp. Peeled, deveined cooked shrimp is often available at many supermarkets.

1 For shrimp, in a large saucepan bring 4 cups water, the 1 teaspoon salt, and ½ teaspoon of the pepper to boiling. Add shrimp. Simmer, uncovered, for 1 to 3 minutes or until shrimp turn pink, stirring occasionally. Rinse under cold running water; drain well and chill.

2 For dressing, in a screw-top jar combine lime juice, tequila, salad oil, marjoram, ¼ teaspoon salt, and the ¼ teaspoon pepper. Cover and shake well.

3 Cut each tomato vertically into 6 slices. Keeping slices loosely together so you can reassemble them easily later on, place in a 2-quart square baking dish. Pour dressing over tomatoes. Cover and chill for 2 to 4 hours.

4 Remove tomatoes from dish, reserving dressing. Place a tomato slice on each of 6 salad plates. Top with about 1 tablespoon of the shredded jicama. Repeat layers, alternately stacking tomatoes and shredded vegetables, and ending with a tomato slice. Top each salad with a cooked shrimp. Drizzle each salad with reserved dressing.

Prep: 30 minutes
Chill: 2 to 4 hours
Makes: 6 side-dish servings

- 6 large shrimp, peeled and deveined
- 1 teaspoon salt
- ½ teaspoon black pepper
- 2 tablespoons lime juice
- 2 tablespoons tequila or orange juice
- 1 tablespoon salad oil
- 2 teaspoons snipped fresh marjoram
- ¼ teaspoon salt
- ¼ teaspoon black pepper
- 3 small yellow, orange, ripe green, and/or red tomatoes (about 12 ounces total), cored
- 1 cup peeled jicama, peeled kohlrabi, yellow summer squash, and/or zucchini, coarsely shredded (about 6 ounces)

Nutrition Facts per serving: 75 cal., 3 g total fat (0 g sat. fat), 28 mg chol., 138 mg sodium, 5 g carbo., 0 g fiber, 5 g pro.

7g
carb

Arugula and Pea Salad

**Don't have a serving platter big enough for this elegant salad?
Make individual salads or toss the mixture in an extra large bowl.**

1 In a medium saucepan cook peas, covered, in a small amount of boiling salted water for 3 minutes. Drain and cool. Arrange peas, green onions, arugula, and Swiss chard in rows on a large platter or in a serving bowl.

2 In a screw-top jar combine the Strawberry Vinegar and salad oil. Cover and shake well. Drizzle over salad. Store any remaining dressing in the refrigerator.

Strawberry Vinegar: In a medium stainless-steel saucepan combine 1 cup chopped fresh strawberries and 1 cup cider vinegar. Bring to boiling; reduce heat. Simmer, uncovered, for 3 minutes. Remove from heat. Pour the vinegar-berry mixture through a fine-mesh strainer; let liquid drain into a bowl. Discard the berries. Transfer vinegar to a jar or bottle. Cover tightly with a nonmetallic lid (or cover with plastic wrap and tightly seal with a metal lid). Chill for at least 1 hour. Store in the refrigerator up to 6 months. Makes 1¼ cups.

Prep: 35 minutes
Chill: 1 hour
Makes: 8 to 10 side-dish servings

2 cups fresh shelled peas (about 1½ pounds unshelled)
1 cup 3- to 4-inch strips green onions
6 cups arugula or baby spinach
4 cups baby Swiss chard, torn red-tip leaf lettuce, or torn romaine lettuce
¼ cup Strawberry Vinegar or purchased raspberry vinegar
¼ cup salad oil

Nutrition Facts per serving: 97 cal., 7 g total fat (1 g sat. fat), 0 mg chol., 38 mg sodium, 7 g carbo., 2 g fiber, 3 g pro.

Asparagus and Carrots with Asian Vinaigrette

The quick chilling in ice water stops the cooking process of the asparagus and carrots so that they don't overcook.

1 In a medium skillet cook carrots, covered, in a small amount of boiling water for 2 minutes. Meanwhile, snap off and discard woody bases from asparagus. If desired, scrape off scales from asparagus. Add asparagus spears to carrots. Cook, covered, for 4 to 6 minutes more or until vegetables are crisp-tender. Drain; immediately plunge vegetables into ice water. Let stand for 1 minute. Drain and pat dry.

2 Line salad plates with lettuce. Arrange carrots, asparagus, and mushrooms on lettuce. Drizzle with Asian Vinaigrette. If desired, sprinkle with sesame seeds.

Asian Vinaigrette: In a small bowl combine ¼ cup bottled Italian salad dressing, 1 tablespoon soy sauce, 1 teaspoon toasted sesame oil, and ¼ teaspoon crushed red pepper.

Nutrition Facts per serving: 128 cal., 9 g total fat (1 g sat. fat), 0 mg chol., 416 mg sodium, 12 g carbo., 3 g fiber, 3 g pro.

Prep: 20 minutes
Cook: 6 minutes
Makes: 4 side-dish servings

- 8 ounces baby carrots with tops, trimmed to 2 inches, or packaged peeled baby carrots
- 12 asparagus spears
- 4 cups torn red-tip leaf lettuce or leaf lettuce
- 1 cup fresh enoki mushrooms
- 1 recipe Asian Vinaigrette
- 2 teaspoons sesame seeds, toasted (optional)

Jicama-Berry Salad

Jicama, a tuberous root vegetable, adds both a crunchy texture and a slightly sweet flavor to this fruit and vegetable salad. Cut any leftover jicama into sticks for a low-fat snack or to serve on veggie trays.

1 Line salad plates with romaine. Arrange the sliced strawberries and jicama on top of romaine leaves.

2 For dressing, in a screw-top jar combine vinegar, orange juice, shallots, mint, oil, and seasoning blend. Cover and shake well. Drizzle dressing over salads. If desired, garnish with whole strawberries.

Nutrition Facts per serving: 89 cal., 4 g total fat (0 g sat. fat), 0 mg chol., 5 mg sodium, 13 g carbo., 2 g fiber, 2 g pro.

Start to Finish: 20 minutes
Makes: 4 side-dish servings

Romaine leaves and/or white
    kale leaves
2 cups sliced fresh strawberries
1 cup peeled jicama cut into thin
    bite-size strips
3 tablespoons white wine vinegar
3 tablespoons orange juice
2 shallots, finely chopped
1 tablespoon snipped fresh mint
    or ½ teaspoon dried mint, crushed
1 tablespoon olive oil or salad oil
    Dash salt-free seasoning blend
    Whole fresh strawberries (optional)

Mesclun with Oranges and Olives

Mesclun is a mixture of young, small salad greens and can include arugula, dandelion, frisée, mâche, mizuna, oak leaf lettuce, radicchio, and sorrel.

1 Place greens in a large salad bowl. For dressing, in a small mixing bowl whisk together the olive oil, orange juice, and vinegar. Pour dressing over greens; gently toss to mix.

2 Divide mixture among salad plates. Top with onion rings, orange sections, and olives. Lightly sprinkle with the salt and pepper.

Nutrition Facts per serving: 103 cal., 7 g total fat (1 g sat. fat), 0 mg chol., 151 mg sodium, 10 g carbo., 3 g fiber, 1 g pro.

Start to Finish: 15 minutes
Makes: 8 side-dish servings

- 12 cups mesclun or other mild salad greens
- 3   tablespoons olive oil
- 2   tablespoons orange juice
- 2   tablespoons balsamic vinegar
- 8   thin slices red onion, separated into rings
- 2   cups orange sections (6 oranges)
- ⅔   cup mixed country olives or kalamata olives
- ⅛   teaspoon salt
- ⅛   teaspoon black pepper

Asparagus Finger Salad

These crisp-tender asparagus and carrot spears are wrapped in lettuce leaves and drizzled with a sour cream-lemon dipping sauce.

1 Snap off and discard woody bases from asparagus. If desired, scrape off scales from asparagus spears. Cook asparagus, covered, in a small amount of boiling water for 2 to 4 minutes or until crisp-tender. Transfer to a bowl filled with ice water. Set aside.

2 For dipping sauce, in a small bowl combine sour cream, chives, lemon juice, tarragon, salt, and pepper. Cover and chill until serving time.

3 To serve, cut center vein from each lettuce leaf, keeping each leaf in one piece. Place lettuce leaves on a serving plate. Pat asparagus dry with paper towels. Cut each carrot half into 4 equal lengthwise strips. Place equal amounts of asparagus and carrot strips across middle of each lettuce leaf. Sprinkle each serving with finely shredded lemon peel. Wrap lettuce around asparagus and carrots. Place each asparagus salad upright in a small cup. Serve or drizzle with dipping sauce.

Prep: 15 minutes
Cook: 2 minutes
Makes: 4 side-dish servings

- 8 ounces asparagus spears
- ⅓ cup light dairy sour cream
- 1 tablespoon snipped fresh chives
- 2 teaspoons lemon juice
- 1 teaspoon snipped fresh tarragon
- ⅛ teaspoon salt
- ⅛ teaspoon black pepper
- 4 large butterhead lettuce or romaine leaves
- 1 small carrot, halved lengthwise
- 2 teaspoons finely shredded lemon peel

Nutrition Facts per serving: 49 cal., 3 g total fat (2 g sat. fat), 8 mg chol., 93 mg sodium, 5 g carbo., 2 g fiber, 2 g pro.

Cranberry-Walnut Cabbage Slaw

Red sweet pepper and dried cranberries add a spark of color to a creamy coleslaw mixture.

1 In a small bowl stir together mayonnaise, pickle relish, honey mustard, honey, pepper, salt, and celery seeds.

2 In a large bowl combine cabbage, walnuts, celery, onion, sweet pepper, and cranberries. Add mayonnaise mixture to cabbage mixture and toss to coat. Cover and chill for 1 to 6 hours.

Nutrition Facts per serving: 124 cal., 9 g total fat (1 g sat. fat), 4 mg chol., 104 mg sodium, 12 g carbo., 2 g fiber, 2 g pro.

Prep: 20 minutes
Chill: 1 to 6 hours
Makes: 8 to 10 side-dish servings

¼ cup mayonnaise or salad dressing
1 tablespoon sweet pickle relish
1 tablespoon honey mustard
1 tablespoon honey
¼ teaspoon white or black pepper
⅛ teaspoon salt
⅛ teaspoon celery seeds
5 cups shredded green cabbage
⅓ cup chopped walnuts
¼ cup finely chopped celery
¼ cup finely chopped onion
¼ cup finely chopped red sweet pepper
¼ cup dried cranberries

Spring Asparagus Slaw

If you're not familiar with radicchio, the leaves have a bitter and peppery taste when eaten alone, but small amounts add a nice flavor and color accent to green tossed salads.

1 Snap off and discard woody bases from asparagus. If desired, scrape off scales from asparagus spears. In a medium saucepan bring 1 inch of water to boiling. Place asparagus in steamer basket. Cover; steam asparagus over the boiling water for 4 to 6 minutes or until crisp-tender. Drain. Gently rinse with cool water.

2 Meanwhile, in a large bowl toss together cabbage, radicchio, carrot, mint, parsley, and onion. Divide asparagus spears among salad plates; top with cabbage mixture.

3 In a screw-top jar combine oil, vinegar, lemon peel, lemon juice, garlic, and pepper. Cover and shake to combine. Pour over cabbage mixture. Sprinkle slaw with Parmesan cheese.

Nutrition Facts per serving: 76 cal., 5 g total fat (1 g sat. fat), 3 mg chol., 56 mg sodium, 6 g carbo., 2 g fiber, 3 g pro.

Start to Finish: 25 minutes
Makes: 8 to 10 side-dish servings

- 1 **pound asparagus spears**
- 4 **cups shredded green cabbage**
- 1 **cup torn radicchio or red cabbage**
- ½ **cup finely shredded carrot**
- ¼ **cup snipped fresh mint**
- ¼ **cup snipped fresh parsley**
- ¼ **of a small red onion, thinly sliced**
- 2 **tablespoons olive oil**
- 2 **tablespoons balsamic vinegar**
- ½ **teaspoon finely shredded lemon peel**
- 1 **tablespoon lemon juice**
- 1 **clove garlic, minced**
- ½ **teaspoon black pepper**
- ¼ **cup shredded Parmesan cheese**

Butternut Squash Salad

Serve this squash salad with grilled or broiled pork chops for an unbeatable fall dinner.

1 In a large skillet cook squash in hot oil over medium heat about 5 minutes or until squash is golden brown, turning slices occasionally. Add broth, sage, salt, and pepper. Cook, covered, for 5 minutes more or until squash is just tender, turning slices once or twice.

2 In a large salad bowl toss greens with apple and onion; set aside. Drizzle Sage Vinaigrette over greens and toss gently. Remove squash with a slotted spoon and place on salad greens. Sprinkle with cheese.

Sage Vinaigrette: In a screw-top jar combine 3 tablespoons balsamic vinegar; 3 tablespoons olive oil; 1 tablespoon snipped fresh sage or 1 teaspoon dried sage, crushed; ¼ teaspoon salt; and ¼ teaspoon black pepper. Cover; shake well.

Nutrition Facts per serving: 130 cal., 9 g total fat (2 g sat. fat), 3 mg chol., 203 mg sodium, 11 g carbo., 2 g fiber, 3 g pro.

Prep: 20 minutes
Cook: 10 minutes
Makes: 8 side-dish servings

1 pound butternut squash, peeled, halved lengthwise, seeded, and cut into ½-inch slices (about 3 cups)
1 tablespoon olive oil
¼ cup chicken broth or vegetable broth
1 tablespoon snipped fresh sage or ½ teaspoon dried sage, crushed
¼ teaspoon salt
¼ teaspoon black pepper
6 cups torn mixed salad greens
1 medium apple, cored and cut into bite-size pieces
½ medium red onion, thinly sliced
1 recipe Sage Vinaigrette
2 ounces goat cheese (chèvre), crumbled

Asian Pea Pod Salad

**To toast sesame seeds, spread them in a single layer in a shallow baking pan.
Bake in a 350°F oven for 5 to 10 minutes or until light golden brown.
Watch them carefully and stir once or twice so they don't burn.**

1 In a large salad bowl toss together the romaine and pea pods. In a small bowl stir together the dressing and hoisin sauce. Pour over romaine mixture and toss to coat. Sprinkle with sesame seeds.

Nutrition Facts per serving: 98 cal., 7 g total fat (1 g sat. fat), 0 mg chol., 153 mg sodium, 6 g carbo., 2 g fiber, 2 g pro.

Start to Finish: 20 minutes
Makes: 6 side-dish servings

- 6 cups torn romaine
- 2 cups fresh pea pods, trimmed and halved crosswise
- ⅓ cup bottled Italian salad dressing
- 1 tablespoon bottled hoisin sauce
- 1 tablespoon sesame seeds, toasted

Sparkling Kumquat Salad

Kumquats have pale orange meat and a combination of sweet and tart flavors. The fruit and the tangy skin are both edible.

1 In a small bowl combine walnut pieces, pomegranate seeds, fennel tops, and 1 tablespoon of the Sparkling Vinaigrette; set aside.

2 In a large salad bowl combine salad greens, sliced fennel, kumquats, salt, and pepper. Drizzle with remaining Sparkling Vinaigrette. Toss gently to coat. Sprinkle the salad with the walnut mixture.

Sparkling Vinaigrette: In a blender container or small food processor bowl combine ½ cup coarsely chopped and seeded kumquats, ½ cup chilled sparkling white wine or chilled alcohol-free sparkling white grape beverage, ¼ cup walnut oil, 1 quartered shallot, ¼ teaspoon salt, ⅛ teaspoon black pepper, and ⅛ teaspoon ground coriander or ground cardamom. Cover and blend or process until nearly smooth.

Nutrition Facts per serving: 130 cal., 8 g total fat (1 g sat. fat), 0 mg chol., 139 mg sodium, 12 g carbo., 4 g fiber, 2 g pro.

Start to Finish: 30 minutes
Makes: 10 side-dish servings

- ⅓ cup walnut pieces, toasted
- ⅓ cup pomegranate seeds
- 2 tablespoons snipped fresh fennel leafy tops
- 1 recipe Sparkling Vinaigrette
- 12 cups torn mixed salad greens
- 1 fennel bulb, trimmed and thinly sliced
- ½ cup kumquats, seeds removed and thinly sliced
- ¼ teaspoon salt
- ⅛ teaspoon black pepper

Big Green Salad with Two-Pepper Dressing

**You can prepare the dressing ahead of time.
Bring it back to room temperature before you toss the salad together.**

1 In a large salad bowl combine lettuce, mint, watercress, daikon, and cilantro. Slowly add Two-Pepper Dressing; toss to coat. Serve immediately.

Two-Pepper Dressing: In a screw-top jar combine ½ cup finely chopped green sweet pepper; ⅓ cup rice vinegar; 3 tablespoons salad oil; 1 fresh Anaheim or jalapeño chile pepper, seeded and finely chopped (see note, page 96); 1 clove garlic, minced; ½ teaspoon sugar; ¼ teaspoon salt; and ¼ teaspoon black pepper. Cover and shake well. Refrigerate until ready to use.

Nutrition Facts per serving: 86 cal., 7 g total fat (1 g sat. fat), 0 mg chol., 112 mg sodium, 4 g carbo., 1 g fiber, 1 g pro.

Start to Finish: 30 minutes
Makes: 6 side-dish servings

- 4 cups torn butterhead lettuce (2 medium heads)
- 1 cup fresh mint sprigs
- 1 cup fresh watercress sprigs
- 1 cup daikon, peeled and cut into 1-inch strips
- ¾ cup fresh cilantro sprigs
- 1 recipe Two-Pepper Dressing

Cantaloupe and Tomato Salad

This salad makes a delightful potluck or picnic dish. Tote the ingredients in separate containers or sealed plastic bags and keep them in a cooler. Toss them together just before it's time to eat.

1 For dressing, in a screw-top jar combine olive oil, balsamic vinegar, green onion, salt, and pepper. Shake well to combine.

2 In a large salad bowl carefully toss together the watercress, cantaloupe wedges, and tomatoes. Sprinkle with goat cheese. Drizzle with dressing. Toss gently to coat.

Nutrition Facts per serving: 149 cal., 11 g total fat (4 g sat. fat), 11 mg chol., 160 mg sodium, 9 g carbo., 1 g fiber, 4 g pro.

Start to Finish: 25 minutes
Makes: 8 side-dish servings

- ¼ cup olive oil
- 2 tablespoons balsamic vinegar
- 1 green onion, finely chopped
- ¼ teaspoon salt
- ¼ teaspoon black pepper
- 2 cups lightly packed watercress
- 1 medium cantaloupe, halved, seeded, peeled, and cut into thin wedges
- 2 cups red and/or yellow pear or cherry tomatoes, halved or quartered
- 4 ounces crumbled goat cheese (chèvre) with garlic and herbs

Confetti Summer Salad

Zucchini, sweet peppers, onion, and corn create this versatile side-dish salad.

1 In a large bowl combine zucchini, sweet peppers, onions, corn, tomatoes, salad dressing, and salsa. Cover and chill for 4 to 24 hours, stirring occasionally. If desired, serve salad on radicchio leaves or garnish with purple flowering kale.

Nutrition Facts per serving: 85 cal., 3 g total fat (0 g sat. fat), 1 mg chol., 310 mg sodium, 16 g carbo., 2 g fiber, 2 g pro.

Prep: 15 minutes
Chill: 4 to 24 hours
Makes: 6 to 8 side-dish servings

½ medium zucchini, halved lengthwise and cut into ¼-inch slices (1 cup)

1 medium sweet yellow pepper, cut into thin strips

1 medium sweet red pepper, cut into thin strips

2 medium green onions, sliced

1 15- to 16-ounce can whole kernel corn, drained

2 medium tomatoes, seeded and cut into ½-inch pieces (1½ cups)

½ cup bottled reduced-calorie Italian salad dressing

½ cup bottled hot salsa

Radicchio leaves or purple flowering kale (optional)

Italian Bean and Artichoke Salad

Toasting nuts brings out their flavor. To toast them, spread the nuts in a single layer in a shallow baking pan. Bake in a 350°F oven for 5 to 10 minutes or until light golden brown, watching carefully. Stir once or twice during baking so the nuts don't burn.

1 In a large bowl combine the drained beans, drained artichoke hearts, and sweet pepper strips. Set aside.

2 For dressing, in a screw-top jar combine oil, vinegar, honey mustard, salt, and cayenne pepper. Cover and shake well. Pour dressing over bean mixture. Stir gently to coat. Cover and chill for 6 to 24 hours, stirring once or twice.

3 To serve, spoon vegetables and marinade over romaine; sprinkle with walnuts.

Nutrition Facts per serving: 141 cal., 10 g total fat (1 g sat. fat), 0 mg chol., 143 mg sodium, 11 g carbo., 5 g fiber, 3 g pro.

Prep: 30 minutes
Chill: 6 to 24 hours
Makes: 6 side-dish servings

1 9-ounce package frozen Italian or cut green beans, cooked and drained
1 8- or 9-ounce package frozen artichoke hearts, cooked and drained
1 medium red sweet pepper, cut into thin bite-size strips
3 tablespoons walnut oil or salad oil
3 tablespoons white wine vinegar
1 tablespoon honey mustard
¼ teaspoon salt
⅛ teaspoon cayenne pepper
4 cups torn romaine
¼ cup chopped walnuts or pecans, toasted

Black Bean Salad

Dried beans contain almost no fat or salt, provide a superior source of fiber, and are good in the protein department too.

1 In a large bowl toss together the beans, sweet peppers, onion, cilantro, and jalapeño pepper. For dressing, in a small bowl combine lemon juice, olive oil, and garlic; add salt and black pepper to taste.

2 Stir dressing into bean mixture until evenly coated. Cover and chill in the refrigerator for 2 to 24 hours.

Nutrition Facts per serving: 91 cal., 3 g total fat (0 g sat. fat), 0 mg chol., 3 mg sodium, 14 g carbo., 4 g fiber, 4 g pro.

*Note: To cook dried beans, in a saucepan bring to boiling ⅔ cup dried beans with water to cover; remove from heat and let stand for 1 hour. Drain beans and add 2 cups fresh water. Cook, covered, over low heat for 1 to 1½ hours or until beans are tender.

Prep: 10 minutes
Chill: 2 to 24 hours
Makes: 6 side-dish servings

- 1½ cups cooked and drained black beans* or one 15-ounce can black beans, rinsed and drained
- ⅓ cup each red, green, and yellow sweet peppers, cut into ½-inch pieces (1 cup total)
- ½ medium red onion, chopped (¼ cup)
- ¼ cup snipped fresh cilantro
- 1 jalapeño pepper, seeded and chopped (see note, page 96)
- 2 tablespoons lemon juice
- 1 tablespoon extra-virgin olive oil
- 1 large clove garlic, minced

Lemony Caesar Salad

The traditional Caesar salad calls for raw egg, a practice that's best left behind. This dressing is cooked to make it safe for any diner.

1 For dressing, in a blender container or food processor bowl combine egg, chicken broth, anchovy fillets, oil, lemon peel, lemon juice, mustard, and Worcestershire sauce. Cover and blend or process until smooth. Transfer dressing to a small saucepan. Cook and stir over low heat for 8 to 10 minutes or until thickened. Do not boil. Transfer dressing to a small bowl. Cover with plastic wrap and chill in the refrigerator for 2 to 24 hours.

2 To serve, rub the inside of a wooden salad bowl with the cut sides of the garlic clove; discard garlic clove. Add romaine, cherry tomatoes, croutons, and Parmesan cheese to salad bowl. Pour dressing over salad. Toss lightly to coat. Transfer to salad plates. Grind peppercorns over each serving.

Nutrition Facts per serving: 139 cal., 10 g total fat (2 g sat. fat), 40 mg chol., 247 mg sodium, 8 g carbo., 2 g fiber, 6 g pro.

Prep: 20 minutes
Cook: 8 minutes
Chill: 2 to 24 hours
Makes: 6 side-dish servings

- 1 egg
- ⅓ cup chicken broth
- 2 anchovy fillets or 1 teaspoon anchovy paste
- 3 tablespoons olive oil
- 1 teaspoon finely shredded lemon peel
- 2 tablespoons lemon juice
- 1 teaspoon Dijon-style mustard
- ¼ teaspoon white wine Worcestershire sauce
- 1 clove garlic, halved
- 10 cups torn romaine
- 6 cherry tomatoes, halved
- 1 cup croutons
- ¼ cup grated Parmesan cheese
  Whole black peppercorns

Orange-Beet Salad

In addition to a wonderful orange flavor, this salad gets a boost from toasted walnuts and walnut oil. Walnut oil is golden in color with a pronounced nut flavor and rich aroma. Look for it at specialty foods stores and large supermarkets.

1 Wash beets well. Cut off and discard root tails and all except 1 inch of stems. Do not peel. Cook, covered, in lightly salted boiling water for 40 to 50 minutes or just until tender. Drain. Let cool until easy to handle. Slip skins off beets under running water. Carefully slice each beet into ¼-inch slices, removing and discarding remaining stem ends.

2 Meanwhile, for dressing, in a screw-top jar combine walnut oil, orange peel, orange juice, and vinegar. Cover and shake well.

3 In a medium bowl gently toss the beet slices with the dressing. Cover and chill for 2 to 4 hours.

4 To serve, let mixture come to room temperature. Gently stir walnuts into beets. Sprinkle with feta cheese and pepper. Serve with a slotted spoon.

**Prep: 15 minutes
Cook: 40 minutes
Chill: 2 to 4 hours
Makes: 4 side-dish servings**

- 3 medium beets (about 9 ounces)
- 3 tablespoons walnut oil or salad oil
- 1 teaspoon shredded orange peel
- 2 tablespoons orange juice
- 1 tablespoon white wine vinegar or white vinegar
- 2 tablespoons broken walnuts, toasted
- 3 tablespoons crumbled feta cheese
- ¼ teaspoon coarsely ground black pepper

Nutrition Facts per serving: 171 cal., 14 g total fat (2 g sat. fat), 5 mg chol., 122 mg sodium, 10 g carbo., 2 g fiber, 3 g pro.

Skillet-Roasted Potato Salad

Although the potatoes are cooked in a skillet, the fat content is about the same as in other marinated potato salads.

1 In a large skillet cook potatoes in hot oil over medium heat about 15 minutes or until tender and brown on all sides, turning occasionally. Spoon potatoes into serving bowl. Sprinkle with the salt and black pepper.

2 To same skillet add summer squash. Cook and stir over medium heat for 3 to 5 minutes or just until tender. Add to the potatoes in the serving bowl. Pour vinaigrette dressing over potatoes and summer squash. Add sweet pepper, tomatoes, parsley, and snipped thyme. Toss gently to mix. Cool.

3 Cover and chill for 4 to 24 hours, stirring salad occasionally. If desired, top with thyme sprigs.

Nutrition Facts per serving: 172 cal., 12 g total fat (2 g sat. fat), 0 mg chol., 103 mg sodium, 15 g carbo., 3 g fiber, 3 g pro.

Prep: 30 minutes
Chill: 4 to 24 hours
Makes: 6 side-dish servings

- 1 pound potatoes, cut into 1-inch pieces (do not peel potatoes)
- 2 tablespoons cooking oil or olive oil
- ¼ teaspoon salt
- ⅛ teaspoon black pepper
- 2 medium summer squash, cut into 1½-inch pieces (8 ounces total)
- ⅓ cup bottled white wine, olive oil, or Italian vinaigrette
- 1 small red sweet pepper, cut into ½- to ¾-inch squares
- 6 cherry tomatoes, halved
- ¼ cup snipped fresh parsley
- 1 teaspoon snipped fresh thyme
  Sprigs of fresh thyme (optional)

Summer Rice Salad

Shorten your prep time by using leftover cooked rice or buy some at the hot foods deli of the supermarket. You'll need 2 cups for this salad.

1 Cook rice according to package directions. Place cooked rice in a colander; rinse with cold water. Drain and set aside.

2 Meanwhile, in a large bowl stir together the lemon peel, lemon juice, water, olive oil, mustard, parsley, dill, and black pepper. Stir in the squash, broccoli, sweet pepper, and green onions. Add the rice; toss to coat. Cover and chill in the refrigerator for 4 to 24 hours.

Nutrition Facts per serving: 99 cal., 4 g total fat (1 g sat. fat), 0 mg chol., 156 mg sodium, 15 g carbo., 2 g fiber, 2 g pro.

Prep: 55 minutes
Chill: 4 to 24 hours
Makes: 8 side-dish servings

- ⅔ cup uncooked regular brown rice
- 1 teaspoon finely shredded lemon peel
- 2 tablespoons lemon juice
- 2 tablespoons water
- 2 tablespoons olive oil
- 1 teaspoon Dijon-style mustard
- 2 tablespoons snipped fresh parsley
- 2 tablespoons snipped fresh dill
- ⅛ teaspoon black pepper
- 1 small yellow summer squash, halved lengthwise and sliced
- 1 cup broccoli florets
- ½ cup chopped red sweet pepper
- 2 green onions, thinly sliced

Vegetable Pasta Salad

Need a recipe that makes plenty of servings? Here's a good one to take along to your next potluck.

1 Cook pasta according to package directions; drain. Rinse with cold water; drain again.

2 In a very large bowl combine the pasta, provolone, zucchini, cherry tomatoes, onion, sweet pepper, olives, Parmesan, and parsley. Add dressing and toss to coat. Cover and chill in the refrigerator for 4 to 24 hours.

Nutrition Facts per serving: 144 cal., 8 g total fat (3 g sat. fat), 10 mg chol., 326 mg sodium, 13 g carbo., 2 g fiber, 6 g pro.

Prep: 25 minutes
Chill: 4 to 24 hours
Makes: 16 side-dish servings

2 cups dried whole wheat pasta (such as penne or rotini)
6 ounces provolone cheese, cut into ¾-inch cubes
1 small zucchini, halved lengthwise and thinly sliced (1 cup)
1 cup halved cherry tomatoes
1 small red onion, thinly sliced and separated into rings
¾ cup chopped red or green sweet pepper
1 2¼-ounce can sliced pitted ripe olives, drained
2 ounces Parmesan cheese, shaved (½ cup)
¼ cup snipped fresh parsley
¾ cup bottled balsamic vinaigrette salad dressing

Eggs

Autumn Frittata   **100**
Baked Brie Strata   **108**
Breakfast Casserole   **106**
Broccoli Omelet Provençale   **99**
Corn and Tomato Bread Pudding   **107**
Egg and Vegetable Salad Wraps   **112**
Egg Cakes with Sweet-and-Sour
    Plum Sauce   **105**
Farmer's Breakfast   **95**
Grecian Quiche   **109**
Moo Shu Vegetable and Egg Crepes   **97**
Poached Eggs on Polenta   **111**
Salmon and Eggs Benedict   **103**
Scrambled Egg Fajitas   **96**
Smoked Chicken-Egg Bake   **104**
Southwestern Breakfast Bake   **102**
Spinach and Cheese Omelet   **98**
Spinach Cheese Puff   **101**
Weekend Scramble   **94**
Zucchini and Swiss Pie   **110**

3 g
carb

Weekend Scramble

**Your family will jump eagerly out of bed for this morning dish.
It's so good and so easy—you can prepare it while you're in your pajamas and slippers.**

1 If desired, remove rind from cheese. Cut cheese into bite-size pieces. In a medium bowl beat together eggs, milk, chives, salt, and pepper with a rotary beater or wire whisk. Set aside.

2 In a large skillet cook pancetta over medium heat until crisp. Drain pancetta on paper towels, reserving 2 tablespoons drippings in skillet. Crumble pancetta and set aside.

3 Add mushrooms to the reserved drippings in skillet. Cook over medium-high heat for 4 to 5 minutes or until tender. Reduce heat to medium. Return pancetta to skillet.

4 Pour egg mixture over mushroom mixture in skillet. Cook over medium heat, without stirring, until egg mixture begins to set on the bottom and around edge. Using a spatula or a large spoon, lift and fold the partially cooked egg mixture so that the uncooked portion flows underneath.

5 Continue cooking over medium heat for 2 to 3 minutes or until egg mixture is cooked through but is still glossy and moist. Sprinkle with cheese. Remove from heat. Cover and let stand for 1 to 2 minutes or until cheese is softened.

Start to Finish: 30 minutes
Makes: 6 servings

- ½ of a 4½- to 5-ounce round Brie or Camembert cheese
- 8 eggs
- 2 tablespoons milk
- 1 tablespoon snipped fresh chives or thinly sliced green onion tops
- ¼ teaspoon salt
- ⅛ teaspoon black pepper
- 2 ounces sliced pancetta or 3 slices bacon
- 1½ cups fresh mushrooms (such as morel, chanterelle, and/or button), sliced
- 4½ cups baby spinach, lightly steamed*

6 To serve, divide spinach among plates and spoon egg mixture alongside.

Nutrition Facts per serving: 203 cal., 16 g total fat (6 g sat. fat), 300 mg chol., 308 mg sodium, 3 g carbo., 1 g fiber, 13 g pro.

*Note: To steam spinach, place a steamer basket in a skillet. Add water to just below bottom of steamer basket. Bring to boiling. Add the spinach to steamer basket. Cover and steam about 1 minute or just until spinach is wilted. Drain well.

Farmer's Breakfast

Many a farmer began the day with this all-American scramble of eggs, potatoes, and ham. With this shortcut version, you can enjoy the same hearty meal whether you toil at a desk or on a tractor.

1 In a medium skillet heat oil over medium heat. Add potatoes in a single layer. Cook, covered, for 5 to 7 minutes or until potatoes are tender, stirring once. Stir in ham.

2 In a small bowl beat together eggs and water with a rotary beater or wire whisk; pour over potato mixture. Cook over medium heat, without stirring, until egg mixture begins to set on the bottom and around edge. Using a spatula or a large spoon, lift and fold the partially cooked egg mixture so that the uncooked portion flows underneath.

3 Continue cooking over medium heat until egg mixture is cooked through but is still glossy and moist. Sprinkle with cheese. Remove from heat. Cover and let stand for 1 to 2 minutes or until cheese is melted.

Nutrition Facts per serving: 306 cal., 19 g total fat (5 g sat. fat), 343 mg chol., 649 mg sodium, 14 g carbo., 0 g fiber, 19 g pro.

Start to Finish: 20 minutes
Makes: 2 servings

1 tablespoon cooking oil
1 cup loose-pack frozen diced hash brown potatoes with onion and peppers, thawed
½ cup coarsely chopped cooked ham
3 eggs
3 tablespoons water
2 tablespoons shredded cheddar cheese

Scrambled Egg Fajitas

Dress is casual and dancing shoes are a must to stay in step with these festive roll-ups and their lively salsa beat. Set out the eggs and tortillas on a buffet table for easy self-service.

1 Wrap the tortillas in foil. Heat in a 350° oven about 10 minutes or until softened. [Or wrap tortillas in microwave-safe paper towels. Microwave on 100-percent power (high) about 30 seconds.]

2 Meanwhile, in a medium bowl beat together eggs, milk, salt, and pepper with a rotary beater or wire whisk; set aside. In a large skillet cook and stir corn and jalapeño pepper in hot oil over medium heat for 2 to 4 minutes or until corn is tender.

3 Pour egg mixture over vegetables in skillet. Cook over medium heat, without stirring, until egg mixture begins to set on the bottom and around edge. Using a spatula or a large spoon, lift and fold the partially cooked egg mixture so that the uncooked portion flows underneath. Sprinkle with cheese. Continue cooking over medium heat until egg mixture is cooked through but is still glossy and moist. Remove from heat. Sprinkle with green onion and cilantro.

4 To serve, fill the warmed tortillas with egg mixture; roll up. Serve with salsa.

Nutrition Facts per serving: 215 cal., 9 g total fat (3 g sat. fat), 220 mg chol., 215 mg sodium, 21 g carbo., 2 g fiber, 13 g pro.

Prep: 15 minutes
Bake: 10 minutes
Oven: 350°F
Makes: 6 servings

6 7-inch whole wheat flour tortillas
6 eggs
⅓ cup milk
⅛ teaspoon salt
⅛ teaspoon black pepper
1 cup frozen whole kernel corn
1 fresh jalapeño chile pepper,
    seeded and finely chopped*
2 teaspoons cooking oil
½ cup shredded reduced-fat Monterey
    Jack or cheddar cheese (2 ounces)
2 tablespoons thinly sliced green onion
2 tablespoons snipped fresh cilantro
    Bottled salsa

*Note: Because hot chile peppers contain volatile oils that can burn your skin and eyes, avoid direct contact with chiles as much as possible. When working with chile peppers, wear plastic or rubber gloves. If your bare hands do touch the chile peppers, wash your hands well with soap and warm water.

Moo Shu Vegetable and Egg Crepes

If there's ever a Chinese take-out Hall of Fame, this menu all-star would surely be in it. A speedy home-cooked rendition, expedited by a sweet-and-sour sauce that starts in a bottle and finishes in a moment, delivers dinner in short order.

1 In a covered large saucepan cook asparagus, carrots, and green onions in a small amount of boiling, lightly salted water for 7 to 9 minutes or until vegetables are crisp-tender; drain. Set aside.

2 Meanwhile, for sauce, in a small bowl stir together sweet-and-sour sauce, orange juice, and ginger; set aside.

3 For egg crepes, in another small bowl beat together eggs and water with a fork until combined but not frothy. In an 8- or 10-inch nonstick skillet with flared sides heat 1 teaspoon of the oil over medium heat until a drop of water sizzles. Lift and tilt skillet to coat sides with oil. Add about ½ cup of the egg mixture to skillet.

4 Cook over medium heat, without stirring, until egg mixture begins to set on the bottom and around edge. Using a spatula or a large spoon, lift and fold the partially cooked egg mixture so that the uncooked portion flows underneath. Continue cooking over medium heat until egg mixture is cooked through but is still glossy and moist. Remove from heat. Transfer egg crepe to a warm plate. Repeat to make two more crepes.

Start to Finish: 30 minutes
Makes: 3 servings

12 asparagus spears, trimmed and
    cut into 3-inch pieces
2 medium carrots, cut into thin
    3-inch strips
2 green onions, cut into 2-inch pieces
3 tablespoons bottled sweet-and-sour
    sauce
1 tablespoon orange juice or
    unsweetened pineapple juice
1 teaspoon grated fresh ginger
5 eggs
¼ cup water
1 tablespoon cooking oil

5 To serve, spread about 2 teaspoons sauce on the center of each crepe. Arrange one-third of the vegetables on one-fourth of the crepe. Fold crepe in half over the vegetables; fold in half again. Serve the egg crepes with the remaining sauce.

Nutrition Facts per serving: 223 cal., 13 g total fat (3 g sat. fat), 355 mg chol., 188 mg sodium, 13 g carbo., 2 g fiber, 12 g pro.

Spinach and Cheese Omelet

A tangy red pepper relish adorns these cheese- and spinach-filled omelets. This breakfast classic makes a quick, easy weeknight supper too.

1 Lightly coat an 8-inch nonstick skillet with flared sides or a crepe pan with cooking spray. Heat skillet over medium-high heat.

2 In a medium bowl beat together eggs, salt, and cayenne pepper with a rotary beater or wire whisk until frothy. Pour into the prepared skillet; cook over medium heat. As egg mixture sets, run a spatula around edge of skillet, lifting egg mixture so that the uncooked portion flows underneath.

3 Continue cooking and lifting edges until egg mixture is set but is still glossy and moist. Sprinkle with cheese and chives. Top with ¾ cup of the spinach and 2 tablespoons of the Red Pepper Relish. Using the spatula, lift and fold an edge of the omelet partially over filling. Top with the remaining ¼ cup spinach and 1 tablespoon of the relish. (Reserve the remaining relish for another use.) Cut the omelet in half.

Red Pepper Relish: In a small bowl combine ⅔ cup chopped red sweet pepper, 2 tablespoons finely chopped onion, 1 tablespoon cider vinegar, and ¼ teaspoon black pepper. Makes about ⅔ cup.

Nutrition Facts per serving: 214 cal., 15 g total fat (6 g sat. fat), 440 mg chol., 303 mg sodium, 3 g carbo., 2 g fiber, 17 g pro.

Start to Finish: 20 minutes
Makes: 2 servings

Nonstick cooking spray
4 eggs or 1 cup refrigerated or frozen egg product, thawed
Dash salt
Dash cayenne pepper
¼ cup shredded sharp cheddar cheese (1 ounce)
1 tablespoon snipped fresh chives, flat-leaf parsley, or chervil
1 cup spinach leaves
1 recipe Red Pepper Relish

Broccoli Omelet Provençale

Steamed broccoli slaw scented with fresh oregano tops these easy-to-make oven omelets. Add a final touch of warmed pasta sauce for colorful and delicious dining.

1 Lightly coat a 15×10×1-inch baking pan with cooking spray; set aside. For omelet, in a medium bowl beat together eggs, water, garlic salt, and pepper with a fork until combined but not frothy.

2 Place the prepared baking pan on an oven rack. Carefully pour egg mixture into the pan. Bake in a 400° oven about 7 minutes or until egg mixture is set but is still glossy and moist.

3 Meanwhile, for filling, place a steamer basket in a medium saucepan. Add water to just below bottom of steamer basket. Bring to boiling. Add the shredded broccoli to steamer basket. Cover and steam for 2 to 3 minutes or until heated through. Drain well. Stir in oregano.

4 To serve, cut the omelet into six 5-inch squares. Divide the filling among omelets, spooning over half of each square. Fold the other omelet half over the filled half, forming a triangle or rectangle. Spoon the warm pasta sauce over omelets.

Prep: 15 minutes
Bake: 7 minutes
Oven: 400°F
Makes: 6 servings

Nonstick cooking spray
12 eggs
¼ cup water
½ teaspoon garlic salt
⅛ teaspoon black pepper
3 cups packaged shredded broccoli (broccoli slaw mix)
2 tablespoons snipped fresh oregano or basil
1 10-ounce container refrigerated roma tomato pasta sauce, heated

Nutrition Facts per serving: 222 cal., 15 g total fat (6 g sat. fat), 439 mg chol., 454 mg sodium, 6 g carbo., 2 g fiber, 14 g pro.

27 g
carb

Autumn Frittata

Along with acorns and blazing leaves, the centerpiece of an autumn brunch should be this delicious dish infused with the seasonal flavors of fennel and sweet potatoes.

1 In a medium bowl beat together eggs, chervil, and salt with a rotary beater or wire whisk; set aside.

2 In a 10-inch ovenproof skillet cook and stir fennel and onion in hot oil for 5 to 7 minutes or until vegetables are tender. Layer sliced sweet potatoes on top of fennel and onion in skillet. Pour the egg mixture over sweet potatoes.

3 Bake in a 350° oven for 18 to 20 minutes or until a knife inserted near the center comes out clean.

Note: To cook sweet potatoes, in a large saucepan combine sweet potatoes and enough water to cover. Bring to boiling; reduce heat. Simmer, covered, for 25 to 35 minutes or until tender. Drain; cool slightly before peeling and slicing.

tion Facts per serving: 283 cal., 14 g total fat (3 g sat. fat), 320 mg chol., 249 mg sodium, 27 g carbo., 9 g fiber, 12 g pro.

Prep: 15 minutes
Bake: 18 minutes
Oven: 350°F
Makes: 4 servings

- 6 eggs
- 1 tablespoon snipped fresh chervil or parsley
- ¼ teaspoon salt
- 1 medium fennel bulb, trimmed and thinly sliced (about 1 cup)
- 1 large sweet onion (such as Vidalia or Walla Walla), thinly sliced
- 2 tablespoons olive oil
- 3 medium sweet potatoes (1 pound), cooked, peeled, and thinly sliced,* or one 16-ounce can sweet potatoes, drained and sliced

Spinach Cheese Puff

Resembling soufflé—only less temperamental—this puff has the consistency of Southern-style spoon bread.

1 Allow egg yolks and egg whites to stand in separate bowls at room temperature for 30 minutes. Grease the bottom and sides of a 1½-quart soufflé dish. Sprinkle inside of dish with 1 tablespoon of the Parmesan; set aside.

2 For sauce, in a saucepan cook shallots and garlic in hot butter for 1 minute. Stir in dried tomatoes, flour, salt, and cayenne pepper. Cook and stir for 1 minute. Add milk. Cook and stir until thickened and bubbly. Remove from heat. Add Swiss cheese and remaining 1 tablespoon Parmesan cheese, a little at a time, stirring until melted.

3 In a bowl beat egg yolks with a fork until combined. Slowly add about half of the cheese sauce to egg yolks, stirring constantly. Return yolk mixture to the saucepan. Stir in drained spinach and prosciutto; set aside.

4 In a large mixing bowl beat egg whites with an electric mixer on medium to high speed until stiff peaks form (tips stand straight). Gently fold about one-third of the egg whites into the sauce. Gradually pour sauce over remaining beaten egg whites, folding to combine. Pour into prepared soufflé dish. Bake in a 375° oven for 40 to 45 minutes or until puffed and a knife inserted near the center comes out clean. Serve immediately.

Prep: 45 minutes
Bake: 40 minutes
Oven: 375°F
Makes: 6 to 8 servings

- 6 egg yolks
- 6 egg whites
- 2 tablespoons grated Parmesan cheese
- ¼ cup finely chopped shallots
- 2 cloves garlic, minced
- 3 tablespoons butter or margarine
- ¼ cup finely snipped dried tomatoes (not oil-packed)
- ¼ cup all-purpose flour
- ¼ teaspoon salt
- ⅛ teaspoon cayenne pepper
- 1 cup milk
- 1 cup shredded Swiss or Gruyère cheese (4 ounces)
- 1 10-ounce package frozen chopped spinach, thawed and well drained
- ¼ cup finely chopped prosciutto

Nutrition Facts per serving: 272 cal., 18 g total fat (10 g sat. fat), 252 mg chol., 477 mg sodium, 12 g carbo., 2 g fiber, 17 g pro.

15 g
carb

Southwestern Breakfast Bake

This puffy egg-topped dish is delicious served as a light dinner or breakfast. For a complete meal, serve with a mixed green salad topped with tomato wedges, chopped avocado, and sliced onions.

1 Grease a 2-quart square baking dish. In the prepared baking dish combine black beans, enchilada sauce, green chile peppers, green onions, hot pepper sauce (if desired), and garlic. Sprinkle with cheese.

2 In a medium mixing bowl beat the egg whites with an electric mixer on medium speed until soft peaks form (tips curl); set aside.

3 In a large bowl combine the egg yolks, flour, and salt. Using a wire whisk, beat mixture until combined (mixture will be stiff). Gradually whisk in milk until smooth. Fold the beaten egg whites and cilantro into egg yolk mixture. Carefully pour the egg mixture over the bean mixture in baking dish.

4 Bake in a 325° oven about 45 minutes or until egg mixture appears set when gently shaken. Let stand for 15 minutes before serving. If desired, serve with salsa.

Nutrition Facts per serving: 163 cal., 8 g total fat (4 g sat. fat), 96 mg chol., 488 mg sodium, 15 g carbo., 4 g fiber, 11 g pro.

Prep: 20 minutes
Bake: 45 minutes
Oven: 325°F
Stand: 15 minutes
Makes: 8 servings

1 15-ounce can black beans, rinsed and drained
¾ cup canned enchilada sauce
2 4½-ounce cans diced green chile peppers, drained
½ cup thinly sliced green onions
  Several dashes bottled hot pepper sauce (optional)
2 cloves garlic, minced
1 cup shredded sharp cheddar cheese and/or shredded Monterey Jack cheese with jalapeño peppers (4 ounces)
3 eggs, separated
2 tablespoons all-purpose flour
¼ teaspoon salt
½ cup milk
1 tablespoon snipped fresh cilantro
  Purchased salsa (optional)

Salmon and Eggs Benedict

With eggs to poach and hollandaise sauce to keep from separating, traditional eggs benedict can be tricky. This easy casserole offers the same much-loved flavors of the classic (and an extra bonus of smoked salmon), but none of the hassle.

1 For sauce, prepare hollandaise sauce mix according to package directions. Stir in capers and lemon peel. Cover and set aside.

2 In a medium bowl beat together eggs, milk, and pepper with a rotary beater or wire whisk. In a large skillet melt 1 tablespoon of the butter over medium heat. Pour in egg mixture. Cook over medium heat, without stirring, until egg mixture begins to set on the bottom and around edge. Using a spatula or a large spoon, lift and fold the partially cooked egg mixture so that the uncooked portion flows underneath. Continue cooking over medium heat for 3 to 4 minutes or until egg mixture is cooked through but is still glossy and moist. Remove skillet from heat.

3 Spread about ½ cup of the sauce over bottom of a 2-quart rectangular baking dish. Arrange English muffins, cut sides up, on top of sauce in dish. Divide smoked salmon into 6 equal portions. Place a portion, folding as necessary, on each muffin half. Spoon cooked eggs onto muffin stacks, dividing evenly. Spoon the remaining sauce over eggs.

4 For crumb topping, melt the remaining 1 tablespoon butter. Add bread crumbs; toss to coat. Sprinkle over muffin stacks.

5 Bake in a 350° oven about 15 minutes or until heated through. If desired, sprinkle with snipped chives.

**Prep: 30 minutes
Bake: 15 minutes
Oven: 350°F
Makes: 6 servings**

1 1⅛-ounce or 0.9-ounce envelope hollandaise sauce mix (to make about 1¼ cups sauce)
2 tablespoons capers, drained
½ teaspoon finely shredded lemon peel
6 eggs
¼ cup milk
⅛ teaspoon black pepper
2 tablespoons butter or margarine
3 whole wheat English muffins, split and toasted
6 ounces thinly sliced smoked salmon (lox-style) or Canadian-style bacon
¾ cup soft bread crumbs (1 slice)
Snipped fresh chives (optional)

Nutrition Facts per serving: 249 cal., 11 g total fat (5 g sat. fat), 231 mg chol., 737 mg sodium, 21 g carbo., 2 g fiber, 15 g pro.

Make-ahead directions: Prepare as above through step 2. Cover and chill sauce and cooked eggs separately up to 24 hours. Prepare crumb topping. Cover; chill up to 24 hours. To serve, assemble egg stacks as directed in step 3. Sprinkle crumb topping over egg stacks. Bake in a 350° oven about 25 minutes or until heated through.

9 g
carb

Smoked Chicken-Egg Bake

Earthy mushrooms and smoked chicken supply the flavor for the rich, creamy sauce in this baked egg dish.

1 For sauce, in a screw-top jar combine milk and flour. Cover and shake well. Pour into a saucepan; cook and stir over medium heat until bubbly. Add cream cheese; cook and stir until melted. Remove from heat; stir in chives.

2 Lightly coat a large skillet with cooking spray. Heat skillet over medium-high heat. Add mushrooms and onion. Cook and stir about 3 minutes or until vegetables are tender. Add the mushroom mixture to sauce. Stir in chicken; set aside.

3 In the same skillet melt butter over medium heat. Add egg product, salt, and pepper. Cook over medium heat, without stirring, until egg mixture begins to set on the bottom and around edge. Using a spatula or a large spoon, lift and fold the partially cooked egg mixture so that the uncooked portion flows underneath. Continue cooking over medium heat until egg mixture is cooked through but is still glossy and moist. Transfer egg mixture to a 2-quart casserole; spoon the sauce over top.

4 Bake in a 400° oven about 15 minutes or until heated through. Let stand for 10 minutes before serving.

Prep: 30 minutes
Bake: 15 minutes
Oven: 400°F
Stand: 10 minutes
Makes: 6 servings

- 1¼ cups milk
- 2 tablespoons all-purpose flour
- 2 ounces reduced-fat cream cheese (Neufchâtel), cubed
- 2 tablespoons snipped fresh chives
  Nonstick cooking spray
- 1½ cups sliced fresh mushrooms, such as morel, shiitake, or crimini
- ¼ cup chopped onion
- 1½ cups coarsely chopped smoked cooked chicken
- 1 tablespoon butter or margarine
- 2½ cups refrigerated or frozen egg product, thawed
- ¼ teaspoon salt
- ⅛ teaspoon black pepper

Nutrition Facts per serving: 263 cal., 15 g total fat (6 g sat. fat), 42 mg chol., 626 mg sodium, 9 g carbo., 0 g fiber, 23 g pro.

Egg Cakes with Sweet-and-Sour Plum Sauce

Make these brunch-size egg cakes Mexican-style by omitting the Sweet-and-Sour Plum Sauce. Instead, sprinkle with shredded cheddar cheese and serve with salsa and sour cream.

1 Lightly coat twelve 2½-inch muffin cups with cooking spray. Press about 1 tablespoon cooked rice into the bottom of each muffin cup; set aside.

2 In a medium nonstick skillet cook ham and green onions in hot oil over medium heat until onions are tender. Spoon ham mixture evenly over rice in muffin cups. In a medium bowl beat together eggs and salt. Divide the egg mixture among muffin cups.

3 Bake in a 375° oven for 12 to 15 minutes or until egg mixture is slightly puffed and golden brown. Let stand for 2 minutes. Run a knife around edges of muffin cups to loosen; remove from cups. Drizzle with Sweet-and-Sour Plum Sauce.

Sweet-and-Sour Plum Sauce: In a small saucepan combine ¼ cup plum jam or preserves, ¼ cup chicken broth, 2 tablespoons red wine vinegar, 2 teaspoons soy sauce, and 1 teaspoon cornstarch. Cook and stir until thickened and bubbly. Cook and stir for 2 minutes more. Makes about ½ cup.

Prep: 20 minutes
Bake: 12 minutes
Oven: 375°F
Makes: 6 servings

Nonstick cooking spray
¾ cup cooked rice
⅔ cup chopped cooked ham
⅓ cup thinly sliced green onions
1 teaspoon cooking oil
8 eggs
½ teaspoon salt
1 recipe Sweet-and-Sour Plum Sauce

Nutrition Facts per serving: 202 cal., 9 g total fat (3 g sat. fat), 293 mg chol., 637 mg sodium, 16 g carbo., 0 g fiber, 12 g pro.

Breakfast Casserole

Fuel up for a day of biking or hiking with this thyme-flavored ham and potato breakfast casserole. For variety, substitute your favorite herb or reduced-fat cheese.

1 In a covered large saucepan cook sliced potatoes in a small amount of boiling, lightly salted water about 10 minutes or just until tender, adding leek the last 5 minutes of cooking. Drain potato mixture.

2 Coat a 2-quart rectangular baking dish with cooking spray. Spread potato mixture in bottom of the prepared baking dish. Sprinkle with ham and Swiss cheese.

3 In a medium bowl stir the milk into the flour until smooth. Stir in the egg product, thyme, and pepper. Pour the egg mixture over potato mixture.

4 Bake in a 350° oven for 35 to 40 minutes or until a knife inserted near the center comes out clean.

Nutrition Facts per serving: 180 cal., 4 g total fat (1 g sat. fat), 16 mg chol., 445 mg sodium, 23 g carbo., 1 g fiber, 13 g pro.

Prep: 25 minutes
Bake: 35 minutes
Oven: 350°F
Makes: 6 servings

1	**pound tiny new potatoes, cut into $\frac{1}{4}$-inch slices**
$\frac{1}{3}$	**cup thinly sliced leek**
	Nonstick cooking spray
$\frac{3}{4}$	**cup chopped reduced-fat, reduced-sodium cooked ham**
3	**ounces reduced-fat Swiss cheese, cut into small pieces**
$1\frac{1}{4}$	**cups milk**
1	**tablespoon all-purpose flour**
$\frac{3}{4}$	**cup refrigerated or frozen egg product, thawed**
2	**teaspoons snipped fresh thyme or $\frac{1}{2}$ teaspoon dried thyme, crushed**
$\frac{1}{4}$	**teaspoon black pepper**

Corn and Tomato Bread Pudding

The classic bread pudding dessert is reinvented as a luscious meatless main course. If using the French bread option, cut cubes from only firm, dry bread, since fresh bread is too soft to soak up all the milk and eggs and hold its shape.

1 Place dried tomatoes in a small bowl; add enough hot water to cover. Let stand about 15 minutes or until softened; drain.

2 Meanwhile, in a medium bowl beat together eggs, milk, and basil; set aside. In a 2-quart square baking dish toss together the softened tomatoes, torn English muffins, corn, and cheese.

3 Carefully pour egg mixture evenly over muffin mixture. Bake in a 375° oven about 30 minutes or until a knife inserted near the center comes out clean. Cool slightly. If desired, serve bread pudding on top of tomatoes.

Nutrition Facts per serving: 268 cal., 9 g total fat (4 g sat. fat), 160 mg chol., 393 mg sodium, 31 g carbo., 3 g fiber, 17 g pro.

*Note: Dry the bread cubes by one of two methods listed here. Use about 5 cups fresh bread cubes to make 4 cups dry cubes. Cut bread into ½-inch slices; cut into cubes. Spread in a single layer in a shallow baking pan. Bake in a 300° oven for 10 to 15 minutes or until dry, stirring twice; cool. (Bread will continue to dry and crisp as it cools.) Or let bread cubes stand, loosely covered, at room temperature for 8 to 12 hours.

Make-ahead directions: Prepare as above through step 2. Cover and chill egg mixture and English muffin mixture separately up to 24 hours. To serve, combine the two mixtures. Bake as above.

Prep: 20 minutes
Bake: 30 minutes
Oven: 375°F
Makes: 6 servings

- 3 tablespoons snipped dried tomatoes (not oil packed)
- 4 eggs
- 1½ cups milk, half-and-half, or light cream
- 1 tablespoon snipped fresh basil or 1 teaspoon dried basil, crushed
- 4 cups torn whole wheat English muffins or dry French bread cubes*
- 1½ cups fresh or frozen whole kernel corn
- 1 cup shredded reduced-fat cheddar cheese or Monterey Jack cheese with jalapeño peppers (4 ounces)
- Thin tomato wedges (optional)

15 g
carb

Baked Brie Strata

Buttery-soft Brie cheese oozes between the layers of crisp-tender zucchini and crusty bread for a sure-to-please brunch casserole. Garnish the plates with melon wedges and tiny bunches of grapes.

1 In a covered small saucepan cook zucchini in a small amount of boiling, lightly salted water for 2 to 3 minutes or just until tender. Drain zucchini and set aside.

2 Meanwhile, coat a 2-quart rectangular baking dish with cooking spray. Arrange bread slices in the bottom of the prepared baking dish, cutting as necessary to fit. Sprinkle with half of the cheese. Arrange zucchini and tomatoes on top of bread. Sprinkle with the remaining cheese.

3 In a medium bowl combine egg product, evaporated milk, onion, dill, salt, and pepper. Pour evenly over vegetables and cheese. Press lightly with the back of a spoon to thoroughly moisten ingredients. Cover with plastic wrap and chill for 4 to 24 hours.

4 Remove plastic wrap from strata; cover with foil. Bake in a 325° oven for 30 minutes. Uncover and bake for 25 to 30 minutes more or until a knife inserted near the center comes out clean. Let stand for 10 minutes before serving.

Nutrition Facts per serving: 189 cal., 9 g total fat (5 g sat. fat), 29 mg chol., 502 mg sodium, 15 g carbo., 2 g fiber, 13 g pro.

Prep: 25 minutes
Chill: 4 to 24 hours
Bake: 55 minutes
Oven: 325°F
Stand: 10 minutes
Makes: 8 servings

2 small zucchini, cut into ¼-inch slices (about 2 cups)
   Nonstick cooking spray
6 ½-inch slices crusty whole wheat sourdough bread
8 ounces Brie cheese, rind removed, cheese cut into ½-inch cubes
2 roma tomatoes, cut lengthwise into ¼-inch slices
6 to 8 cherry tomatoes, halved
1 cup refrigerated or frozen egg product, thawed
⅔ cup evaporated milk
⅓ cup finely chopped onion
3 tablespoons snipped fresh dill
½ teaspoon salt
⅛ teaspoon black pepper

Grecian Quiche

Kalamata olives and feta cheese lend quintessential Greek touches to the classic quiche. Serve this delightful quiche with fruit salad for brunch or with a mixed greens salad for a lunch or light supper.

1 Prepare Herb Crust. Roll dough into a 12-inch circle. Place in a 9-inch fluted tart pan with a removable bottom. Press dough into sides; trim edges. Line with a double thickness of foil. Bake in a 450° oven for 8 minutes. Remove foil; bake about 10 minutes more. Cool. Reduce oven temperature to 375°.

2 In a large skillet melt butter over medium-high heat. Add mushrooms; cook and stir for 4 to 5 minutes or until tender. Remove from heat. Stir in pimiento, shallots, and olives. Spoon the mixture evenly into prebaked tart shell; set aside.

3 In a small bowl beat together eggs, milk, dry mustard, salt, and pepper. Carefully pour over mushroom mixture. Bake in the 375° oven for 20 to 25 minutes or just until set and a knife inserted near the center comes out clean. If desired, sprinkle with cheese. Let stand for 5 minutes before serving.

Herb Crust: In a medium bowl stir together 1½ cups all-purpose flour; 2 teaspoons dried herbes de Provence, crushed; and ½ teaspoon salt. Using a pastry blender, cut in ½ cup cold butter until pieces are pea-size. Add 5 to 6 tablespoons cold water, 1 tablespoon at a time, tossing gently until all the flour mixture is moistened. Form dough into a ball.

Prep: 35 minutes
Bake: 18 minutes + 20 minutes
Oven: 450°F; 375°F
Stand: 5 minutes
Makes: 8 servings

- 1 recipe Herb Crust
- 1 tablespoon butter or margarine
- 2½ cups sliced fresh mushrooms
- 1 4-ounce jar sliced pimiento, drained
- ¼ cup finely chopped shallots
- ¼ cup chopped pitted kalamata olives
- 2 eggs
- ½ cup milk
- ½ teaspoon dry mustard
- ¼ teaspoon salt
- ¼ teaspoon black pepper
- ½ cup crumbled feta cheese (2 ounces) (optional)

Nutrition Facts per serving: 247 cal., 17 g total fat (9 g sat. fat), 91 mg chol., 431 mg sodium, 20 g carbo., 1 g fiber, 6 g pro.

Tip: Be sure to use cold butter and cold water when making the crust for a dough that is easier to roll. If the dough is too soft, cover with plastic wrap and chill for 15 minutes for easier rolling.

23 g
carb

Zucchini and Swiss Pie

Use Parmesan cheese to flavor and enrich a hash brown potato crust. It's a delicious base for a vegetable-custard filling.

1 Grease a 9-inch pie plate; set aside. For crust, in a large bowl combine ¼ cup of the egg product, the onion, and Parmesan cheese. Stir in potatoes. Transfer mixture to the prepared pie plate; pat mixture into the bottom and up the sides.

2 Bake in a 400° oven for 35 to 40 minutes or until golden brown. Cool the crust slightly on a wire rack. Reduce oven temperature to 350°.

3 In a large skillet cook zucchini and garlic in hot oil until zucchini is crisp-tender; cool slightly. Place cheese slices in bottom of crust, tearing to fit. Arrange zucchini mixture over cheese.

4 In a small bowl combine the remaining ¾ cup egg product, the milk, oregano, pepper, and salt. Pour the egg mixture over zucchini mixture.

5 Bake in the 350° oven for 25 to 30 minutes or until filling appears set when gently shaken. Let stand for 10 minutes before serving.

Prep: 20 minutes
Bake: 35 minutes + 25 minutes
Oven: 400°F; 350°F
Stand: 10 minutes
Makes: 6 servings

1 cup refrigerated or frozen egg product, thawed
¼ cup chopped onion
¼ cup grated Parmesan cheese
½ of a 20-ounce package refrigerated shredded hash brown potatoes (about 3 cups)
2 medium zucchini, thinly sliced (2½ cups)
1 clove garlic, minced
1 teaspoon cooking oil
3 ounces sliced Swiss cheese
¼ cup milk
2 teaspoons snipped fresh oregano or ½ teaspoon dried oregano, crushed
¼ teaspoon black pepper
⅛ teaspoon salt

Nutrition Facts per serving: 197 cal., 6 g total fat (2 g sat. fat), 11 mg chol., 401 mg sodium, 23 g carbo., 3 g fiber, 13 g pro.

Poached Eggs on Polenta

You don't need a fancy egg-poaching pan to perfectly poach eggs. Simply break each egg into a measuring cup and carefully slide it into a skillet of simmering water, holding the lip of the cup as close to the water as possible to avoid breaking the egg.

1 For polenta, lightly grease a 9×5×3-inch loaf pan; set aside. In a large saucepan bring 1½ cups water and butter to a simmer over medium heat. Combine milk and cornmeal; add to simmering mixture, stirring constantly. Reduce heat to low. Cook for 10 to 15 minutes or until mixture is very thick, stirring occasionally. Remove from heat; stir in the ½ cup Parmesan cheese. Spread polenta in prepared loaf pan. Cool. Cover and chill at least 1 hour.

2 For sauce, in a large skillet cook onion and garlic in hot oil over medium heat about 5 minutes or until onion is tender. Stir in tomatoes. Cook, uncovered, for 5 minutes more. Remove from heat; stir in basil and the ½ teaspoon salt. Cover and keep warm.

3 Preheat broiler. Remove polenta from pan and cut into 12 slices. Arrange slices on a baking sheet. Broil polenta about 4 inches from the heat for 8 to 10 minutes or until golden brown, turning once halfway through broiling. Keep warm.

4 Meanwhile, for eggs, lightly grease a 12-inch skillet. Add 5 cups water, vinegar, and the ⅛ teaspoon salt. Bring to boiling; reduce heat to simmering. Add eggs to simmering water, allowing each egg an equal amount of space. Simmer eggs, uncovered, for 3 to 5 minutes or until the whites are completely set and the yolks begin to thicken but are not hard. Remove eggs with a slotted spoon.

Prep: 35 minutes
Cook: 21 minutes
Chill: 1 hour
Makes: 6 servings

- 1 tablespoon butter or margarine
- 1½ cups milk
- 1 cup yellow cornmeal
- ½ cup finely shredded Parmesan cheese
- 1 cup finely chopped onion
- 4 cloves garlic, minced (2 teaspoons)
- 2 tablespoons olive oil
- 1¾ pounds roma tomatoes, seeded and chopped (4 cups)
- ¼ cup snipped fresh basil
- ½ teaspoon salt
- ¼ cup vinegar
- ⅛ teaspoon salt
- 6 eggs
- ⅓ cup finely shredded Parmesan cheese
  Freshly ground black pepper

5 To serve, arrange 2 polenta slices on each plate. Top with sauce and poached eggs. Sprinkle with the ⅓ cup Parmesan cheese and pepper.

Nutrition Facts per serving: 350 cal., 18 g total fat (7 g sat. fat), 237 mg chol., 546 mg sodium, 31 g carbo., 4 g fiber, 17 g pro.

Egg and Vegetable Salad Wraps

Need an energy boost? High-protein eggs wrapped with crisp, refreshing veggies are the perfect solution. Enjoy these healthful sandwiches for lunch or a light supper.

1 In a large bowl combine eggs, cucumber, zucchini, red onion, and carrot. For dressing, in a small bowl stir together mayonnaise dressing, Dijon mustard, milk, tarragon, and paprika. Pour the dressing over egg mixture; toss gently to coat.

2 For each sandwich, place a lettuce leaf on a tortilla. Place 3 or 4 tomato slices on top of the lettuce, slightly off center. Spoon about ⅔ cup of the egg mixture on top of the tomato slices. Fold in two opposite sides of the tortilla; roll up from the bottom. Cut the tortilla rolls in half diagonally.

Nutrition Facts per sandwich: 149 cal., 4 g total fat (1 g sat. fat), 141 mg chol., 340 mg sodium, 19 g carbo., 11 g fiber, 8 g pro.

Start to Finish: 30 minutes
Makes: 6 sandwiches

- 4 hard-cooked eggs, chopped
- 1 cup chopped cucumber
- 1 cup chopped zucchini or yellow summer squash
- ½ cup chopped red onion
- ½ cup shredded carrot
- ¼ cup fat-free or light mayonnaise dressing or salad dressing
- 2 tablespoons Dijon-style mustard
- 1 tablespoon milk
- 1 teaspoon snipped fresh tarragon or basil
- ⅛ teaspoon paprika
- 6 leaf lettuce leaves
- 6 10-inch whole wheat, spinach, or vegetable flour tortillas
- 2 roma tomatoes, thinly sliced

Meat

Asian Beef and Noodle Bowl	128
Beef Roast with Vegetables	123
Beef Tenderloin Fillets with Horseradish Chili	115
Beef-Vegetable Ragout	127
Braised Short Ribs with Beets	125
Filet Mignon with Portobello Sauce	114
French Beef Stew	126
Gingered Pork and Cabbage Soup	142
Grilled Mango-Berry "Chalsa" with Pork	140
Grilled Mustard-Glazed Pork Tenderloin	139
Grilled Pork Chops with Mushroom Stuffing	133
Grilled Veal Chops with Pesto Mushrooms	131
Grilled Vegetables and Beef Kabobs	120
Herbed Beef Tenderloin	124
Italian Steak Sandwiches	122
Italian Wedding Soup	129
Lamb Chops and Peppers	145
Lemony Flank Steak	119
Moroccan Lamb Roast	146
Pizza-Topped Meat Loaf	130
Pork and Mango Picadillo	143
Pork and Pear au Jus	134
Pork Chops in Creamy Vegetable Sauce	136
Pork Medallions with Cherry Sauce	138
Sage Pork Roast with Apple	141
Skillet Veal Scaloppine with Marsala	132
Spice-Rubbed Pork Chops	135
Spicy Steak Tortillas	121
Spinach and Ham Lasagna	144
Spinach-Stuffed Flank Steak	118
Steak with Roasted Garlic and Herbs	117
Sweet Pepper and Olive Pork	137
Top Sirloin with Smoky Pepper Sauce	116

4 g
carb

Filet Mignon with Portobello Sauce

Just a splash of Madeira or port wine makes this buttery, meltingly tender steak and mushroom dish simply marvelous. Madeira and port are both slightly sweet Spanish wines flavored with a bit of brandy.

1 Trim fat from steaks. Rub both sides of steaks with oil and pepper. Grill steaks on the rack of an uncovered grill directly over medium coals to desired doneness, turning once halfway through grilling. Allow 8 to 12 minutes for medium-rare (145°F) and 12 to 15 minutes for medium (160°F).

2 Meanwhile, for sauce, in a large skillet cook and stir mushrooms and onions in hot butter over medium heat about 5 minutes or until vegetables are tender. Stir in broth and Madeira. Bring to boiling. Remove from heat. Thinly slice steaks diagonally and serve with sauce.

Nutrition Facts per serving: 260 cal., 13 g total fat (5 g sat. fat), 88 mg chol., 128 mg sodium, 4 g carbo., 1 g fiber, 29 g pro.

Prep: 15 minutes
Grill: 8 minutes
Makes: 4 servings

4 beef tenderloin steaks, cut 1 inch thick (about 1¼ pounds total)
1 teaspoon olive oil
¼ teaspoon black pepper
2 large portobello mushrooms, halved and sliced
8 green onions, cut into 1-inch pieces
1 tablespoon butter or margarine
⅓ cup reduced-sodium beef broth
2 tablespoons Madeira or port wine or reduced-sodium beef broth

Beef Tenderloin Fillets with Horseradish Chili

A bold dry rub seals in the flavor of these thick and juicy steaks. The horseradish chili is a surefire wake-up call for your palate.

1 Trim fat from meat. Rub both sides of meat with sage, pepper, and salt; set aside.

2 In a heavy skillet heat the oil over medium-high heat. Add tomatoes, chili seasoning, and garlic to skillet; cook for 1 to 2 minutes or just until tomatoes start to soften. Reduce heat to medium-low. Add beans and horseradish. Cook and stir for 2 minutes more. Cover loosely; keep warm.

3 Lightly coat a nonstick 12-inch skillet with cooking spray. Heat skillet over medium heat. Add meat to skillet; cook for 14 to 16 minutes for medium-rare (145°F) to medium (160°F), turning once halfway through cooking. To serve, place meat on dinner plates; spoon warm tomato mixture over meat. If desired, garnish with sage leaves.

Nutrition Facts per serving: 347 cal., 14 g total fat (5 g sat. fat), 96 mg chol., 759 mg sodium, 18 g carbo., 1 g fiber, 37 g pro.

Prep: 25 minutes
Cook: 17 minutes
Makes: 4 servings

1½   pounds beef tenderloin, cut into about 1¼-inch slices
2   teaspoons snipped fresh sage or ½ teaspoon dried sage, crushed
¼   to 1 teaspoon coarsely ground white or black pepper
¼   teaspoon salt
2   teaspoons cooking oil
1   cup coarsely chopped tomatoes
2   tablespoons chili seasoning mix
2   cloves garlic, minced
½   cup canned red beans, rinsed and drained
¼   to ½ cup grated fresh horseradish root or prepared horseradish
  Nonstick cooking spray
  Fresh sage leaves (optional)

Top Sirloin with Smoky Pepper Sauce

Chipotle chile peppers are actually smoked jalapeños; they have a smoky, slightly sweet, spicy flavor.

1 For sauce, in a medium bowl place dried tomatoes and chile peppers; add boiling water. Let stand about 30 minutes or until vegetables are softened. Drain, reserving liquid.

2 Cut up tomatoes; place in a blender container or food processor bowl. Trim stems from chiles; scrape out seeds. Cut up chile peppers; add chile peppers, ¼ cup of the reserved soaking liquid, the wine, onion, brown sugar, lime juice, black pepper, and garlic. Cover and blend or process until nearly smooth.

3 Trim fat from meat. Place meat in a shallow glass dish; pour sauce over meat. Cover and marinate in the refrigerator for 2 to 8 hours, turning meat occasionally. Drain, reserving marinade.

4 Preheat broiler. Lightly coat the unheated rack of a broiler pan with cooking spray. Place meat on rack. Broil 3 to 4 inches from heat, turning and brushing with marinade halfway through broiling. Allow 15 to 17 minutes for medium-rare (145°F) and 20 to 22 minutes for medium (160°F). In a small saucepan heat remaining marinade until boiling; pass with meat.

Nutrition Facts per serving: 240 cal., 8 g total fat (3 g sat. fat), 57 mg chol., 105 mg sodium, 12 g carbo., 1 g fiber, 21 g pro.

Prep: 15 minutes
Stand: 30 minutes
Marinate: 2 to 8 hours
Broil: 15 minutes
Makes: 4 servings

- 12 dried tomato halves (not oil packed)
- 1 to 3 dried chipotle chile peppers (see note, page 96)
- 1 cup boiling water
- 1 cup dry red or white wine or 1 cup water plus ½ teaspoon instant beef bouillon granules
- ½ cup chopped onion
- 1 tablespoon brown sugar
- 1 tablespoon lime or lemon juice
- ¼ teaspoon black pepper
- 2 cloves garlic, quartered
  Nonstick cooking spray
- 12 ounces boneless beef top sirloin steak, cut 1 inch thick

Steak with Roasted Garlic and Herbs

Whole bulbs of garlic are soft and sweet after roasting, making them a fantastic flavor treat to spread on grilled steak or to toss with steamed vegetables.

1 Remove papery outer layers from garlic bulb(s), leaving the individual garlic cloves attached to bulb(s). Cut off about ½ inch from top(s) of bulb(s) and discard. Fold a 20×18-inch piece of heavy foil in half crosswise. Trim into a 10-inch square. Place garlic bulb(s), cut side(s) up, in center of foil square. Bring foil up around garlic, forming a shallow bowl. Sprinkle with basil and rosemary; drizzle with oil. Completely enclose garlic in foil, twisting ends of foil on top.

2 Grill garlic on the rack of an uncovered grill over medium coals about 30 minutes or until garlic cloves are soft, turning garlic occasionally. Remove garlic from foil packet, reserving oil mixture. Cool slightly.

3 Meanwhile, trim fat from meat. In a small bowl combine pepper and salt; rub onto both sides of meat. While garlic is grilling, add meat to grill. Grill to desired doneness, turning once halfway through grilling. For sirloin steak, allow 14 to 18 minutes for medium-rare (145°F) and 18 to 22 minutes for medium (160°F). For ribeye steaks, allow 11 to 15 minutes for medium-rare (145°F) and 14 to 18 minutes for medium (160°F).

Prep: 15 minutes
Grill: 30 minutes
Makes: 6 servings

- 1 or 2 whole garlic bulb(s)
- 3 to 4 teaspoons snipped fresh basil or 1 teaspoon dried basil, crushed
- 1 tablespoon snipped fresh rosemary or 1 teaspoon dried rosemary, crushed
- 1 tablespoon olive oil or cooking oil
- 1½ pounds boneless beef sirloin steak or ribeye steaks, cut 1 inch thick
- 1 to 2 teaspoons cracked black pepper
- ½ teaspoon salt
- Fresh oregano sprigs (optional)

4 To serve, cut meat into serving-size pieces. Squeeze garlic pulp from each clove onto the steak. Mash pulp slightly with a fork; spread over meat. Drizzle with reserved oil mixture. If desired, garnish with fresh oregano.

Nutrition Facts per serving: 251 cal., 15 g total fat (5 g sat. fat), 76 mg chol., 235 mg sodium, 2 g carbo., 0 g fiber, 26 g pro.

Spinach-Stuffed Flank Steak

Lean flank steak is a good choice for health-wise steak lovers. This steak is scored with a sharp knife and rolled into spinach-and-tomato-filled spirals.

1 In a small bowl soak dried tomatoes in enough hot water to cover for 10 minutes. Drain. Snip into small pieces.

2 Meanwhile, trim fat from meat. Score meat on both sides by making shallow cuts at 1-inch intervals in a diamond pattern. Place meat between 2 pieces of plastic wrap. Pound into a 12×8-inch rectangle. Remove plastic wrap.

3 Spread the spinach over the meat. Sprinkle with the tomatoes, cheese, and basil. Starting from a short side, roll up meat. Secure with wooden toothpicks at 1-inch intervals, starting ½ inch from one end. Cut between the toothpicks into eight 1-inch slices.

4 Preheat broiler. Place meat slices, cut sides down, on the unheated rack of a broiler pan. Broil 3 to 4 inches from the heat for 12 to 16 minutes for medium (160°F), turning once halfway through broiling. Remove the toothpicks.

Prep: 20 minutes
Broil: 12 minutes
Makes: 4 servings

¼ cup dried tomatoes (not oil packed)
1 1-pound beef flank steak or
   top round steak
1 10-ounce package frozen chopped
   spinach, thawed and well drained
2 tablespoons grated Parmesan cheese
2 tablespoons snipped fresh basil

Nutrition Facts per serving: 281 cal., 9 g total fat (4 g sat. fat), 45 mg chol., 521 mg sodium, 18 g carbo., 12 g fiber, 37 g pro.

Lemony Flank Steak

Though it's rare to utter the words "light" and "beef" in the same breath, this refreshingly different dish is undeniably both. Lots of fresh lemon flavors the super-lean flank steak or top sirloin. Serve it with a side of grilled or steamed asparagus.

1 Trim fat from meat. Score meat on both sides by making shallow cuts at 1-inch intervals in a diamond pattern. Place meat in a resealable plastic bag set in a shallow dish. For marinade, combine the lemon peel, lemon juice, sugar, soy sauce, oregano, and pepper. Pour over meat; close bag. Marinate in the refrigerator for 2 to 24 hours. Drain meat, reserving marinade.

2 Preheat broiler. Place meat on the unheated rack of a broiler pan. Broil 4 to 5 inches from the heat for 15 to 18 minutes for medium (160°F), turning and brushing once with marinade halfway through broiling. Discard any remaining marinade.

3 To serve, thinly slice meat diagonally across the grain. If desired, garnish with lemon slices and fresh oregano leaves.

Prep: 15 minutes
Marinate: 2 to 24 hours
Broil: 15 minutes
Makes: 6 servings

1   1½-pound beef flank steak or
      boneless beef top sirloin steak
1   teaspoon finely shredded lemon peel
½   cup lemon juice
2   tablespoons sugar
2   tablespoons reduced-sodium
      soy sauce
2   teaspoons snipped fresh oregano
      or ½ teaspoon dried oregano,
      crushed
⅛   teaspoon black pepper
      Lemon slices (optional)
      Fresh oregano leaves (optional)

Nutrition Facts per serving: 201 cal., 8 g total fat (3 g sat. fat), 46 mg chol., 367 mg sodium, 6 g carbo., 0 g fiber, 26 g pro.

12 g
carb

Grilled Vegetables and Beef Kabobs

A light lemon-basil marinade flavors the grilled steak and complements the summer vegetables. Serve with hot cooked brown rice or couscous.

1 Trim fat from meat. Cut meat into 1-inch cubes. Place in a resealable plastic bag set in a shallow bowl.

2 For marinade, in a small bowl stir together lemon peel, lemon juice, oil, honey, basil, pepper, and garlic salt. Pour half of marinade over meat in bag; seal bag. Marinate in the refrigerator for 2 to 4 hours, turning bag occasionally. Cover and chill remaining marinade.

3 Meanwhile, in a covered medium saucepan cook the carrots in a small amount of boiling water for 3 minutes. Drain. Cut zucchini in half lengthwise; cut into ½-inch slices.

4 Drain meat, discarding marinade. On 8 long metal skewers, alternately thread meat, carrots, and zucchini.

5 Grill kabobs on the rack of an uncovered grill directly over medium coals for 12 to 14 minutes or until meat is of desired doneness, turning once and brushing kabobs often with marinade.

Nutrition Facts per serving: 264 cal., 15 g total fat (4 g sat. fat), 57 mg chol., 170 mg sodium, 12 g carbo., 2 g fiber, 20 g pro.

Prep: 20 minutes
Marinate: 2 to 4 hours
Grill: 12 minutes
Makes: 4 servings

12	ounces boneless beef sirloin, cut 1 inch thick
2	teaspoons finely shredded lemon peel
⅓	cup lemon juice
3	tablespoons olive oil or cooking oil
1	tablespoon honey
1½	teaspoons snipped fresh basil or ½ teaspoon dried basil, crushed
1	teaspoon coarsely cracked black pepper
¼	teaspoon garlic salt
8	ounces baby carrots, peeled, or packaged, peeled baby carrots
1	medium zucchini

Spicy Steak Tortillas

These beef-filled tortillas spotlight the smoky-spicy flavor of chipotle peppers. Look for canned chipotle peppers in adobo sauce in the Mexican food section of your supermarket or at a Mexican grocery store.

1 In a small bowl combine garlic salt, cumin, and oregano. In a large skillet heat 1 tablespoon of the oil over medium-high heat. Add 2 teaspoons of the garlic salt mixture, the sweet pepper, onion, and chipotle peppers. Cook and stir for 2 to 3 minutes or just until vegetables are tender. Using a slotted spoon, remove vegetables from skillet; keep warm.

2 Add the remaining 1 tablespoon oil, remaining garlic salt mixture, and the meat to same skillet. Cook meat over medium-high heat about 8 minutes or until meat is slightly pink in the center, turning once. Transfer meat to a serving platter, reserving drippings in skillet. Thinly slice meat; cover and keep warm.

3 Return cooked vegetables to skillet. Stir in tomato; heat through. Spoon vegetables over meat. To serve, fill tortillas with meat-vegetable mixture; roll up. If desired, serve with guacamole and garnish with fresh cilantro.

Start to Finish: 25 minutes
Makes: 4 servings

- 1   teaspoon garlic salt
- 1   teaspoon ground cumin
- 1   teaspoon dried oregano, crushed
- 2   tablespoons olive oil
- 1   medium red sweet pepper, cut into thin bite-size strips (1 cup)
- ½   cup chopped onion
- 1   or 2 chipotle peppers in adobo sauce, drained and chopped (see note, page 96)
- 1   pound boneless beef top loin steak, cut ¾ inch thick
- 1   medium tomato, seeded and chopped
- 4   8-inch whole wheat flour tortillas, warmed
     Purchased guacamole (optional)
     Fresh cilantro sprigs (optional)

Nutrition Facts per serving: 341 cal., 15 g total fat (3 g sat. fat), 65 mg chol., 772 mg sodium, 25 g carbo., 1 g fiber, 26 g pro.

Italian Steak Sandwiches

Flavors of Italian cuisine dominate in this sandwich. The intensely flavorful, garlicky sauce elevates the steak sandwich from ordinary to outstanding.

1 For sauce, in a blender container or food processor bowl combine parsley, olive oil, lemon juice, capers, salt, hot pepper sauce, and garlic. Cover and blend or process until nearly smooth, stopping and scraping sides as necessary. Set aside.

2 Preheat broiler. Trim fat from meat. Place meat on the unheated rack of a broiler pan. Broil 3 to 4 inches from the heat for 15 to 17 minutes for medium-rare (145°F) and 20 to 22 minutes for medium (160°F), turning once halfway through broiling.

3 Thinly slice meat. To serve, arrange onion rings and mesclun on toasted bread slices; top with meat slices. Drizzle with sauce.

Nutrition Facts per serving: 211 cal., 13 g total fat (2 g sat. fat), 13 mg chol., 244 mg sodium, 17 g carbo., 1 g fiber, 7 g pro.

Prep: 20 minutes
Broil: 15 minutes
Makes: 4 servings

- 1 cup loosely packed fresh flat-leaf parsley
- 3 tablespoons olive oil
- 4 teaspoons lemon juice
- 1 tablespoon capers, drained
  Dash salt
  Dash bottled hot pepper sauce
- 2 cloves garlic, minced
- 1 1-pound boneless beef sirloin steak, cut 1 inch thick
- 1 medium onion, thinly sliced and separated into rings
- 1 cup mesclun
- 4 1-inch slices sourdough bread, toasted

Beef Roast with Vegetables

Roasting the fall vegetables with the meat gives them a slightly caramelized flavor.

1 Combine rosemary, salt, and pepper; rub half the mixture onto meat. Reserve remaining rosemary mixture. Place meat, fat side up, on a rack in a shallow roasting pan. Insert an oven-going meat thermometer into center of meat. Roast in a 350° oven. For medium-rare, roast, uncovered, for 1½ to 2 hours or until thermometer registers 135°F. Cover and let stand 15 minutes. Temperature of the meat after standing should be 145°F. (For medium, roast for 2 to 2½ hours or until the meat thermometer registers 150°F. Cover and let stand 15 minutes. Temperature after standing should be 160°F.)

2 Meanwhile, in a covered large Dutch oven cook sweet potatoes, turnips, and onions in boiling water for 3 minutes. Drain. Add remaining rosemary mixture, oil, and garlic to vegetables; toss gently to combine. During last 45 minutes of roasting, arrange the vegetables around the meat.

3 Carve roast. Serve the sliced meat with roasted vegetables.

Nutrition Facts per serving: 328 cal., 15 g total fat (5 g sat. fat), 67 mg chol., 229 mg sodium, 24 g carbo., 5 g fiber, 25 g pro.

Prep: 30 minutes
Roast: 1½ hours
Oven: 350°F
Stand: 15 minutes
Makes: 8 servings

2 tablespoons snipped fresh rosemary or 2 teaspoon dried rosemary, crushed
1 teaspoon salt
1 teaspoon coarsely ground black pepper
1 4- to 6-pound boneless beef ribeye roast
3 large sweet potatoes, peeled and cut into 1-inch pieces (about 1½ pounds)
3 turnips, peeled and cut into ½-inch cubes
3 medium onions, cut into thin wedges
2 tablespoons olive oil or cooking oil
2 cloves garlic, minced

Herbed Beef Tenderloin

Stir fresh parsley, rosemary, and thyme into Dijon-style mustard to make a flavorful herb rub for this fork-tender roast beef. Mustard-spiked sour cream makes a refreshing condiment.

1 Trim fat from meat. In small bowl stir together parsley, the 2 tablespoons mustard, the rosemary, thyme, oil, pepper, and garlic. Rub over top and sides of meat.

2 Place meat on a rack in a shallow roasting pan. Insert an oven-going meat thermometer into center of meat. Roast in a 325° oven for 30 to 45 minutes or until meat thermometer registers 135°F. Cover with foil and let stand 15 minutes. The temperature of meat after standing should be 145°F.

3 Meanwhile, for sauce, stir together sour cream and the 2 teaspoons mustard. Thinly slice meat. Serve with sauce. If desired, sprinkle with additional black pepper.

Nutrition Facts per serving: 189 cal., 9 g total fat (3 g sat. fat), 66 mg chol., 193 mg sodium, 3 g carbo., 0 g fiber, 23 g pro.

Prep: 5 minutes
Roast: 30 minutes
Oven: 325°F
Stand: 15 minutes
Makes: 8 servings

1	2-pound beef tenderloin roast
¼	cup snipped fresh parsley
2	tablespoons Dijon-style mustard
1	tablespoon snipped fresh rosemary
2	teaspoons snipped fresh thyme
1	teaspoon olive oil or cooking oil
½	teaspoon coarsely ground black pepper
2	cloves garlic, minced
½	cup light dairy sour cream
2	teaspoons Dijon-style mustard

Braised Short Ribs with Beets

Plain red beets will turn the sauce a deep red. To make a lighter colored sauce, cook red beets separately, or use pink or golden varieties.

1 Cut meat into 8 serving-size pieces. In a Dutch oven brown meat in hot oil over medium-high heat. Drain off fat. Add broth, pepper, rosemary, thyme, and salt. Bring to boiling; reduce heat. Simmer, covered, for 1 hour.

2 Meanwhile, for beets, remove roots and all but 1 inch of stems; wash beets well. Do not peel. Cut in half lengthwise.

3 For leeks, remove any tough outer leaves. Trim roots from base. Cut away tops, leaving white portion. Slit leeks lengthwise and wash well. Cut crosswise into 2-inch slices.

4 Add beets and lemon peel to meat mixture. Return to boiling; reduce heat. Simmer, covered, for 20 minutes. Add mushrooms and leeks. Simmer, covered, about 10 minutes more or until vegetables and meat are tender. Using a slotted spoon, remove meat and vegetables. Cover with foil to keep warm.

5 Measure 1 cup cooking liquid. If necessary, add additional reduced-sodium chicken broth to make 1 cup. Return to Dutch oven. In a small bowl stir together sour cream and flour. Stir into cooking liquid. Cook and stir until slightly thickened and bubbly; cook and stir for 1 minute more. Spoon meat and vegetables into serving bowls. Ladle sauce over meat and vegetables.

Prep: 20 minutes
Cook: 1½ hours
Makes: 8 servings

- 2 pounds boneless beef short ribs
- 1 tablespoon cooking oil
- ¾ cup reduced-sodium chicken broth
- ½ teaspoon black pepper
- ½ teaspoon dried rosemary, crushed
- ½ teaspoon dried thyme, crushed
- ¼ teaspoon salt
- 16 baby pink or golden beets, or 4 medium carrots, cut into 1-inch pieces
- 4 medium leeks
- 2 teaspoons finely shredded lemon peel
- 8 ounces fresh mushrooms, halved
- ⅓ cup light dairy sour cream
- 1 tablespoon all-purpose flour

Nutrition Facts per serving: 263 cal., 13 g total fat (5 g sat. fat), 55 mg chol., 290 mg sodium, 12 g carbo., 2 g fiber, 26 g pro.

French Beef Stew

Herbes de Provence, niçoise olives, and capers give this dish its country French accent. Long, slow simmering tenderizes the meat.

1 In a Dutch oven brown half of the meat in hot oil on all sides. Remove meat from pan using a slotted spoon. Add remaining meat and chopped onion to drippings in pan. Cook for 3 to 5 minutes or until meat is brown and onion is tender. Drain off fat. Return all of the meat to the Dutch oven.

2 Add wine to the Dutch oven, stirring to scrape up the browned bits from bottom of pan. Add herbes de Provence, salt, pepper, and the water. Bring to boiling; reduce heat. Simmer, covered, for 1¼ hours or until meat is nearly tender. Add the potatoes and pearl onions. Return to boiling; reduce heat. Simmer, covered, about 30 minutes or until meat and vegetables are tender. Stir in tomato, olives, and capers; heat through.

3 Meanwhile, in a covered medium saucepan cook haricots verts in a small amount of boiling water for 5 to 7 minutes or until tender. Drain.

4 To serve, spoon the stew into soup bowls. Serve with haricots verts and garnish with parsley.

Nutrition Facts per serving: 289 cal., 8 g total fat (2 g sat. fat), 65 mg chol., 399 mg sodium, 17 g carbo., 4 g fiber, 28 g pro.

Prep: 15 minutes
Cook: 1¾ hours
Makes: 4 servings

- 1 **pound lean, boneless beef round, cut into 1-inch cubes**
- 1 **tablespoon olive oil**
- ¼ **cup chopped onion**
- 1 **cup dry white wine or beef broth**
- 1 **teaspoon dried herbes de Provence, crushed**
- ¼ **teaspoon salt**
- ¼ **teaspoon black pepper**
- 2 **cups water**
- 8 **small new potatoes (about 6 ounces)**
- 8 **pearl onions, peeled**
- 1 **large tomato, peeled, cored, seeded, and chopped**
- ¼ **cup niçoise olives, pitted, or pitted kalamata olives**
- 2 **tablespoon drained capers**
- 8 **ounces haricots verts or small green beans, trimmed and cut into 3-inch lengths**
- 1 **tablespoon chopped fresh flat-leaf parsley**

Beef-Vegetable Ragout

This recipe fits the bill for casual get-togethers, and it's ready to eat in only 30 minutes.

1 Cut beef into ¾-inch pieces. In a large nonstick skillet heat oil. Cook and stir meat in hot oil for 2 to 3 minutes or until meat is of desired doneness. Remove meat; set aside. In the same skillet cook mushrooms, onion, and garlic until tender.

2 Stir in flour, salt, and pepper. Add broth and wine. Cook and stir until thickened and bubbly. Stir in sugar snap peas; cook and stir for 2 to 3 minutes more or until peas are tender. Stir in meat and tomatoes; heat through.

Tip: Sugar snap peas (also called sugar peas), those wonderfully sweet peas encased in an edible pod, should not be confused with snow peas. While both have edible pods, the peas inside the snow pea are tiny, and the pod is almost translucent. The peas inside the sugar snap pea are larger. Each legume yields different flavors and textures.

Nutrition Facts per serving: 252 cal., 9 g total fat (3 g sat. fat), 48 mg chol., 481 mg sodium, 17 g carbo., 3 g fiber, 21 g pro.

Start to Finish: 30 minutes
Makes: 4 servings

- 12 ounces beef tenderloin
- 1 tablespoon olive oil or cooking oil
- 1½ cups sliced fresh shiitake or button mushrooms (4 ounces)
- ½ cup chopped onion
- 2 cloves garlic, minced
- 3 tablespoons all-purpose flour
- ½ teaspoon salt
- ¼ teaspoon black pepper
- 1 14-ounce can reduced-sodium beef broth
- ¼ cup port wine, dry sherry, or reduced-sodium beef broth
- 2 cups sugar snap peas or one 10-ounce package frozen sugar snap peas, thawed
- 1 cup cherry tomatoes, halved

Asian Beef and Noodle Bowl

Much loved in Chinese cookery, chile oil adds a good amount of heat with just a small dose. This fiery concoction can be found wherever Asian foods are sold. Store it in the refrigerator.

1 In a large saucepan bring 4 cups of water to boiling. If desired, break up noodles; drop noodles into the boiling water. (Do not use the flavor packets.) Return to boiling; boil for 2 to 3 minutes or just until noodles are tender but firm, stirring occasionally. Drain noodles.

2 Cut beef into bite-size strips. In a wok or large skillet heat oil over medium-high heat. Cook and stir beef, ginger, and garlic in hot oil for 2 to 3 minutes or to desired doneness. Push beef from center of wok. Add broth and soy sauce. Bring to boiling; reduce heat. Stir meat into broth mixture. Cook and stir for 1 to 2 minutes more or until heated through.

3 Add noodles, spinach, carrots, and mint to mixture in wok; toss to combine. Ladle mixture into soup bowls. If desired, sprinkle with chopped peanuts.

Start to Finish: 30 minutes
Makes: 4 servings

- 2 3-ounce packages ramen noodles
- 12 ounces beef flank steak or beef top round steak
- 2 teaspoons chile oil or
    - 2 teaspoons cooking oil plus
    - 1/8 to 1/4 teaspoon cayenne pepper
- 1 teaspoon grated fresh ginger
- 2 cloves garlic, minced
- 1 cup reduced-sodium beef broth
- 1 tablespoon reduced-sodium soy sauce
- 2 cups torn fresh spinach
- 1 cup shredded carrots
- 1/4 cup snipped fresh mint or cilantro
- Chopped peanuts (optional)

Nutrition Facts per serving: 337 cal., 10 g total fat (3 g sat. fat), 75 mg chol., 333 mg sodium, 34 g carbo., 3 g fiber, 26 g pro.

Italian Wedding Soup

Orzo pasta, sometimes called "rosamarina," is small, rice-shape pasta. If orzo is not available, you can substitute spaghetti or linguine that has been broken into ¼- to ½-inch pieces.

1 In a large saucepan cook beef, fennel, onion, and garlic, uncovered, over medium-high heat for 5 minutes or until meat is brown and vegetables are nearly tender, stirring occasionally. Drain off fat, if necessary.

2 Add broth, water, oregano, bay leaves, and pepper. Bring to boiling; reduce heat. Simmer, covered, for 10 minutes. Remove and discard bay leaves.

3 Stir in orzo. Return to boiling; reduce heat to medium. Boil gently, uncovered, about 10 minutes or just until pasta is tender, stirring occasionally. Remove from heat; stir in escarole.

4 To serve, if desired, place wedge of cheese in 4 soup bowls. Ladle hot soup into bowls.

Prep: 5 minutes
Cook: 25 minutes
Makes: 4 servings

12 ounces lean ground beef or lean ground lamb
1 small fennel bulb, trimmed and chopped (about ⅔ cup)
½ cup chopped onion
2 cloves garlic, minced
4 cups reduced-sodium beef broth
2 cups water
1 teaspoon dried oregano, crushed
2 bay leaves
¼ teaspoon cracked black pepper
½ cup dried orzo pasta (rosamarina)
4 cups shredded escarole, curly endive, and/or spinach
3 ounces Parmigiano-Reggiano or domestic Parmesan cheese with rind, cut into 4 wedges (optional)

Nutrition Facts per serving: 262 cal., 10 g total fat (4 g sat. fat), 54 mg chol., 493 mg sodium, 22 g carbo., 7 g fiber, 21 g pro.

Pizza-Topped Meat Loaf

To shape meat loaf, line a 9-inch pie plate or round cake pan with plastic wrap and press the meat mixture into the pie plate. Turn meat loaf out onto the rack of a broiler pan or roasting pan with rack. Remove pan and plastic wrap.

1 In a large bowl combine egg, bread crumbs, milk, Parmesan cheese, parsley, salt, and garlic. Add ground beef and Italian sausage; mix lightly. Shape meat mixture into a round loaf, 9 inches in diameter. Transfer loaf to the unheated rack of a broiler pan or roasting pan with rack.

2 Bake in a 375° oven for 25 to 30 minutes or until a thermometer inserted into the middle of the loaf registers 160° and juices run clear. Remove from oven. Top with sliced tomatoes; sprinkle with cheese. Bake about 5 minutes more or until cheese is melted. Transfer to a serving platter; sprinkle with basil chiffonade. Cut into wedges to serve.

Nutrition Facts per serving: 269 cal., 12 g total fat (7 g sat. fat), 103 mg chol., 482 mg sodium, 7 g carbo., 1 g fiber, 21 g pro.

*Note: To make basil chiffonade, stack fresh basil leaves. Starting at a long edge, roll the leaves up. With a sharp knife, slice the roll into thin strips.

Prep: 20 minutes
Bake: 30 minutes
Oven: 375°F
Makes: 6 servings

- 1 beaten egg
- 1 cup soft bread crumbs (about 1½ slices)
- ½ cup milk
- 2 tablespoons grated Parmesan cheese
- 2 tablespoons snipped fresh flat-leaf parsley or parsley
- ⅛ teaspoon salt
- 2 cloves garlic, minced
- 12 ounces lean ground beef
- 8 ounces bulk hot Italian sausage
- 2 roma tomatoes, thinly sliced
- ½ cup shredded Italian blend cheese or shredded mozzarella cheese
- 2 tablespoons basil chiffonade*

Grilled Veal Chops with Pesto Mushrooms

Short on time tonight? Briefly soak tender veal chops in a white wine-sage marinade and toss them on the grill. Short on time tomorrow? Marinate the meat overnight for a dinner in no time and for more flavorful chops too.

1 Trim fat from chops. Place chops in a resealable plastic bag set in a shallow dish. For marinade, in a small bowl combine white wine, sage, Worcestershire sauce, oil, and garlic. Pour over chops; seal bag. Marinate in the refrigerator for 6 to 24 hours, turning bag occasionally.

2 Drain veal chops, reserving marinade. Sprinkle chops with black pepper. Grill chops on the rack of an uncovered grill directly over medium coals to desired doneness, turning and brushing with marinade halfway through cooking. Allow 12 to 14 minutes for medium-rare (145°F) and 15 to 17 minutes for medium (160°F).

3 Meanwhile, carefully remove stems from mushrooms; reserve stems for another use or discard. Brush mushroom caps with reserved marinade; place mushrooms, stem sides down, on grill rack. Grill for 4 minutes. Turn stem sides up; carefully spoon some pesto into each cap. Grill about 4 minutes more or until heated through.

Prep: 10 minutes
Marinate: 6 to 24 hours
Grill: 12 minutes
Makes: 4 servings

- 4 veal loin chops, cut ¾ inch thick
- ¼ cup dry white wine
- 1 tablespoon snipped fresh sage or thyme
- 1 tablespoon white wine Worcestershire sauce
- 1 tablespoon olive oil
- 3 large cloves garlic, minced
- 8 large fresh mushrooms (2 to 2½ inches in diameter)
- 2 to 3 tablespoons prepared pesto

Nutrition Facts per serving: 285 cal., 16 g total fat (2 g sat. fat), 100 mg chol., 157 mg sodium, 4 g carbo., 1 g fiber, 28 g pro.

6 g
carb

Skillet Veal Scaloppine with Marsala

Ready in minutes, this richly flavored entrée is perfect for spur-of-the-moment celebrations. If veal isn't available, chicken makes a delicious substitute.

1 In a 12-inch skillet cook mushrooms and green onions in 2 teaspoons of the butter for 4 to 5 minutes or until tender. Remove from skillet, reserving drippings. Set aside.

2 Meanwhile, cut veal into 2 serving-size pieces. Place each piece of veal or chicken between 2 sheets of plastic wrap. Working from center to edges, pound lightly with the flat side of a meat mallet to about ⅛-inch thickness. Remove the plastic wrap.

3 Sprinkle veal with salt and pepper. In the same skillet cook veal in the remaining 2 teaspoons butter over medium-high heat about 2 minutes or until cooked through, turning once. Transfer to dinner plates. Keep warm.

4 Add Marsala and broth to drippings in skillet. Bring to boiling. Boil gently, uncovered, about 1 minute, scraping up any browned bits. Return mushroom mixture to skillet; add parsley. Heat through. To serve, spoon the mushroom mixture over meat.

Start to Finish: 15 minutes
Makes: 2 servings

1½ cups fresh mushrooms (such as
     crimini, porcini, morel, shiitake, or
     button), quartered, halved, or sliced
  2 green onions, sliced (¼ cup)
  4 teaspoons butter or margarine
  8 ounces veal leg round steak
     or veal sirloin steak
     or 2 medium skinless, boneless
     chicken breast halves (about
     8 ounces total)
  ⅛ teaspoon salt
  ⅛ teaspoon black pepper
  ⅓ cup dry Marsala wine or dry sherry
  ¼ cup reduced-sodium chicken broth
  1 tablespoon snipped fresh parsley

Nutrition Facts per serving: 283 cal., 12 g total fat (6 g sat. fat), 112 mg chol., 364 mg sodium, 6 g carbo., 1 g fiber, 27 g pro.

Grilled Pork Chops with Mushroom Stuffing

There's a surprise inside the pocket of these quick-cooking boneless pork chops—a mouthwatering mushroom stuffing. Instead of white button mushrooms, try using brown crimini mushrooms for even more mushroom flavor.

1 For stuffing, in a large skillet heat oil over medium heat. Add green onions and cook for 1 minute. Stir in mushrooms, rosemary, salt, and pepper. Cook and stir for 2 to 3 minutes more or until mushrooms are tender. Remove from heat.

2 Trim fat from chops. Make a pocket in each chop by cutting from fat side almost to, but not through, the opposite side. Spoon stuffing into pockets in chops. If necessary, secure with wooden toothpicks.

3 Brush chops with Worcestershire sauce. Season chops lightly with additional salt and black pepper. Grill chops on the rack of an uncovered grill directly over medium coals for 12 to 15 minutes or until done (160°F) and juices run clear, turning once. To serve, remove wooden toothpicks.

Prep: 15 minutes
Grill: 12 minutes
Makes: 4 servings

- 2 teaspoons olive oil
- 2 tablespoons thinly sliced green onions
- 1 8-ounce package fresh mushrooms, coarsely chopped
- 2 teaspoons snipped fresh rosemary or oregano
- ⅛ teaspoon salt
- ⅛ teaspoon black pepper
- 4 boneless pork loin chops, cut ¾ to 1 inch thick
- 2 teaspoons Worcestershire sauce

Nutrition Facts per serving: 241 cal., 14 g total fat (4 g sat. fat), 77 mg chol., 218 mg sodium, 4 g carbo., 1 g fiber, 25 g pro.

Pork and Pear au Jus

**Another time, use firm cooking apples in place of the pears.
Either fruit makes a sweet, mellow complement to the peppery panbroiled chops.**

1 In a medium saucepan combine pear wedges, pear nectar, ginger, and cinnamon. Bring to boiling; reduce heat. Simmer, covered, for 2 to 3 minutes or until pears are tender. Remove pears with slotted spoon, reserving liquid. Pour liquid into a glass measure. If necessary, add additional pear nectar to make 1¼ cups total liquid. Set aside.

2 Trim fat from chops. Use your fingers to press pepper onto both sides of chops. Sprinkle with salt. In a large skillet cook chops in hot oil over medium-high heat for 8 to 10 minutes or until done (160°F) and juices run clear, turning once. Remove chops from skillet. Keep warm, reserving drippings in skillet.

3 For the sauce, stir cornstarch into reserved drippings in the skillet. Stir in reserved pear cooking liquid. Cook and stir until thickened and bubbly. Add pears. Cook and stir for 2 minutes more. Serve pears with chops; drizzle sauce over chops.

Start to Finish: 35 minutes
Makes: 4 servings

- 2 small pears, cored and cut into 8 wedges each
- 1 cup pear nectar or apple juice
- 2 teaspoons grated fresh ginger
- ¼ teaspoon ground cinnamon
- 4 pork loin rib chops, cut ¾ inch thick
- 2 teaspoons cracked black pepper
- ¼ teaspoon salt
- 1 tablespoon cooking oil
- 2 teaspoons cornstarch

Nutrition Facts per serving: 354 cal., 14 g total fat (4 g sat. fat), 98 mg chol., 226 mg sodium, 25 g carbo., 3 g fiber, 32 g pro.

Spice-Rubbed Pork Chops

Big, meaty chops pair well with full-flavored ingredients. This lime and chili powder marinade is just the ticket. Add more or less of the hot pepper sauce to suit your taste.

1 Trim fat from chops. Place chops in a plastic bag set in a shallow dish. For the marinade, in a small bowl stir together the lime juice, chili powder, olive oil, cumin, cinnamon, hot pepper sauce, salt, and garlic. Pour over chops; seal bag. Marinate in the refrigerator for 4 to 24 hours, turning bag occasionally. Drain chops, discarding marinade.

2 Preheat broiler. Place chops on the unheated rack of a broiler pan. Broil 3 to 4 inches from the heat for 6 to 8 minutes or until done (160°F) and juices run clear, turning once halfway through broiling.

Nutrition Facts per serving: 163 cal., 10 g total fat (3 g sat. fat), 51 mg chol., 128 mg sodium, 3 g carbo., 1 g fiber, 17 g pro.

Prep: 15 minutes
Marinate: 4 to 24 hours
Broil: 6 minutes
Makes: 4 servings

- 4 boneless pork loin chops, cut ½ inch thick
- ¼ cup lime juice
- 2 tablespoons chili powder
- 1 tablespoon olive oil
- 1½ teaspoons ground cumin
- 1½ teaspoons ground cinnamon
- ½ teaspoon bottled hot pepper sauce
- ¼ teaspoon salt
- 1 clove garlic, minced

Pork Chops in Creamy Vegetable Sauce

This cream sauce combines reduced-fat soup and fat-free sour cream, providing a seemingly high-fat richness that won't give away its secret.

1 Trim fat from chops. Coat a 12-inch nonstick skillet with cooking spray. Heat over medium heat. Add pork chops; cook for 6 minutes. Turn chops; add mushrooms and sweet pepper. Cook about 6 minutes more or until done (160°F) and juices run clear. Remove the chops and vegetables.

2 For sauce, in a small bowl stir together the soup, sour cream, milk, and paprika. Stir the mixture into skillet; bring to boiling.

3 Return the chops and cooked vegetables to skillet. Cook, covered, for 5 minutes. Add tomato. Cook about 1 to 2 minutes more or until heated through.

Nutrition Facts per serving: 193 cal., 9 g total fat (3 g sat. fat), 50 mg chol., 264 mg sodium, 11 g carbo., 1 g fiber, 17 g pro.

Start to Finish: 25 minutes
Makes: 6 servings

- 6 pork rib chops, cut ½ inch thick
  Nonstick cooking spray
- 1½ cups sliced fresh mushrooms
- 1 medium green or red sweet pepper, cut into thin strips
- 1 10¾-ounce can condensed reduced-fat and reduced-sodium cream of mushroom soup
- ½ cup fat-free dairy sour cream
- ¼ cup milk
- 1 teaspoon paprika
- 1 medium tomato, seeded and chopped

Sweet Pepper and Olive Pork

A family favorite gets a Latino twist. Pimiento-stuffed olives are often sold already chopped for ease. Look for "salad olives" on the label.

1 Place each pork slice between 2 sheets of plastic wrap. Using the heel of your hand, press lightly to ⅛-inch thickness. Remove plastic wrap. Season the pork slices with salt and pepper.

2 Lightly coat a large nonstick skillet with cooking spray; heat over medium-high heat. Cook half of the pork slices at a time in skillet for 2 to 3 minutes or until meat is brown and juices run clear, turning once. Remove meat from skillet; keep warm.

3 Add oil to skillet; heat over medium-high heat. Cook onions, sweet peppers, mushrooms, cumin, and garlic in hot oil about 4 minutes or until crisp-tender.

4 Stir in olives; heat through. Serve vegetable mixture with pork slices.

Prep: 15 minutes
Cook: 8 minutes
Makes: 4 servings

- 1 12-ounce pork tenderloin, cut into 8 slices
- ⅛ teaspoon salt
- ⅛ teaspoon black pepper
  Nonstick cooking spray
- 2 teaspoons olive oil
- 2 medium onions, cut into thin wedges
- 2 medium green sweet peppers, cut into thin bite-size strips
- ½ cup sliced fresh mushrooms
- ½ teaspoon ground cumin
- 2 cloves garlic, minced
- ⅓ cup chopped pimento-stuffed green olives

Nutrition Facts per serving: 171 cal., 9 g total fat (2 g sat. fat), 38 mg chol., 342 mg sodium, 9 g carbo., 2 g fiber, 14 g pro.

Pork Medallions with Cherry Sauce

During the autumn months, pork is often prepared with fruit such as prunes or apples. These quick-seared medallions cloaked in a delightful sweet cherry sauce provide a whole new reason—and season—to pair pork with fruit.

1 Trim fat from pork. Cut pork crosswise into 1-inch slices. Place each slice between 2 pieces of plastic wrap. With the heel of your hand, press each slice into a ½-inch-thick medallion. Remove plastic wrap. Sprinkle lightly with salt and black pepper.

2 Coat a large nonstick skillet with cooking spray. Heat skillet over medium-high heat. Add pork; cook for 6 minutes or until pork is slightly pink in center and juices run clear, turning once. Transfer to a serving platter; keep warm.

3 Combine cranberry juice, mustard, and cornstarch; add to skillet. Cook and stir until thickened and bubbly. Cook and stir for 2 minutes more. Stir cherries into cranberry juice mixture in skillet. Serve over pork.

Start to Finish: 20 minutes
Makes: 4 servings

1 pound pork tenderloin
  Nonstick cooking spray
¾ cup cranberry juice cocktail or
    apple juice
2 teaspoons spicy brown mustard
1 teaspoon cornstarch
1 cup sweet cherries (such as Rainier
    or Bing), halved and pitted,
    or 1 cup frozen unsweetened pitted
    dark sweet cherries, thawed

Nutrition Facts per serving: 197 cal., 5 g total fat (2 g sat. fat), 81 mg chol., 127 mg sodium, 12 g carbo., 0 g fiber, 26 g pro.

7 g
carb

Grilled Mustard-Glazed Pork Tenderloin

This express-lane dinner gives you time to slow down as soon as you walk in the door. Simply mix up the marinade and pour it over the pork. Let it marinate in the refrigerator while you unwind. Grill about 20 minutes and dinner's done.

1 Trim fat from meat. Place meat in a resealable plastic bag set in a shallow dish. For marinade, combine apple juice, vinegar, shallots, mustard, oil, brown sugar, soy sauce, and pepper. Pour over meat; seal bag. Marinate in the refrigerator for 30 minutes, turning bag occasionally.

2 Drain meat, reserving marinade. Arrange medium-hot coals around a drip pan. Place meat on the grill rack directly over coals. Grill for 8 minutes, turning once to brown both sides. Test for medium heat above drip pan. Move meat directly over drip pan; insert oven-going meat thermometer into center of thickest tenderloin. Cover and grill for 15 to 20 minutes more or until meat thermometer registers 160°F.

3 Meanwhile, for sauce, pour reserved marinade into a medium saucepan. Bring to boiling; reduce heat. Simmer, covered, about 8 minutes or until reduced to ⅔ cup. Slice the meat across the grain. Serve with the sauce. If desired, sprinkle with chives.

Prep: 10 minutes
Marinate: 30 minutes
Grill: 23 minutes
Makes: 6 servings

- 2 12- to 14-ounce pork tenderloins
- ½ cup apple juice
- ¼ cup cider vinegar
- 2 large shallots, minced
- ¼ cup coarse-grain brown mustard
- 2 tablespoons olive oil
- 1 tablespoon brown sugar
- 1½ teaspoons soy sauce
- Dash black pepper
- Snipped fresh chives (optional)

Nutrition Facts per serving: 215 cal., 9 g total fat (2 g sat. fat), 81 mg chol., 280 mg sodium, 7 g carbo., 0 g fiber, 26 g pro.

Grilled Mango-Berry "Chalsa" with Pork

Pop this pork onto the grill and ignore it until it's done. Serve it with the chunky sauce that combines the best qualities of chutney and salsa.

1 Combine soy sauce, black pepper, and garlic. Trim fat from meat. Use a sharp knife to score top and bottom of roast in a diamond pattern, making cuts ¼ inch deep. Rub garlic mixture onto meat. Insert an oven-going meat thermometer near center of roast.

2 Arrange medium coals around a drip pan. Test for medium-low heat above pan. Place meat on a rack in a roasting pan on grill rack. Cover and grill about 1 hour or until the meat thermometer registers 155°F. Remove meat from grill. Cover meat with foil and let stand 15 minutes. The temperature of the meat after standing should be 160°F.

3 Meanwhile, combine half of the mango, the onion, brown sugar, banana pepper, lime peel, lime juice, and salt. Tear off a 24×18-inch piece of heavy foil. Fold in half to make an 18×12-inch rectangle. Spoon mixture onto center of foil. Bring up 2 opposite edges; fold foil to enclose the mixture, leaving space for steam to build.

4 Grill packet on the rack of an uncovered grill directly over medium coals about 10 minutes or until heated through. Transfer mango mixture to a medium bowl. Gently stir in remaining mango and the raspberries. Serve with pork and, if desired, lime.

Prep: 25 minutes
Grill: 1 hour
Stand: 15 minutes
Makes: 6 servings

- 1 tablespoon reduced-sodium soy sauce
- ¼ teaspoon black pepper
- 3 cloves garlic, minced
- 1 1½- to 2-pound boneless pork top loin roast (single loin)
- 1 mango, seeded, peeled, and chopped (1 cup)
- ¼ cup chopped onion
- 2 tablespoons brown sugar
- 1 finely chopped small, fresh banana pepper (see note, page 96) (1 to 2 tablespoons)
- ½ teaspoon finely shredded lime peel
- 1 tablespoon lime juice
- ⅛ teaspoon salt
- 1 cup fresh raspberries
  Lime wedges (optional)

Nutrition Facts per serving: 189 cal., 8 g total fat (3 g sat. fat), 51 mg chol., 257 mg sodium, 14 g carbo., 2 g fiber, 17 g pro.

Sage Pork Roast with Apple

It's generally known that pork and applesauce go together like bread and butter. Here the accompanying apple and onion compote roasts right alongside the meat.

1 Rub the roast with the snipped sage and 1 teaspoon of the pepper. Place roast, rib side down, in a shallow roasting pan. Place bacon slices across top of roast. Insert an oven-going meat thermometer into center of roast. Roast in a 325° oven for 1 to 1¼ hours or until meat thermometer registers 130°F.

2 Remove pan from oven. Add apples, onion, garlic, and the whole sage leaves to roasting pan. Sprinkle with salt and remaining ½ teaspoon pepper. Stir fruit and vegetables to coat with pan juices. Return to oven and roast for 25 to 30 minutes more or until apples and onion are golden and tender and meat thermometer registers 155°F, stirring apple and onion mixture several times during roasting.

3 Transfer the pork to a serving platter. Cover with foil; let stand for 15 minutes. (The temperature of the meat after standing should be 160°F.)

4 Using a slotted spoon, transfer the apple and onion mixture to a large bowl; cover and keep warm. Pour drippings from the roasting pan into a small saucepan, scraping out, and including, the crusty browned bits. Stir in apple juice. Bring mixture just to boiling over medium heat. Pour over the apple mixture, tossing to coat.

Prep: 30 minutes
Roast: 1 hour 25 minutes
Oven: 325°F
Stand: 15 minutes
Makes: 6 to 8 servings

1   3½- to 4-pound pork loin center rib roast, backbone loosened
2   teaspoons snipped fresh sage
1½ teaspoons coarsely ground black pepper
3   slices bacon
6   medium cooking apples, cored and cut into bite-size chunks
1   large red onion, cut into thin wedges
3   large cloves garlic, peeled and thinly sliced
8   whole sage leaves
¼   teaspoon salt
⅓   cup apple juice
    Fresh sage sprigs (optional)

5 To serve, spoon the apple mixture around the pork roast. If desired, garnish with additional sage sprigs.

Nutrition Facts per serving: 341 cal., 11 g total fat (4 g sat. fat), 82 mg chol., 202 mg sodium, 27 g carbo., 5 g fiber, 34 g pro.

13 g
carb

Gingered Pork and Cabbage Soup

Fresh ginger and Chinese cabbage lend Asian flavors to this hearty soup.

1 In a medium saucepan bring the 6 cups chicken broth to boiling. Meanwhile, trim fat from pork. Cut pork into ½-inch cubes.

2 In a large saucepan cook pork cubes, onion, ginger, and garlic in hot oil until pork is brown.

3 Add hot chicken broth. Bring to boiling. Stir in tomatoes and carrots. Return to boiling; reduce heat. Simmer, covered, for 15 minutes.

4 Stir in the pasta and cook for 6 to 8 minutes more or until pasta is tender but still firm. Stir in sliced Chinese cabbage and mint.

Nutrition Facts per serving: 118 cal., 3 g total fat (1 g sat. fat), 18 mg chol., 493 mg sodium, 13 g carbo., 3 g fiber, 10 g pro.

Start to Finish: 40 minutes
Makes: 8 servings

6 cups reduced-sodium chicken broth
8 ounces boneless pork sirloin, cut ½ inch thick
1 cup chopped onion
2 teaspoons grated fresh ginger
4 cloves garlic, minced
1 tablespoon cooking oil
3 small tomatoes, chopped
2 medium carrots, finely chopped
½ cup dried anelli pasta or other small pasta
4 cups thinly sliced Chinese cabbage (napa cabbage)
¼ cup snipped fresh mint

Pork and Mango Picadillo

Pronounced pee-kah-DEE-yoh, this dish can be found in many Spanish-speaking countries. While most all versions contain the tomatoes, spices, onions, garlic, and ground meat found here, this version adds mango to complement the spicy flavors.

1 In a large skillet cook meat over medium-high heat until no longer pink. Drain off fat. Stir in green onions, cinnamon, coriander, cumin, oregano, thyme, and garlic. Cook and stir for 2 minutes more.

2 Gently stir in salsa and mango. Cook, covered, for 1 to 2 minutes or until heated through. Spoon into serving dish. Sprinkle with almonds and cilantro. If desired, serve with rice.

Nutrition Facts per serving: 223 cal., 12 g total fat (4 g sat. fat), 53 mg chol., 268 mg sodium, 16 g carbo., 2 g fiber, 16 g pro.

Start to Finish: 30 minutes
Makes: 4 servings

- 1 pound lean ground pork
- ⅓ cup thinly sliced green onions
- 1 teaspoon ground cinnamon
- 1 teaspoon ground coriander
- 1 teaspoon ground cumin
- 1 teaspoon dried oregano, crushed
- 1 teaspoon dried thyme, crushed
- 2 cloves garlic, minced
- 1 cup thick-and-chunky salsa
- 1 mango, peeled, pitted, and cubed
- 2 tablespoons smoked almonds or whole almonds, chopped
- 2 tablespoons snipped fresh cilantro
  Hot cooked brown or yellow rice (optional)

26 g carb

Spinach and Ham Lasagna

Deviate from the traditional red-sauced lasagna. This luscious lasagna is layered with spinach, ham, cheese, and a lightened "cream" sauce. Ham adds a tasty smoky flavor.

1 Cook the lasagna noodles according to package directions, except omit oil. Drain. Rinse with cold water; drain again. Set aside.

2 Meanwhile, cook the spinach according to package directions; drain well. Set spinach aside.

3 For sauce, in a medium saucepan combine the milk, onion, and cornstarch. Cook and stir until thickened and bubbly. Cook and stir for 2 minutes more.

4 Spread 2 tablespoons of the sauce evenly on the bottom of a 2-quart rectangular baking dish. Stir ham and Italian seasoning into remaining sauce.

5 Arrange 3 lasagna noodles in the dish. Spread with one-third of the remaining sauce. Layer the spinach on top. Layer another one-third of the sauce, the cottage cheese, and half of the mozzarella cheese over the spinach. Place remaining noodles on top. Top with remaining sauce and mozzarella.

6 Bake in a 375° oven for 30 to 35 minutes or until heated through. Let stand 10 minutes before serving.

Prep: 40 minutes
Bake: 30 minutes
Oven: 375°F
Stand: 10 minutes
Makes: 6 servings

- 6 packaged dried lasagna noodles (4 ounces)
- 1 10-ounce package frozen chopped spinach
- 2 cups milk
- ¼ cup chopped onion
- 3 tablespoons cornstarch
- 1½ cups diced lower-fat, lower-sodium cooked ham (8 ounces)
- ½ teaspoon dried Italian seasoning, crushed
- 1 cup low-fat cottage cheese
- 1 cup shredded mozzarella cheese (4 ounces)

Nutrition Facts per serving: 241 cal., 5 g total fat (2 g sat. fat), 30 mg chol., 724 mg sodium, 26 g carbo., 0 g fiber, 22 g pro.

8 g
carb

Lamb Chops and Peppers

Enjoy this quick-cooking skillet dish in the summertime when sweet peppers and zucchini are at their peak.

1 Trim fat from chops. Lightly coat a large nonstick skillet with cooking spray. Heat over medium-high heat. Cook the chops in the skillet about 4 minutes or until brown, turning once. Remove chops from skillet. Add the sweet peppers, zucchini, leek, and garlic to the skillet and cook for 3 minutes. Return the chops to skillet.

2 In a small bowl stir together wine, bouillon granules, basil, oregano, and black pepper. Add to chops and vegetables. Bring to boiling; reduce heat. Simmer, covered, for 6 to 8 minutes or until chops are slightly pink in the center and juices run clear.

Nutrition Facts per serving: 181 cal., 6 g total fat (2 g sat. fat), 58 mg chol., 268 mg sodium, 8 g carbo., 2 g fiber, 19 g pro.

Start to Finish: 30 minutes
Makes: 4 servings

4 lamb leg sirloin chops, cut ¾ inch thick (about 1¼ pounds total)
 Nonstick cooking spray
1 cup green sweet pepper cut into thin bite-size strips
1 cup red or yellow sweet pepper cut into thin bite-size strips
1 cup zucchini cut into thin bite-size strips
½ cup thinly sliced leek
1 clove garlic, minced
½ cup dry white wine or water
1 teaspoon instant beef bouillon granules
1 teaspoon dried basil, crushed
½ teaspoon dried oregano, crushed
⅛ teaspoon black pepper

Moroccan Lamb Roast

For an easy side dish, place an assortment of cut-up vegetables (such as carrots, turnips, and sweet peppers) in the roasting pan for the last 45 minutes of roasting.

1 Trim fat from meat. Cut several ½-inch-wide slits randomly in top and sides of roast. Insert garlic slivers into slits. In a small bowl stir together coriander seeds, lemon peel, olive oil, cumin seeds, salt, and pepper. Rub surface of meat with spice mixture. If desired, cover and chill for several hours or overnight.

2 Insert an oven-going meat thermometer into center of roast. The thermometer should not touch bone. Roast in a 325° oven. For medium-rare, roast for 1¾ to 2¼ hours or until meat thermometer registers 140°F. Cover with foil and let stand 15 minutes. The temperature of the meat after standing should register 145°F. (For medium, roast for 2¼ to 2¾ hours or until meat thermometer registers 155°F. Cover and let stand 15 minutes. The temperature of the meat after standing should be 160°F.)

Prep: 15 minutes
Roast: 1¾ hours
Oven: 325°F
Stand: 15 minutes
Makes: 10 servings

- 1 5- to 7-pound leg of lamb (with bone)
- 4 to 8 cloves garlic, cut into slivers
- 2 tablespoons coriander seeds, crushed
- 2 tablespoons finely shredded lemon peel
- 1 tablespoon olive oil
- 1 teaspoon cumin seeds, crushed
- ½ teaspoon salt
- ½ teaspoon whole black pepper, crushed

Nutrition Facts per serving: 235 cal., 10 g total fat (3 g sat. fat), 101 mg chol., 185 mg sodium, 1 g carbo., 0 g fiber, 32 g pro.

Chicken & Turkey

Apple-Glazed Chicken with Spinach	153
Beer-Brined Turkey	166
Braised Chicken with Beans and Squash	156
Chicken and Broccoli Stir-Fry	159
Chicken and Dumplings	162
Chicken with Chipotle Barbecue Sauce	154
Curried Turkey and Couscous Pie	174
Grilled Citrus Chicken	155
Grilled Curried Lime Chicken Kabobs	157
Grilled Fiery Chicken and Potato Fingers	160
Grilled Turkey Steaks with Sweet Pepper-Citrus Salsa	170
Grilled Turkey with Pepper Sauce	169
Kale, Lentil, and Chicken Soup	165
Maple-Mustard-Glazed Chicken and Winter Squash	149
Mediterranean Chicken and Pasta	161
Mexican-Style Turkey Soup	180
Pasta with Arugula and Sausage	178
Pineapple-Rum Turkey Kabobs	173
Popover Pizza Casserole	177
Roasted Italian Chicken	148
Roasted Tarragon Chicken	150
Savory Turkey-Mushroom Burgers	176
Spanish-Style Chicken	151
Summer Chicken and Mushroom Pasta	158
Sweet and Spicy Turkey Skillet	172
Tandoori Chicken Burgers	163
Turkey and Asparagus Stir-Fry	175
Turkey Breast with Roasted Asparagus	167
Turkey Enchiladas	179
Turkey Mushroom Marsala	171
Turkey with Cranberry Sauce	168
Vegetable-Stuffed Chicken	152
Wild Rice Chicken Soup	164

2 g
carb

Roasted Italian Chicken

Roasted chicken tastes better if something flavorful, such as an herb, is placed under its skin. The under-the-skin rub used in this recipe contributes a lot of flavor while working like a marinade.

1 In a small bowl whisk together vinegar, oil, oregano, basil, lemon juice, thyme, salt, pepper, and garlic. Set aside.

2 Rinse inside of chicken; pat dry with paper towels. Tie legs to tail. Twist wing tips under back. Slip your fingers between the skin and the breast and leg meat of the chicken, forming a pocket. Spoon herb mixture into pocket. Place chicken, breast side up, on a rack in a shallow roasting pan. If desired, insert an oven-going meat thermometer into center of an inside thigh muscle, making sure it doesn't touch bone.

3 Roast in a 375° oven for 1¼ to 1½ hours or until drumsticks move easily in their sockets and chicken is no longer pink (180°). Remove chicken from oven. Cover with foil and let stand for 10 minutes before carving.

Nutrition Facts per serving: 266 cal., 17 g total fat (4 g sat. fat), 79 mg chol., 268 mg sodium, 2 g carbo., 0 g fiber, 25 g pro.

Prep: 15 minutes
Roast: 1¼ hours
Oven: 375°F
Stand: 10 minutes
Makes: 6 servings

- 2 tablespoons balsamic vinegar
- 2 tablespoons olive oil
- 1 tablespoon snipped fresh oregano or
    1 teaspoon dried oregano, crushed
- 1 tablespoon snipped fresh basil or
    1 teaspoon dried basil, crushed
- 1 tablespoon lemon juice
- 1½ teaspoons snipped fresh thyme or
    ½ teaspoon dried thyme, crushed
- ½ teaspoon salt
- ½ teaspoon black pepper
- 3 cloves garlic, minced
- 1 3- to 3½-pound whole broiler-fryer
    chicken

Maple-Mustard-Glazed Chicken and Winter Squash

Roasted chicken and vegetables may sound like Sunday-dinner fare, but this lovely maple-glazed version calls for chicken pieces (rather than the whole bird) to save roasting time. It's too good—and too quick—to save for weekends only!

1 Remove skin from chicken. Arrange chicken in a single layer in a 2- or 3-quart rectangular baking dish.

2 For glaze, in a small bowl combine the 2 tablespoons maple syrup, whiskey, Dijon mustard, parsley, and pepper. Brush the glaze over chicken.

3 If desired, peel squash. Cut squash into serving-size pieces, removing seeds. Place squash in a 2-quart casserole; cover. In a small bowl combine softened butter, pecans, brown sugar, the 1 tablespoon maple syrup, and salt; set aside.

4 Bake chicken, uncovered, and squash, covered, in a 375° oven for 35 minutes. Spoon juices over chicken. Dot squash with butter mixture. Bake chicken and squash, uncovered, about 15 minutes more or until chicken is no longer pink (170° for breasts; 180° for thighs and drumsticks) and squash is tender.

5 Serve the chicken with squash, spooning maple-flavored pan juices over each.

Prep: 20 minutes
Bake: 50 minutes
Oven: 375°F
Makes: 6 servings

2½ to 3 pounds meaty chicken pieces (breast halves, thighs, and drumsticks)
2 tablespoons maple syrup
2 tablespoons whiskey or orange juice
1 tablespoon Dijon-style mustard
1 tablespoon snipped fresh parsley
½ teaspoon black pepper
1 1½- to 2-pound butternut squash
2 tablespoons butter or margarine, softened
2 tablespoons chopped pecans, toasted
1 tablespoon brown sugar
1 tablespoon maple syrup
¼ teaspoon salt

Nutrition Facts per serving: 302 cal., 12 g total fat (4 g sat. fat), 88 mg chol., 227 mg sodium, 20 g carbo., 2 g fiber, 26 g pro.

5 g
carb

Roasted Tarragon Chicken

Tarragon's bold, aniselike flavor complements the sweetness of the roasted tomatoes and shallots. If tarragon is too strong for your taste buds, try rosemary or thyme instead.

1 In a medium bowl stir together oil, tarragon, pepper, salt, and garlic. Add tomatoes and shallots; toss gently to coat. Using a slotted spoon, remove tomatoes and shallots from bowl, reserving the oil mixture.

2 If desired, remove skin from chicken. Arrange chicken in a single layer in a shallow roasting pan. Brush with the reserved oil mixture.

3 Roast the chicken in a 375° oven for 20 minutes. Add shallots; roast for 15 minutes. Add tomatoes; roast for 10 to 12 minutes more or until chicken is no longer pink (170° for breasts; 180° for thighs and drumsticks) and vegetables are tender.

Prep: 15 minutes
Roast: 45 minutes
Oven: 375°F
Makes: 6 servings

  3 tablespoons olive oil
2½ teaspoons dried tarragon, crushed
  ½ teaspoon black pepper
  ¼ teaspoon salt
  2 cloves garlic, minced
  1 pound cherry tomatoes
  8 small shallots
2½ to 3 pounds meaty chicken pieces
      (breast halves, thighs, and
      drumsticks)

Nutrition Facts per serving: 227 cal., 13 g total fat (2 g sat. fat), 67 mg chol., 170 mg sodium, 5 g carbo., 1 g fiber, 23 g pro.

Spanish-Style Chicken

An old Spanish saying claims that in Spain, food is generally fried in the south, roasted in the middle of the country, and stewed in the north. If so, that means this dish, a quick version of stew, is reminiscent of northern Spain.

1 Remove skin from chicken. In a large plastic bag combine flour, salt, and cayenne pepper. Add chicken, a few pieces at a time, shaking to coat. In a 4-quart Dutch oven cook chicken in hot oil over medium-high heat about 10 minutes or until light brown, turning chicken to brown evenly.

2 Add undrained tomatoes, potatoes, onion, olives, wine, capers (if desired), dried herbs (if using), and garlic. Bring to boiling; reduce heat. Simmer, covered, for 35 to 40 minutes or until chicken is no longer pink (170° for breasts; 180° for thighs and drumsticks). Transfer chicken to a serving dish; cover and keep warm.

3 In a small bowl combine the water and cornstarch; stir into tomato mixture in Dutch oven. Cook and stir until thickened and bubbly. Cook and stir for 2 minutes more. If using, stir in fresh herbs. Pour the tomato mixture over chicken.

Nutrition Facts per serving: 354 cal., 12 g total fat (3 g sat. fat), 77 mg chol., 566 mg sodium, 28 g carbo., 4 g fiber, 29 g pro.

Prep: 25 minutes
Cook: 35 minutes
Makes: 6 servings

- 3 to 3½ pounds meaty chicken pieces (breast halves, thighs, and drumsticks)
- ¼ cup all-purpose flour
- ½ teaspoon salt
- ¼ teaspoon cayenne pepper
- 2 tablespoons olive oil
- 1 28-ounce can whole Italian-style tomatoes, undrained and cut up
- 4 medium potatoes, cut into ½-inch pieces (4 cups)
- 1 medium onion, sliced
- ½ cup halved pitted ripe olives
- ½ cup dry red wine or chicken broth
- 2 tablespoons capers, drained (optional)
- 1 tablespoon snipped fresh basil or 1 teaspoon dried basil, crushed
- 2 teaspoons snipped fresh oregano or ½ teaspoon dried oregano, crushed
- 2 cloves garlic, minced
- 1 tablespoon cold water
- 2 teaspoons cornstarch

4 g
carb

Vegetable-Stuffed Chicken

A simple Madeira wine sauce complements this elegant mushroom-and-cheese-stuffed chicken. If you like a more earthy flavor, use wild mushrooms such as shiitake, chanterelle, or porcini.

1 For stuffing, coat a large nonstick skillet with cooking spray. Heat skillet over medium heat. Add mushrooms and garlic; cook until mushrooms are tender. Stir in roasted pepper and marjoram. Remove from heat.

2 Cut a horizontal slit in the thickest portion of each chicken piece, forming a pocket. Place a slice of cheese and some of the stuffing in each pocket. Secure with wooden toothpicks.

3 In a large skillet cook chicken in hot oil over medium heat about 4 minutes or until light brown, turning once. Pour broth and wine into skillet. Bring to boiling; reduce heat. Simmer, uncovered, about 8 minutes or until chicken is no longer pink (170°). Transfer chicken to a serving platter.

4 Strain pan juices; measure juices and return to skillet. If necessary, boil gently, uncovered, until liquid is reduced to ¾ cup. In a small bowl combine water and cornstarch; stir into liquid in skillet. Cook and stir until thickened and bubbly. Return chicken to skillet; cook about 2 minutes more or until heated through. Remove toothpicks from chicken. Sprinkle with parsley.

Nutrition Facts per serving: 208 cal., 8 g total fat (3 g sat. fat), 71 mg chol., 199 mg sodium, 4 g carbo., 1 g fiber, 26 g pro.

Start to Finish: 35 minutes
Makes: 4 servings

Nonstick cooking spray
1½ cups chopped fresh mushrooms
1 clove garlic, minced
2 tablespoons chopped roasted red sweet pepper
¼ teaspoon dried marjoram, crushed
4 skinless, boneless chicken breast halves (about 1 pound total)
1½ ounces Gruyère cheese, cut into 4 slices
1 teaspoon olive oil
⅔ cup reduced-sodium chicken broth
⅓ cup Madeira wine or reduced-sodium chicken broth
1 tablespoon cold water
2 teaspoons cornstarch
1 tablespoon snipped fresh parsley

Apple-Glazed Chicken with Spinach

Apple jelly is the secret ingredient that replaces fat for basting the chicken and flavors the spinach. Wild rice makes a perfect side dish.

1 For glaze, in a small saucepan heat apple jelly, soy sauce, thyme, lemon peel, and ginger just until jelly is melted. Set aside ¼ cup of the glaze.

2 Preheat broiler. Place chicken on the unheated rack of a broiler pan. Broil 4 to 5 inches from the heat for 12 to 15 minutes or until chicken is no longer pink (170°), turning once and brushing with the remaining glaze the last 5 minutes of broiling. (Or place chicken on the rack of an uncovered grill directly over medium coals. Grill for 12 to 15 minutes, turning once and brushing with the remaining glaze the last 5 minutes of grilling.)

3 Meanwhile, lightly coat a large saucepan or Dutch oven with cooking spray. Heat saucepan over medium heat. Add apples, leek, and garlic; cook for 3 minutes. Add the reserved ¼ cup glaze and apple cider; bring to boiling. Add spinach; toss just until wilted. Season to taste with salt and black pepper.

4 To serve, cut each chicken piece crosswise into 6 to 8 slices. Divide the spinach mixture among dinner plates. Top with sliced chicken.

Prep: 20 minutes
Broil: 12 minutes
Makes: 4 servings

½ cup apple jelly
2 tablespoons soy sauce
1 tablespoon snipped fresh thyme
1 teaspoon finely shredded lemon peel
1 teaspoon grated fresh ginger
4 skinless, boneless chicken breast
halves (about 1 pound total)
Nonstick cooking spray
2 medium apples, peeled, cored,
and chopped
⅓ cup sliced leek
2 cloves garlic, minced
2 tablespoons apple cider or
chicken broth
1 10-ounce package prewashed
spinach, trimmed (about 8 cups)

Nutrition Facts per serving: 263 cal., 3 g total fat (1 g sat. fat), 45 mg chol., 654 mg sodium, 42 g carbo. 4 g fiber, 19 g pro.

36 g
carb

Chicken with Chipotle Barbecue Sauce

Chipotle chile peppers are dried, smoked jalapeño peppers with a smoky, sweet, almost chocolaty flavor. Here, they lend their distinctive spicy taste to a molasses-sweetened barbecue sauce.

1 For sauce, remove any stems from chipotle peppers. Place peppers and adobo sauce in a blender container. Cover and blend until smooth; set aside.

2 Lightly coat a medium saucepan with cooking spray. Heat saucepan over medium heat. Add onion and garlic; cook until onion is tender. Stir in pureed chipotle peppers, catsup, vinegar, molasses, and Worcestershire sauce. Bring to boiling; reduce heat. Simmer, uncovered, about 10 minutes or until sauce is slightly thickened.

3 Place chicken on the rack of an uncovered grill directly over medium coals. Grill for 12 to 15 minutes or until chicken is no longer pink (170°), turning once and brushing occasionally with some of the sauce the last 5 minutes of grilling.

4 To serve, reheat the remaining sauce. Serve the chicken with sauce.

Prep: 30 minutes
Grill: 12 minutes
Makes: 6 servings

¼ cup canned chipotle chile peppers in adobo sauce (see note, page 96)
   Nonstick cooking spray
⅓ cup finely chopped onion
3 cloves garlic, minced
1 cup catsup
3 tablespoons white wine vinegar
3 tablespoons molasses or sorghum
1 tablespoon Worcestershire sauce
6 skinless, boneless chicken breast halves (about 1½ pounds total)

Nutrition Facts per serving: 291 cal., 6 g total fat (1 g sat. fat), 59 mg chol., 1,399 mg sodium, 36 g carbo., 1 g fiber, 23 g pro.

Grilled Citrus Chicken

**Prepare your ingredients for this grilled dish the night before.
The next day, relax by the grill while the chicken cooks.**

1 Place chicken in a resealable plastic bag set in a shallow dish. Pour 1 cup of the Citrus-Spice Marinade over chicken and add orange slices; seal bag. Marinate in the refrigerator for 6 to 24 hours, turning bag occasionally. Cover and chill the remaining marinade for basting.

2 Drain chicken, discarding marinade. Place chicken and vegetables on the rack of an uncovered grill directly over medium coals. Grill chicken for 12 to 15 minutes or until no longer pink (170°), turning and brushing once with some of the reserved marinade halfway through grilling. Grill vegetables for 8 to 10 minutes or until tender, turning and brushing occasionally with the reserved marinade. Season vegetables to taste with salt and black pepper.

Citrus-Spice Marinade: In a screw-top jar combine ¾ cup orange juice, ¼ cup lemon juice, 3 tablespoons cooking oil, 2 tablespoons Worcestershire sauce, ¾ teaspoon ground cumin, ½ teaspoon onion powder, ¼ teaspoon salt, ¼ teaspoon black pepper, and 2 cloves garlic, minced. Cover and shake well.

Nutrition Facts per serving: 304 cal., 14 g total fat (2 g sat. fat), 59 mg chol., 268 mg sodium, 22 g carbo., 5 g fiber, 24 g pro.

Prep: 20 minutes
Marinate: 6 to 24 hours
Grill: 12 minutes
Makes: 4 servings

4 skinless, boneless chicken breast
   halves (about 1 pound total)
1 recipe Citrus-Spice Marinade
1 medium orange, sliced
1 small eggplant, cut into 1-inch slices
1 large red sweet pepper, cut into
   1-inch strips
1 medium zucchini or yellow summer
   squash, quartered lengthwise
1 small sweet onion (such as Vidalia or
   Walla Walla), cut into ½-inch slices

Braised Chicken with Beans and Squash

White kidney beans, sometimes called "cannellini beans," are popular in the Tuscany region of Italy. As American chefs become increasingly interested in Tuscan cooking, the beans are becoming much loved stateside too.

1 In a large skillet cook chicken in hot oil over medium-high heat until light brown, turning to brown evenly. Remove chicken from skillet. Drain off fat.

2 Add wine, bouillon granules, and garlic to skillet. Bring to boiling; reduce heat. Boil gently, uncovered, about 3 minutes or until liquid is reduced by about half, scraping up any crusty browned bits from bottom of skillet.

3 Stir in dried herbs (if using) and pepper. Return chicken to skillet. Add squash. Bring to boiling; reduce heat. Simmer, covered, for 15 to 20 minutes or until chicken is no longer pink (180°) and squash is nearly tender. Stir in beans, undrained tomatoes, and, if using, fresh oregano, thyme, and savory. Simmer, uncovered, about 5 minutes more or until bean mixture is slightly thickened.

4 To serve, spoon the bean mixture into shallow bowls. Place chicken on top of bean mixture. Sprinkle with parsley.

Nutrition Facts per serving: 190 cal., 7 g total fat (1 g sat. fat), 36 mg chol., 454 mg sodium, 18 g carbo., 5 g fiber, 16 g pro.

Prep: 15 minutes
Cook: 20 minutes
Makes: 6 servings

- 6 skinless, boneless chicken thighs (about 1 pound total)
- 1 tablespoon cooking oil or olive oil
- ½ cup dry white wine or water
- 1 teaspoon instant chicken bouillon granules
- 2 cloves garlic, minced
- 1 teaspoon dried oregano, crushed, or 1 tablespoon snipped fresh oregano
- ¾ teaspoon dried thyme, crushed, or 2 teaspoons snipped fresh thyme
- ½ teaspoon dried savory, crushed, or 1 teaspoon snipped fresh savory
- ⅛ teaspoon black pepper
- 1 pound banana, buttercup, or butternut squash, peeled, seeded, and cut into ½-inch pieces (about 2½ cups)
- 1 15-ounce can white kidney (cannellini) beans, rinsed and drained
- 1 14½-ounce can diced tomatoes
- 2 tablespoons snipped fresh parsley

Grilled Curried Lime Chicken Kabobs

Authentic curry powders blend up to 20 spices, herbs, and seeds. Other flavors in this marinade include honey, mustard, and garlic. Lime peel brings a fresh spark, and yogurt adds a creamy tang.

1 Place chicken in a resealable plastic bag set in a shallow dish. For marinade, in a small bowl stir together yogurt, cilantro, lime peel, lime juice, oil, honey, Dijon mustard, curry powder, salt, black pepper, and garlic. Pour over chicken; seal bag. Marinate in the refrigerator for 4 to 24 hours, turning bag occasionally. Drain chicken, reserving marinade.

2 On eight 10- to 12-inch metal skewers, alternately thread chicken, sweet peppers, and zucchini, leaving ¼ inch between pieces. Brush vegetables with marinade. Discard any remaining marinade.

3 In a grill with a cover arrange medium-hot coals around a drip pan. Test for medium heat above the pan. Place kabobs on the grill rack over drip pan. Cover and grill for 18 to 20 minutes or until chicken is no longer pink (170°), turning once halfway through grilling. Place a cherry tomato on the end of each skewer the last 1 minute of grilling.

Nutrition Facts per serving: 261 cal., 9 g total fat (2 g sat. fat), 68 mg chol., 256 mg sodium, 15 g carbo., 2 g fiber, 30 g pro.

Prep: 20 minutes
Marinate: 4 to 24 hours
Grill: 18 minutes
Makes: 4 servings

- 1 **pound skinless, boneless chicken breast halves, cut into 1½-inch pieces**
- ½ **cup plain yogurt**
- ¼ **cup snipped fresh cilantro**
- 1 **teaspoon finely shredded lime peel**
- 2 **tablespoons lime juice**
- 2 **tablespoons olive oil or cooking oil**
- 1 **tablespoon honey**
- 1 **tablespoon Dijon-style mustard**
- ½ **teaspoon curry powder**
- ¼ **teaspoon salt**
- ¼ **teaspoon black pepper**
- 2 **cloves garlic, minced**
- 2 **medium green and/or red sweet peppers, cut into 1-inch pieces**
- 1 **medium zucchini, cut into ½-inch slices**
- 8 **cherry tomatoes**

Summer Chicken and Mushroom Pasta

Healthy doses of garlic and white wine perk up this herbed mushroom and pasta combination. Light and fresh, it is perfect for dinner on a warm summer evening.

1 Cook pasta in boiling, lightly salted water according to package directions; drain. Return pasta to saucepan; cover and keep warm.

2 Meanwhile, sprinkle chicken with salt and ⅛ teaspoon pepper. In a large skillet heat 1 tablespoon of the oil over medium-high heat. Add chicken and garlic; cook and stir for 3 to 4 minutes or until chicken is no longer pink. Remove from skillet; cover and keep warm.

3 Add the remaining 1 tablespoon oil to skillet. Add mushrooms and onion; cook just until tender, stirring occasionally. Carefully add broth and white wine. Bring to boiling; reduce heat. Boil gently, uncovered, about 2 minutes or until liquid is reduced by half. Remove skillet from heat.

4 Add cooked pasta, chicken, cherry tomatoes, basil, and oregano to mushroom mixture; toss gently to coat. Transfer to a serving dish; sprinkle with Parmesan cheese and ⅛ teaspoon pepper.

Start to Finish: 30 minutes
Makes: 6 servings

- 8 ounces dried whole wheat penne pasta
- 12 ounces skinless, boneless chicken breast halves, cut into bite-size strips
- ¼ teaspoon salt
- ⅛ teaspoon black pepper
- 2 tablespoons olive oil or cooking oil
- 3 large cloves garlic, minced
- 3 cups sliced fresh mushrooms
- 1 medium onion, thinly sliced
- ½ cup chicken broth
- ¼ cup dry white wine or chicken broth
- 1 cup cherry tomatoes, halved
- ¼ cup finely shredded fresh basil
- 3 tablespoons snipped fresh oregano
- ¼ cup shaved Parmesan cheese
- ⅛ teaspoon black pepper

Nutrition Facts per serving: 286 cal., 8 g total fat (2 g sat. fat), 35 mg chol., 256 mg sodium, 33 g carbo., 4 g fiber, 22 g pro.

Chicken and Broccoli Stir-Fry

Thirty minutes to a fresh, hot, homemade stir-fry—that beats takeout any day! Super-convenient hoisin sauce and sesame oil bring complex, aromatic flavors to this dish.

1 For sauce, in a small bowl stir together water, soy sauce, hoisin sauce, cornstarch, ginger, and sesame oil; set aside.

2 Cut florets from broccoli stems and separate florets into small pieces. Cut broccoli stems into ¼-inch slices. Cut sweet pepper into thin bite-size strips.

3 Pour 1 tablespoon of the cooking oil into a wok or large skillet. Heat wok over medium-high heat. Add broccoli stems to wok; cook and stir for 1 minute. Add broccoli florets and sweet pepper; cook and stir for 3 to 4 minutes or until vegetables are crisp-tender. Remove vegetables from wok.

4 Add the remaining 1 tablespoon cooking oil to wok. Add chicken; cook and stir for 2 to 3 minutes or until chicken is no longer pink. Push chicken from center of wok. Stir sauce; add to center of wok. Cook and stir until thickened and bubbly. Return vegetables to wok. Cook and stir about 1 minute more or until heated through. Serve over chow mein noodles. If desired, sprinkle with toasted sesame seeds and serve with additional hoisin sauce.

Nutrition Facts per serving: 378 cal., 16 g total fat (3 g sat. fat), 49 mg chol., 877 mg sodium, 31 g carbo., 6 g fiber, 29 g pro.

Start to Finish: 30 minutes
Makes: 4 servings

½ cup water
2 tablespoons soy sauce
2 tablespoons bottled hoisin sauce
2 teaspoons cornstarch
1 teaspoon grated fresh ginger
1 teaspoon toasted sesame oil
1 pound broccoli
1 yellow sweet pepper
2 tablespoons cooking oil
12 ounces skinless, boneless chicken breast halves or thighs, cut into bite-size pieces
2 cups chow mein noodles or hot cooked brown rice
Sesame seeds, toasted (optional)

Grilled Fiery Chicken and Potato Fingers

Stay outdoors and keep the stove and oven off—grill thick slices of zucchini for a great side dish to this hot-and-sweet combo.

1 Cut each chicken piece lengthwise into 3 strips. Place chicken in a resealable plastic bag set in a shallow dish. For marinade, in a small bowl stir together oil, hot pepper sauce, parsley (if desired), honey, salt, cayenne pepper, black pepper, and garlic. Pour 2 tablespoons of the marinade over chicken; seal bag. Marinate in the refrigerator for 30 minutes to 24 hours, turning bag occasionally. Cover and chill the remaining marinade for basting.

2 Drain chicken, discarding marinade. Just before grilling, cut each potato lengthwise into 8 wedges. Lightly brush wedges with some of the reserved marinade.

3 Place potatoes on the rack of an uncovered grill directly over medium coals. Grill for 15 minutes. Turn potatoes. Place chicken on grill rack next to potatoes. Grill for 9 to 12 minutes more or until chicken is no longer pink (170°) and potatoes are tender, turning and brushing chicken once with the reserved marinade halfway through grilling.

Prep: 20 minutes
Marinate: 30 minutes to 24 hours
Grill: 24 minutes
Makes: 4 servings

- 4 skinless, boneless chicken breast halves (about 1 pound total)
- 3 tablespoons olive oil
- 3 tablespoons bottled hot pepper sauce
- 2 tablespoons snipped fresh parsley (optional)
- 1 tablespoon honey or brown sugar
- ½ teaspoon salt
- ½ teaspoon cayenne pepper
- ½ teaspoon cracked black pepper
- 3 cloves garlic, minced
- 2 large baking potatoes (about 1 pound)

Nutrition Facts per serving: 335 cal., 12 g total fat (2 g sat. fat), 59 mg chol., 340 mg sodium, 32 g carbo., 1 g fiber, 25 g pro.

Mediterranean Chicken and Pasta

Travelers to the Mediterranean are apt to describe their dining experiences there as simple and sublime. With its oregano, garlic, and feta cheese (a favorite flavor trio found in the Mediterranean), this chicken dish is likely to elicit similar praise.

1 Drain artichokes, reserving marinade. Set aside. In a large skillet heat oil over medium-high heat. Add chicken and garlic; cook and stir until chicken is light brown. Add the reserved artichoke marinade, broth, wine, and, if using, dried oregano.

2 Bring to boiling; reduce heat. Simmer, covered, for 10 minutes. Stir in the artichokes, roasted peppers, olives, and, if using, fresh oregano. Heat through.

3 To serve, spoon the chicken mixture over pasta. If desired, sprinkle with feta cheese.

Nutrition Facts per serving: 330 cal., 9 g total fat (1 g sat. fat), 49 mg chol., 326 mg sodium, 36 g carbo., 4 g fiber, 27 g pro.

Start to Finish: 30 minutes
Makes: 4 servings

- 1 6-ounce jar marinated artichoke hearts
- 1 tablespoon olive oil
- 12 ounces skinless, boneless chicken breast halves, cut into ¾-inch pieces
- 3 cloves garlic, thinly sliced
- ¼ cup chicken broth
- ¼ cup dry white wine or chicken broth
- 1 tablespoon small fresh oregano leaves or 1 teaspoon dried oregano, crushed
- 1 7-ounce jar roasted red sweet peppers, drained and cut into strips
- ¼ cup pitted kalamata olives
- 3 cups hot cooked whole wheat penne or rotini pasta
- ¼ cup crumbled feta cheese (optional)

Chicken and Dumplings

When was the last time you had a comforting meal of chicken and dumplings? Perhaps back when someone had time to cook it! Try this up-to-date version that takes uses a couple of shortcuts: condensed soup and ready-to-bake buttermilk biscuits.

1 Place flour in a plastic bag. Add chicken pieces and shake to coat. In a large saucepan cook chicken, celery, carrot, and onion in hot butter for 2 to 3 minutes or until chicken is light brown.

2 Stir in broth, condensed soup, and pepper. Bring to boiling; reduce heat. Simmer, covered, about 20 minutes or until chicken and vegetables are tender.

3 Meanwhile, separate biscuits. Cut each biscuit into quarters. Stir peas into chicken mixture; return to boiling. Place biscuit pieces on top of chicken mixture. Cook, covered, over medium-low heat for 10 to 15 minutes or until a wooden toothpick inserted in centers of biscuits comes out clean.

Nutrition Facts per serving: 338 cal., 11 g total fat (4 g sat. fat), 71 mg chol., 1,194 mg sodium, 31 g carbo., 4 g fiber, 28 g pro.

*Note: If you like, substitute drop biscuits for the refrigerated biscuits. To prepare biscuits, in a medium bowl combine 1 cup packaged biscuit mix and ⅓ cup milk. Drop mixture by teaspoonfuls to form 8 dumplings on hot chicken mixture. Cook, covered, as above.

Prep: 15 minutes
Cook: 30 minutes
Makes: 4 servings

- 1 tablespoon all-purpose flour
- 12 ounces skinless, boneless chicken breast halves or thighs, cut into 1-inch pieces
- 1 stalk celery, sliced
- 1 medium carrot, chopped
- 1 medium onion, cut into wedges
- 2 tablespoons butter or margarine
- 1¼ cups chicken broth
- 1 10¾-ounce can condensed cream of chicken with herbs soup
- ⅛ teaspoon black pepper
- 1 4.5-ounce package (6) refrigerated buttermilk biscuits*
- 1 cup frozen peas

Tandoori Chicken Burgers

Feel free to separate the onions from the cucumbers before piling them onto your burgers. That way, those who aren't fond of onions can share with those who are.

1 In a large bowl combine bread crumbs, garam masala, salt, and cayenne pepper. Add ground chicken and yogurt; mix well. Shape chicken mixture into four ¾-inch-thick patties.

2 Place patties on the rack of an uncovered grill directly over medium coals. Grill for 14 to 18 minutes or until patties are no longer pink (165°), turning once halfway through grilling. Serve burgers on toasted buns with Minty Cucumbers and kale leaves.

Minty Cucumbers: In a medium bowl combine 1 thinly sliced cucumber, ½ cup thinly sliced red onion, ¼ cup snipped fresh mint, 1 tablespoon bottled balsamic vinaigrette, and ¼ teaspoon salt.

Nutrition Facts per serving: 329 cal., 13 g total fat (1 g sat. fat), 0 mg chol., 728 mg sodium, 27 g carbo., 2 g fiber, 25 g pro.

*Note: If you ask your butcher to prepare ground chicken, be sure to request coarsely ground.

Prep: 25 minutes
Grill: 14 minutes
Makes: 4 servings

- ¼ cup fine dry bread crumbs
- 2 teaspoons garam masala or curry powder
- ¼ teaspoon salt
- ¼ teaspoon cayenne pepper
- 1 pound uncooked ground chicken*
- 2 tablespoons plain yogurt
- 4 multigrain hamburger buns or kaiser rolls, split and toasted
- 1 recipe Minty Cucumbers
  Kale or lettuce leaves

31 g
carb

Wild Rice Chicken Soup

Garlic and a splash of Madeira give this chicken and rice soup a high intensity flavor. It's a sunny twist on old-fashioned chicken and rice soup.

1 Prepare rice mix according to package directions, except omit the seasoning packet and margarine.

2 Meanwhile, in a Dutch oven combine chicken broth, dried thyme (if using), and garlic. Bring to boiling. Stir in tomatoes, chicken, zucchini, pepper, and, if using, fresh thyme.

3 Return to boiling; reduce heat. Simmer, covered, for 5 minutes. Stir in cooked rice and, if desired, Madeira. Heat through.

Nutrition Facts per serving: 236 cal., 5 g total fat (1 g sat. fat), 38 mg chol., 440 mg sodium, 31 g carbo., 2 g fiber, 18 g pro.

Start to Finish: 25 minutes
Makes: 6 servings

- 1 6.2-ounce package quick-cooking long grain and wild rice mix
- 2 14-ounce cans reduced-sodium chicken broth
- 1 tablespoon snipped fresh thyme or 1 teaspoon dried thyme, crushed
- 4 cloves garlic, minced
- 4 cups chopped tomatoes
- 1 9-ounce package frozen chopped cooked chicken breast
- 1 cup finely chopped zucchini
- ¼ teaspoon black pepper
- 1 tablespoon Madeira wine or dry sherry (optional)

Kale, Lentil, and Chicken Soup

Chicken soup is made even better by adding kale, lentils, and tomato. This home-style soup is packed with flavor and nutrients, which supply many health advantages.

1 In a large saucepan heat olive oil over medium-low heat. Add onion, carrots, and garlic. Cook, covered, for 5 to 7 minutes or until the vegetables are nearly tender, stirring occasionally.

2 Add chicken broth and, if using, dried basil to vegetable mixture. Bring to boiling; reduce heat. Simmer, covered, for 10 minutes. Stir in kale, salt, and pepper. Return to boiling; reduce heat. Simmer, covered, for 10 minutes.

3 Stir in chicken, tomato, lentils, and, if using, fresh basil. Simmer, covered, for 5 to 10 minutes more or until kale and lentils are tender.

Nutrition Facts per serving: 199 cal., 5 g total fat (1 g sat. fat), 31 mg chol., 871 mg sodium, 20 g carbo., 7 g fiber, 20 g pro.

Prep: 25 minutes
Cook: 25 minutes
Makes: 6 servings

- 1   tablespoon olive oil
- 1   cup chopped onion
- 1   cup coarsely chopped carrots
- 2   cloves garlic, minced
- 6   cups reduced-sodium chicken broth
- 1   tablespoon snipped fresh basil or
        1 teaspoon dried basil, crushed
- 4   cups coarsely chopped kale
        (about 8 ounces)
- ½   teaspoon salt
- ⅛   teaspoon black pepper
- 1½ cups cubed cooked chicken or turkey
- 1   medium tomato, seeded and chopped
- ½   cup red lentils, rinsed and drained

Beer-Brined Turkey

Soaking turkey overnight in beer, salt, and herbs boosts the flavor before roasting.

1 Place turkey in a very large bowl. Pour beer over turkey. Add salt, bay leaves, rosemary sprigs, and sliced garlic. If necessary, add just enough water to cover turkey. Cover and marinate in the refrigerator for 24 hours.

2 Drain turkey, discarding beer mixture. Place turkey, bone side down, on a rack in a shallow roasting pan. In a small bowl stir together the melted butter and minced garlic; brush over turkey. In another small bowl stir together the paprika, thyme, onion powder, sage, and pepper. Sprinkle evenly over entire surface of turkey; rub in with your fingers.

3 Insert an oven-going meat thermometer into thickest part of the breast, making sure it doesn't touch bone. Roast in a 325° oven for 1¼ to 1½ hours or until juices run clear and turkey is no longer pink (170°). Remove turkey from oven. Cover with foil and let stand for 10 to 15 minutes before carving.

Nutrition Facts per serving: 198 cal., 10 g total fat (3 g sat. fat), 78 mg chol., 846 mg sodium, 1 g carbo., 1 g fiber, 25 g pro.

Prep: 25 minutes
Marinate: 24 hours
Roast: 1¼ hours
Oven: 325°F
Stand: 10 minutes
Makes: 6 servings

- 1 1¾- to 2-pound turkey breast portion with bone
- 3 12-ounce cans beer
- ¼ cup coarse salt
- 6 bay leaves
- 4 fresh rosemary sprigs
- 4 cloves garlic, sliced
- 1 tablespoon butter or margarine, melted
- 2 cloves garlic, minced
- 1 teaspoon paprika
- 1 teaspoon dried thyme, crushed
- ½ teaspoon onion powder
- ½ teaspoon ground sage
- ¼ teaspoon black pepper

Turkey Breast with Roasted Asparagus

Remember this recipe when spring's first tender shoots of asparagus begin to appear at farmers' markets. You'll love the flavor-pairing of tarragon and Dijon mustard.

1 In a small bowl combine softened butter, Dijon mustard, tarragon, ¼ teaspoon salt, and black pepper; set aside.

2 Remove skin from turkey; set skin aside. Lay one turkey breast half, boned side up, on work surface. Make 4 or 5 shallow cuts in thickest part of the breast (do not cut through). Place turkey breast between two pieces of plastic wrap. Using the flat side of a meat mallet, lightly pound turkey breast to a uniform ¾-inch thickness. Remove plastic wrap. Repeat with the remaining turkey breast half. Dot turkey with half of the butter mixture; set the remaining mixture aside. Top turkey evenly with roasted peppers and parsley. Starting from a short side, roll up each turkey breast into a spiral. Wrap the reserved skin around each roll; tie with 100-percent-cotton string. Place on a rack in a shallow roasting pan.

3 Melt the remaining butter mixture; brush over surface of turkey. Insert an oven-going meat thermometer into center of one of the turkey rolls. Roast in a 325° oven for 1½ to 1¾ hours or until juices run clear and turkey is no longer pink (170°).

4 Meanwhile, in a large bowl toss together asparagus, oil, and ¼ teaspoon salt. Place asparagus in the roasting pan next to turkey the last 15 to 20 minutes of roasting.

5 Cover turkey and asparagus with foil and let stand for 10 to 15 minutes before slicing. Serve turkey with asparagus.

Prep: 30 minutes
Roast: 1½ hours
Oven: 325°F
Stand: 10 minutes
Makes: 10 to 12 servings

¼ cup butter or margarine, softened
2 teaspoons Dijon-style mustard
¾ teaspoon dried tarragon, crushed
¼ teaspoon salt
⅛ teaspoon black pepper
2 1¼- to 1½-pound boneless turkey breast halves (with skin on)
1 7-ounce jar roasted red sweet peppers, drained and coarsely chopped
½ cup snipped fresh parsley
1½ pounds asparagus spears, trimmed
1 tablespoon olive oil
¼ teaspoon salt

Nutrition Facts per serving: 212 cal., 9 g total fat (4 g sat. fat), 92 mg chol., 220 mg sodium, 2 g carbo., 1 g fiber, 28 g pro.

Turkey with Cranberry Sauce

This ruby-red sauce, flecked with carrot and sweetened with orange juice, is the perfect match for succulent roasted turkey. Another time, try this sauce paired with grilled pork chops or baked ham.

1 Remove skin from turkey. Place turkey, bone side down, on a rack in a shallow roasting pan. Insert an oven-going meat thermometer into thickest part of the breast, making sure it doesn't touch bone. Cover turkey loosely with foil.

2 Roast in a 325° oven for 2½ to 3 hours or until juices run clear and turkey is no longer pink (170°), removing foil the last 30 minutes of roasting. Remove turkey from oven. Cover with foil and let stand for 10 to 15 minutes before carving.

3 Meanwhile, for sauce, in a small saucepan combine cranberries, carrot, orange peel, orange juice, sugar, raisins, and cloves. Bring to boiling; reduce heat. Simmer, uncovered, for 3 to 4 minutes or until cranberry skins pop.

4 In a small bowl combine cold water and cornstarch; stir into cranberry mixture. Cook and stir until thickened and bubbly. Cook and stir for 2 minutes more. Serve the turkey with sauce.

Prep: 10 minutes
Roast: 2½ hours
Oven: 325°F
Stand: 10 minutes
Makes: 8 servings

1   2½- to 3-pound turkey breast
      half with bone
1½ cups cranberries
½   cup coarsely shredded carrot
½   teaspoon finely shredded orange peel
½   cup orange juice
2   tablespoons sugar
2   tablespoons raisins
    Dash ground cloves
1   tablespoon cold water
2   teaspoons cornstarch

Nutrition Facts per serving: 154 cal., 2 g total fat (1 g sat. fat), 50 mg chol., 49 mg sodium, 11 g carbo., 1 g fiber, 22 g pro.

Grilled Turkey with Pepper Sauce

Red or yellow sweet peppers add natural sweetness to the savory sauce on top of these grilled turkey steaks.

1 For sauce, in a large skillet heat 1 tablespoon of the oil over medium heat. Add sweet peppers and onion. Cook about 10 minutes or until vegetables are very tender, stirring occasionally. Transfer vegetables to a food processor bowl or blender container; add broth, salt, and black pepper. Cover and process or blend until mixture is smooth. Return to skillet; set aside.

2 In a small bowl combine the remaining 1 tablespoon oil and garlic. Brush oil mixture over turkey.

3 In a grill with a cover, arrange medium-hot coals around a drip pan. Test for medium heat above the drip pan. Place turkey on the grill rack over drip pan. Cover and grill for 25 to 30 minutes or until turkey is no longer pink (170°).

4 Cut the turkey into slices. Reheat the sauce. Serve the turkey and sauce over hot cooked pasta. Sprinkle with basil.

Prep: 20 minutes
Grill: 25 minutes
Makes: 4 servings

- 2 tablespoons olive oil or cooking oil
- 2 medium red or yellow sweet peppers, chopped
- ½ cup finely chopped onion
- ¾ cup chicken broth
- ¼ teaspoon salt
- ¼ teaspoon black pepper
- 2 cloves garlic, minced
- 2 turkey breast tenderloins (about 1 pound total)
- 3 cups hot cooked whole wheat fettuccine
- 2 tablespoons finely shredded fresh basil

Nutrition Facts per serving: 353 cal., 9 g total fat (2 g sat. fat), 68 mg chol., 350 mg sodium, 34 g carbo., 6 g fiber, 34 g pro.

Grilled Turkey Steaks with Sweet Pepper-Citrus Salsa

Turkey steak is a meaty, full-flavored cut that's as versatile as its bovine counterpart. Like beef steak, turkey steak is terrific grilled, broiled, and pan-fried.

1 Place turkey in a resealable plastic bag set in a shallow dish. For marinade, in a small bowl combine oil, lemon juice, orange peel, orange juice, salt, pepper, and garlic. Pour marinade over turkey; seal bag. Marinate in the refrigerator for 2 to 4 hours, turning occasionally. Drain turkey, reserving marinade.

2 Place turkey on the rack of an uncovered grill directly over medium coals. Grill for 12 to 15 minutes or until turkey is no longer pink (170°), turning once halfway through grilling and brushing occasionally with marinade the first 6 minutes of grilling. Discard any remaining marinade. Serve turkey with Sweet Pepper-Citrus Salsa.

Sweet Pepper-Citrus Salsa: In a small bowl combine one 7-ounce jar roasted red sweet peppers, drained and chopped; 1 orange, peeled, seeded, and cut up; 2 green onions, sliced; 2 tablespoons balsamic vinegar; and 1 tablespoon snipped fresh basil or 1 teaspoon dried basil, crushed. Cover and chill until ready to serve. Makes 1½ cups.

Nutrition Facts per serving: 262 cal., 13 g total fat (2 g sat. fat), 70 mg chol., 141 mg sodium, 8 g carbo., 1 g fiber, 29 g pro.

*Note: Precut turkey breast tenderloin steaks are available in some areas. If you find only the large whole tenderloins, slice them horizontally into ½-inch-thick steaks.

Prep: 20 minutes
Marinate: 2 to 4 hours
Grill: 12 minutes
Makes: 6 servings

- 6 turkey breast tenderloin steaks, cut ½ inch thick (about 1½ pounds total)*
- ⅓ cup olive oil
- ¼ cup lemon juice
- 1 teaspoon finely shredded orange peel
- ¼ cup orange juice
- ¼ teaspoon salt
- ¼ teaspoon black pepper
- 4 cloves garlic, minced
- 1 recipe Sweet Pepper-Citrus Salsa

Turkey Mushroom Marsala

A rich shiitake mushroom-wine sauce adorns these turkey steaks. Discard the mushroom stems and use only the caps. If you like, serve the turkey with whole wheat linguine (a ¾-cup serving has about 130 calories and 28 grams carbohydrate).

1 Place turkey in a resealable plastic bag set in a shallow dish. For marinade, in a small bowl combine shiitake mushrooms, Marsala, ⅓ cup water, thyme, rosemary, salt, and pepper. Pour over turkey; seal bag. Marinate in the refrigerator for 30 minutes to 2 hours, turning bag occasionally.

2 Drain turkey, reserving marinade. Pat turkey dry with paper towels. In a large skillet heat oil over medium heat. Add turkey; cook for 8 to 10 minutes or until turkey is no longer pink (170°), turning once. Remove turkey from skillet; cover and keep warm.

3 Pour the marinade into skillet. Bring to boiling; reduce heat. Simmer, covered, for 2 minutes.

4 In a small bowl combine the 2 teaspoons water and cornstarch; stir into marinade in skillet. Cook and stir over medium heat until thickened and bubbly. Cook and stir for 2 minutes more. If desired, serve the turkey and mushroom mixture over hot cooked linguine.

Nutrition Facts per serving: 151 cal., 5 g total fat (1 g sat. fat), 50 mg chol., 114 mg sodium, 1 g carbo., 0 g fiber, 22 g pro.

Prep: 20 minutes
Marinate: 30 minutes to 2 hours
Cook: 8 minutes
Makes: 4 servings

- 4 turkey breast tenderloin steaks, cut ½ inch thick (about 1 pound total)
- 1 cup sliced fresh shiitake mushrooms
- ⅓ cup dry Marsala wine or dry sherry
- 1½ teaspoons snipped fresh thyme or ½ teaspoon dried thyme, crushed
- 1 teaspoon snipped fresh rosemary or ¼ teaspoon dried rosemary, crushed
- ⅛ teaspoon salt
- ⅛ teaspoon black pepper
- 2 teaspoons olive oil or cooking oil
- 2 teaspoons cold water
- 1 teaspoon cornstarch
  Hot cooked whole wheat linguine (optional)

22 g
carb

Sweet and Spicy Turkey Skillet

Ready in 30 minutes, this lively yet simple dish allows you to dine in style any night of the week. The spicy apple and sweet pepper sauce is the perfect partner to the pan-fried turkey steaks.

1. In a small bowl combine apple juice, hoisin sauce, grated ginger, salt, and cayenne pepper; set aside.

2. In a large skillet cook sweet peppers and onion in hot oil over medium-high heat for 4 to 5 minutes or until nearly tender. Remove vegetables, reserving oil in skillet. Add turkey to skillet; cook about 4 minutes or until light brown, turning once.

3. Return vegetables to skillet; add apple juice mixture. Bring to boiling; reduce heat. Simmer, covered, for 8 to 10 minutes or until turkey is no longer pink (170°).

4. Using a slotted spoon, transfer turkey and vegetables to a serving platter; cover and keep warm.

5. In a small bowl combine water and cornstarch; stir into liquid in skillet. Cook and stir over medium heat until thickened and bubbly. Stir in apple wedges. Cook, covered, about 3 minutes more or just until apple wedges are slightly softened. Serve over turkey and vegetables.

Start to Finish: 30 minutes
Makes: 4 servings

- ½ cup apple juice
- ¼ cup bottled hoisin sauce
- 1 teaspoon grated fresh ginger
- ¼ teaspoon salt
- ⅛ teaspoon cayenne pepper
- 2 small red, green, and/or yellow sweet peppers, cut into bite-size strips
- 1 medium onion, cut into thin wedges
- 2 tablespoons cooking oil
- 4 turkey breast tenderloin steaks, cut ½ inch thick (about 1 pound total)
- 1 tablespoon cold water
- 2 teaspoons cornstarch
- 1 small apple or pear, cored and cut into wedges

Nutrition Facts per serving: 289 cal., 9 g total fat (2 g sat. fat), 68 mg chol., 534 mg sodium, 22 g carbo., 2 g fiber, 27 g pro.

Pineapple-Rum Turkey Kabobs

Rum lends a Caribbean flavor, while lemongrass tastes distinctly Asian. And then there's the pineapple-brown sugar twist so loved in the South Seas. So is it more east than west, or vice versa? You decide! (Or simply dig in and call it delicious.)

1 Cut turkey into 1-inch pieces. Place turkey in a resealable plastic bag set in a shallow dish. For marinade, in a small bowl combine pineapple juice, rum, brown sugar, lemongrass, and oil. Pour over turkey; seal bag. Marinate in the refrigerator for 4 to 24 hours, turning bag occasionally.

2 Drain turkey, reserving marinade. In a small saucepan bring marinade to boiling. Boil gently, uncovered, for 1 minute. Remove from heat. On four 12-inch metal skewers, alternately thread turkey and onion, leaving ¼ inch between pieces. On four additional 12-inch metal skewers, alternately thread plums and pineapple. Brush onion and fruit with some of the marinade.

3 Place turkey and fruit kabobs on the rack of an uncovered grill directly over medium coals. Grill until turkey is no longer pink, onion is tender, and fruit is heated through, turning once halfway through grilling and brushing occasionally with marinade the last half of grilling. (Allow 12 to 14 minutes for turkey and onion and about 5 minutes for fruit.)

4 If desired, serve the turkey, onion, and fruit with hot cooked rice.

Prep: 20 minutes
Marinate: 4 to 24 hours
Grill: 12 minutes
Makes: 4 servings

- 12 **ounces turkey breast tenderloin or boneless turkey breast**
- ⅓ **cup unsweetened pineapple juice**
- 3 **tablespoons rum or unsweetened pineapple juice**
- 1 **tablespoon brown sugar**
- 1 **tablespoon finely chopped lemongrass or 2 teaspoons finely shredded lemon peel**
- 1 **tablespoon olive oil**
- 1 **medium red onion, cut into thin wedges**
- 3 **plums or 2 nectarines, pitted and cut into thick slices**
- 2 **cups fresh or canned pineapple chunks**
  Hot cooked brown rice (optional)

Nutrition Facts per serving: 235 cal., 6 g total fat (1 g sat. fat), 37 mg chol., 37 mg sodium, 24 g carbo., 2 g fiber, 17 g pro.

Curried Turkey and Couscous Pie

You've probably experienced the paper-thin layers in the Greek classic dessert baklava, but phyllo often is used in savory dishes as well. Here it makes a golden crust for this turkey pie. Phyllo dough is located in the frozen food aisles of most grocery stores.

1 Cut turkey into ½-inch pieces. Lightly coat a large nonstick skillet with cooking spray. Heat skillet over medium heat. Add turkey and garlic; cook and stir for 1 minute. Sprinkle curry powder, salt, and cayenne pepper over turkey; cook and stir for 1 to 2 minutes more or until turkey is no longer pink.

2 Add broth and peas to turkey mixture. Bring to boiling. Remove from heat; stir in couscous. Cover and let stand about 5 minutes or until liquid is absorbed. Stir in cilantro, fluffing couscous mixture with a fork.

3 Place 1 phyllo sheet on a work surface; lightly coat with cooking spray. Top with 2 more phyllo sheets, lightly coating each layer with cooking spray. Coat a 9-inch springform pan with cooking spray. Place the layered sheets in prepared pan, extending it from just off-center over side of pan. Repeat with remaining phyllo dough, making 3 more stacks; arrange stacks spoke-fashion evenly around pan and overlapping in center. Spoon turkey mixture into pan, spreading evenly. Fold the overhanging phyllo dough over the top to cover the filling. Coat top of pie with cooking spray.

4 Bake in a 350° oven for 30 to 35 minutes or until golden brown. If phyllo is browning too quickly, cover loosely with foil. Let stand for 5 minutes before serving. If desired, serve with yogurt and chutney.

Prep: 40 minutes
Bake: 30 minutes
Oven: 350°F
Stand: 5 minutes
Makes: 6 to 8 servings

- 1 **pound turkey breast tenderloin or skinless, boneless chicken breast halves**
- **Nonstick cooking spray**
- 2 **cloves garlic, minced**
- 1½ **teaspoons curry powder**
- ⅛ **teaspoon salt**
- ⅛ **teaspoon cayenne pepper**
- 1 **14-ounce can chicken or vegetable broth**
- 1 **cup frozen peas**
- 1 **cup quick-cooking couscous**
- ¼ **cup snipped fresh cilantro**
- 12 **sheets frozen phyllo dough (9×14-inch rectangles), thawed**
- **Plain low-fat yogurt (optional)**
- **Cranberry or mango chutney (optional)**

Nutrition Facts per serving: 278 cal., 4 g total fat (1 g sat. fat), 33 mg chol., 406 mg sodium, 38 g carbo., 6 g fiber, 22 g pro.

Turkey and Asparagus Stir-Fry

When buying asparagus for this colorful stir-fry, look for firm, bright green stalks with tight tips. To store asparagus, wrap the bases in wet paper towels and keep in the refrigerator up to four days.

1 Cut turkey into thin bite-size strips. For sauce, in a small bowl combine the water, white wine, soy sauce, cornstarch, honey, and bouillon granules. Set aside.

2 Pour oil into a wok or large skillet. (Add more oil as necessary during cooking.) Heat wok over medium-high heat. Add ginger to wok; cook and stir for 15 seconds. Add asparagus and carrot; cook and stir for 3 minutes. Add green onions; cook and stir about 1 minute more or until vegetables are crisp-tender. Remove vegetables from wok.

3 Add turkey to wok; cook and stir for 2 to 3 minutes or until turkey is no longer pink. Push turkey from center of wok.

4 Stir sauce; add to center of wok. Cook and stir until thickened and bubbly. Return vegetables to wok. Cook, covered, about 1 minute or until heated through. Serve over hot cooked couscous. If desired, sprinkle with nuts.

Nutrition Facts per serving: 318 cal., 8 g total fat (1 g sat. fat), 53 mg chol., 728 mg sodium, 32 g carbo., 4 g fiber, 28 g pro.

Start to Finish: 30 minutes
Makes: 2 servings

- 6 ounces turkey breast tenderloin or skinless, boneless chicken breast halves
- ⅓ cup water
- 2 tablespoons dry white wine or water
- 1 tablespoon soy sauce
- 2 teaspoons cornstarch
- 1 teaspoon honey
- ½ teaspoon instant chicken bouillon granules
- 1 tablespoon cooking oil
- 1 teaspoon grated fresh ginger
- 8 ounces asparagus spears, trimmed and cut into 1-inch pieces (1½ cups), or ½ of a 10-ounce package frozen cut asparagus, thawed
- 1 medium carrot, thinly bias-sliced
- 2 green onions, sliced
- 1 cup hot cooked couscous, orzo pasta (rosamarina), or brown rice
- 2 tablespoons coarsely chopped walnuts or pecans (optional)

27 g
carb

Savory Turkey-Mushroom Burgers

These large burgers are a mushroom-lover's delight. Not only are mushrooms heaped on top, they're also packed into each juicy ground turkey patty.

1 Remove stems and finely chop half of the mushroom caps (should have 1 cup); slice the remaining mushroom caps and set aside. In a small saucepan cook the finely chopped mushrooms and garlic in ½ cup of the broth for 4 to 5 minutes or until tender. Stir in bulgur. Bring to boiling; reduce heat to low. Cook, covered, about 10 minutes or until bulgur is tender and liquid is absorbed. Cool slightly.

2 Meanwhile, in a large bowl combine the ground turkey, green onion, Worcestershire sauce, and pepper. Add bulgur mixture; mix well. Shape into four ¾-inch-thick patties.

3 Place patties on the greased rack of an uncovered grill directly over medium coals. Grill for 14 to 18 minutes or until patties are no longer pink (165°), turning once halfway through grilling.

4 Meanwhile, in a small saucepan cook the sliced mushrooms, covered, in the remaining ¼ cup broth for 4 to 5 minutes or until tender.

5 To serve, if desired, spread mustard on bottom halves of buns. Add burgers, grilled onion slices (if desired), and sliced mushrooms; replace top halves of buns.

Prep: 30 minutes
Grill: 14 minutes
Makes: 4 servings

- 7 ounces fresh mushrooms (such as chanterelle, porcini, shiitake, or button)
- 2 cloves garlic, minced
- ¾ cup chicken broth
- 3 tablespoons bulgur
- 12 ounces uncooked ground turkey breast
- 2 tablespoons thinly sliced green onion
- 2 teaspoons Worcestershire sauce
- ¼ teaspoon black pepper
  Dijon-style mustard (optional)
- 4 multigrain hamburger buns, split and toasted
  Red onion slices, grilled (optional)

Nutrition Facts per serving: 293 cal., 10 g total fat (2 g sat. fat), 55 mg chol., 412 mg sodium, 27 g carbo., 3 g fiber, 26 g pro.

Popover Pizza Casserole

Here a saucy mix of ground turkey and pepperoni is topped with a layer of mozzarella cheese and then a popover batter that puffs as it bakes. It has all the beloved flavors of pizza.

1 In a large skillet cook ground turkey, onion, and sweet pepper until meat is brown and vegetables are tender. Drain off fat.

2 Cut the pepperoni slices in half. Stir pepperoni, pizza sauce, mushrooms, fennel seeds, oregano, and basil into meat mixture. Bring to boiling; reduce heat. Simmer, uncovered, for 10 minutes, stirring occasionally.

3 Meanwhile, grease the sides of a 3-quart rectangular baking dish; set aside. For topping, in a medium mixing bowl combine eggs, milk, and oil. Beat with an electric mixer on medium speed for 1 minute. Add flour; beat about 1 minute more or until smooth. Spoon the hot meat mixture into the prepared baking dish. Arrange mozzarella cheese on top of meat mixture. Pour topping over mozzarella cheese, covering completely. Sprinkle with Parmesan cheese.

4 Bake in a 400° oven about 30 minutes or until topping is puffed and golden brown. Serve immediately.

Prep: 30 minutes
Bake: 30 minutes
Oven: 400°F
Makes: 8 servings

- 1 **pound uncooked ground turkey**
- 1 **cup chopped onion**
- 1 **cup chopped green sweet pepper**
- ½ **of a 3½-ounce package sliced pepperoni**
- 1 **15½-ounce jar pizza sauce**
- 1 **4-ounce can mushroom stems and pieces, drained**
- ½ **teaspoon fennel seeds, crushed**
- ½ **teaspoon dried oregano, crushed**
- ½ **teaspoon dried basil, crushed**
- 2 **eggs**
- 1 **cup milk**
- 1 **tablespoon cooking oil**
- 1 **cup all-purpose flour**
- 6 **ounces thinly sliced mozzarella cheese**
- ¼ **cup grated Parmesan cheese**

Nutrition Facts per serving: 328 cal., 16 g total fat (7 g sat. fat), 124 mg chol., 683 mg sodium, 22 g carbo., 2 g fiber, 22 g pro.

Pasta with Arugula and Sausage

Not a meek or mild green, arugula is somewhat bitter with a peppery mustard flavor. Substitute spinach for those with more delicate taste buds.

1 Cook pasta according to package directions; drain. Return pasta to saucepan; cover and keep warm.

2 Meanwhile, cut sausage lengthwise into quarters; cut into ¼-inch pieces. In a large skillet cook leek and garlic in hot oil until tender. Stir in sausage pieces, broth, and roasted peppers. Bring to boiling; reduce heat. Add arugula; cook for 1 to 2 minutes or just until arugula is wilted.

3 Add the sausage mixture, basil, Parmesan cheese, and black pepper to cooked pasta; toss gently to combine.

Nutrition Facts per serving: 267 cal., 6 g total fat (2 g sat. fat), 24 mg chol., 473 mg sodium, 38 g carbo., 2 g fiber, 15 g pro.

Start to Finish: 30 minutes
Makes: 4 servings

6   ounces dried medium bow tie pasta
4   ounces cooked smoked turkey or chicken sausage links
1   large leek, cut into ¼-inch slices
2   cloves garlic, minced
1   teaspoon olive oil
⅔   cup reduced-sodium chicken broth
½   of a 7-ounce jar roasted red sweet peppers, drained and cut into bite-size strips
8   cups torn arugula or spinach
¼   cup snipped fresh basil
¼   cup finely shredded Parmesan cheese
½   teaspoon coarsely cracked black pepper

Turkey Enchiladas

Yes, you can have the whole enchilada and honor your goal to eat healthfully too—light and reduced-fat dairy products are the keys.

1 For filling, in a covered small saucepan cook onion in a small amount of water until tender; drain. In a medium bowl stir together cream cheese, 1 tablespoon water, cumin, black pepper, and salt. Stir in cooked onion, turkey, and pecans. Wrap tortillas in foil. Heat in a 350° oven about 10 minutes or until softened. [Or wrap tortillas in microwave-safe paper towels. Microwave on 100-percent power (high) about 30 seconds.]

2 Meanwhile, coat a 3-quart rectangular baking dish with cooking spray. For each enchilada, spoon about ¼ cup of the filling onto a tortilla; roll up. Place tortilla, seam side down, in the prepared baking dish. Repeat with remaining filling and tortillas.

3 For sauce, in a bowl stir together soup, sour cream, milk, and jalapeño peppers. Pour sauce over enchiladas. Cover and bake in a 350° oven about 40 minutes or until heated through. Sprinkle with cheddar cheese. Bake, uncovered, 4 to 5 minutes more or until cheese is melted.

Nutrition Facts per serving: 246 cal., 9 g total fat (4 g sat. fat), 55 mg chol., 475 mg sodium, 18 g carbo., 9 g fiber, 21 g pro.

Prep: 35 minutes
Bake: 44 minutes
Oven: 350°F
Makes: 12 servings

- ½ cup chopped onion
- ½ of an 8-ounce package reduced-fat cream cheese (Neufchâtel), softened
- 1 teaspoon ground cumin
- ¼ teaspoon black pepper
- ⅛ teaspoon salt
- 4 cups chopped cooked turkey breast
- ¼ cup chopped pecans, toasted
- 12 7- to 8-inch whole wheat flour tortillas
  Nonstick cooking spray
- 1 10¾-ounce can reduced-sodium condensed cream of chicken soup
- 1 8-ounce carton light dairy sour cream
- 1 cup milk
- 2 to 4 tablespoons finely chopped pickled jalapeño chile peppers (see note, page 96)
- ½ cup shredded reduced-fat sharp cheddar cheese (2 ounces)

17 g
carb

Mexican-Style Turkey Soup

Red sweet pepper, winter squash, and cilantro brighten this spicy soup, making this one-dish meal the perfect family dinner. Accompany with a fresh fruit salad and warm crusty bread.

1 In a Dutch oven cook onion and sweet pepper in hot oil over medium heat about 5 minutes or until tender, stirring occasionally. Stir in cumin, chili powder, and paprika; cook and stir for 30 seconds.

2 Add broth, squash, tomato, salt, and black pepper. Bring to boiling; reduce heat. Simmer, covered, about 20 minutes or until squash is tender, stirring occasionally. Stir in turkey, corn, and cilantro. Heat through.

Nutrition Facts per serving: 205 cal., 6 g total fat (1 g sat. fat), 43 mg chol., 790 mg sodium, 17 g carbo., 3 g fiber, 22 g pro.

Prep: 20 minutes
Cook: 20 minutes
Makes: 5 or 6 servings

   1 cup chopped onion
   1 large red sweet pepper, chopped
   1 tablespoon cooking oil
   1 teaspoon ground cumin
   1 teaspoon chili powder
   ½ teaspoon paprika
   5 cups reduced-sodium chicken broth
1½ cups cubed, peeled winter squash
   1 large tomato, chopped
   ¼ teaspoon salt
   ¼ teaspoon black pepper
   2 cups chopped cooked turkey or
       chicken
   1 cup frozen whole kernel corn
   2 tablespoons snipped fresh cilantro

Fish & Seafood

Asian Glazed Salmon	**186**
Basil Halibut Steaks	**184**
Broiled Fish Steaks with Tarragon Cheese Sauce	**190**
Easy Citrus Salmon Steaks	**188**
Fiery Southwestern Seafood Skewers	**205**
Fish Fillets with Roasted Red Pepper Sauce	**183**
Fish Fillets with Spinach, Red Pepper, and Onion	**191**
Ginger Scallion Fish	**187**
Grilled Tuna with Peanut Sauce	**193**
Lemon and Parmesan Fish	**195**
Lemon-Herb Swordfish Steaks	**189**
Lime-Marinated Swordfish with Southwestern Pesto	**199**
Mahi Mahi with Vegetable Slaw	**194**
Mustard-Glazed Halibut Steaks	**192**
Pecan-Crusted Fish with Vegetables	**182**
Salmon Chowder	**202**
Salmon-Vegetable Packets	**198**
Smoked Pepper Halibut	**196**
Snapper Veracruz	**185**
Sole with Feta and Tomatoes	**200**
Spicy Seafood Stew	**203**
Tangy Thyme Fish	**197**
Thai-Spiced Scallops	**204**
Tuna-Vegetable Salad	**201**
Zucchini Crab Cakes	**206**

Pecan-Crusted Fish with Vegetables

A crunchy pecan coating is the perfect foil for mild fish. The nuts and colorful vegetables provide health-protective plant compounds such as vitamin E, vitamin C, carotenoids, and fiber.

1 Thaw fish, if frozen. Rinse fish; pat dry with paper towels. Cut fish into 4 serving-size pieces; set aside. Line a 15×10×1-inch baking pan with foil. Lightly coat the foil with cooking spray; set aside.

2 In a shallow dish stir together pecans, cornmeal, and onion salt. In another shallow dish stir together flour and cayenne pepper. In a small bowl beat together egg and water. Dip each piece of fish in flour mixture to lightly coat, shaking off any excess. Dip fish in egg mixture, then in pecan mixture to coat. Place coated fish in the prepared baking pan, tucking under any thin edges.

3 In a large bowl combine sweet peppers, zucchini, and summer squash. Add oil and seasoned salt; toss to coat. Arrange vegetables around fish, overlapping as needed to fit into the pan.

4 Bake, uncovered, in a 425° oven for 20 to 25 minutes or until fish flakes easily when tested with a fork and vegetables are tender.

Prep: 15 minutes
Bake: 20 minutes
Oven: 425°F
Makes: 4 servings

12 ounces fresh or frozen skinless catfish, whitefish, or orange roughy fillets, about ½ inch thick
    Nonstick cooking spray
½ cup finely chopped pecans
⅓ cup yellow cornmeal
½ teaspoon onion salt
¼ cup all-purpose flour
¼ teaspoon cayenne pepper
1 egg
1 tablespoon water
2 small red and/or orange sweet peppers, quartered
1 medium zucchini, bias-sliced ½ inch thick
1 medium yellow summer squash, bias-sliced ½ inch thick
1 tablespoon cooking oil
¼ teaspoon seasoned salt

Nutrition Facts per serving: 302 cal., 15 g total fat (2 g sat. fat), 98 mg chol., 367 mg sodium, 21 g carbo., 3 g fiber, 21 g pro.

Fish Fillets with Roasted Red Pepper Sauce

The sauce comes together easily with ingredients you can keep on hand.

1 For sauce, in a blender container or food processor bowl combine peppers and garlic; cover and process until nearly smooth. Add ½ cup of the water, the basil, tomato paste, vinegar, sugar, the ⅛ teaspoon salt, and cayenne pepper. Cover and blend or process with several on-off turns until mixture is nearly smooth. Transfer to a small saucepan; cook over medium heat, stirring frequently, until heated through.

2 Meanwhile, rinse fish; pat dry with paper towels. Measure thickness of fish. Cut fish into 4 serving-size pieces. In a large skillet bring the remaining ½ cup water and half of the lemon slices just to boiling. Carefully add fish. Return just to boiling; reduce heat. Simmer, covered, for 4 to 6 minutes per ½-inch thickness of fish or until fish flakes easily when tested with a fork. Gently pat tops of fish dry with paper towels. Sprinkle fish lightly with the ¼ teaspoon salt and lemon-pepper seasoning.

3 Spoon the sauce onto dinner plates. Place the fish on top of sauce. Garnish with remaining lemon slices.

Start to Finish: 25 minutes
Makes: 4 servings

- 1 12-ounce jar roasted red sweet peppers, drained
- 2 cloves garlic, minced
- 1 cup water
- 2 teaspoons dried basil, crushed
- 2 tablespoons tomato paste
- 1 tablespoon red wine vinegar
- ½ teaspoon sugar
- ⅛ teaspoon salt
  Dash cayenne pepper
- 1 pound fresh orange roughy or cod fish fillets
- 1 lemon, sliced
- ¼ teaspoon salt
- ¼ teaspoon lemon-pepper seasoning

Nutrition Facts per serving: 109 cal., 1 g total fat (0 g sat. fat), 23 mg chol., 358 mg sodium, 7 g carbo., 2 g fiber, 18 g pro.

Basil Halibut Steaks

Fresh tomatoes and basil make a sensational sauce for grilled fish.

1 Thaw fish, if frozen. Rinse fish; pat dry with paper towels. If necessary, cut fish into 4 serving-size pieces. Set aside. In a medium skillet cook onion and garlic in hot oil until tender. Stir in tomatoes, salt, and pepper. Bring to boiling; reduce heat. Simmer, uncovered, for 15 minutes. Stir in 2 tablespoons of the basil.

2 Meanwhile, combine melted butter and remaining 2 tablespoons basil; brush over one side of the fish steaks.

3 Grill fish, brushed side up, on the lightly greased rack of an uncovered grill directly over medium coals for 5 minutes. Turn fish; grill 3 to 7 minutes more or until fish flakes easily when tested with a fork. (Or place fish, brushed side up, on the greased unheated rack of a broiler pan. Broil 4 inches from heat for 8 to 12 minutes or until fish flakes easily when tested with fork, turning once.)

4 Season fish to taste with additional salt and pepper. Serve with tomato mixture.

Prep: 25 minutes
Grill: 8 minutes
Makes: 4 servings

- 4   6-ounce fresh or frozen halibut steaks, cut 1 inch thick
- 1   medium onion, chopped
- 1   clove garlic, minced
- 2   tablespoons olive oil
- 2   to 3 cups chopped, peeled tomatoes
- ¼   teaspoon salt
- ¼   teaspoon black pepper
- ¼   cup snipped fresh basil
- 1   tablespoon butter or margarine, melted

Nutrition Facts per serving: 302 cal., 14 g total fat (3 g sat. fat), 62 mg chol., 265 mg sodium, 7 g carbo., 2 g fiber, 37 g pro.

Snapper Veracruz

Snapper Veracruz, one of Mexico's best-known fish recipes, is a melding of flavors— Spanish green olives and capers with jalapeño peppers from nearby Jalapa, the capital of Veracruz.

1 Thaw fish, if frozen. Rinse fish; pat dry with paper towels. Cut fish into 6 serving-size pieces. Sprinkle fish with salt and black pepper.

2 For sauce, in a large skillet cook onion and garlic in hot oil until onion is tender. Stir in tomatoes, olives, wine, capers, jalapeño peppers, sugar, and bay leaf. Bring to boiling. Add fish to skillet. Return to boiling; reduce heat. Simmer, covered, for 6 to 10 minutes or until fish flakes easily when tested with a fork. Use a slotted spatula to carefully transfer fish to a serving platter. Cover and keep warm.

3 Boil sauce in skillet for 5 to 6 minutes or until reduced to about 2 cups, stirring occasionally. Discard bay leaf. Spoon sauce over fish. Sprinkle with parsley.

Nutrition Facts per serving: 174 cal., 5 g total fat (1 g sat. fat), 42 mg chol., 260 mg sodium, 7 g carbo., 6 g fiber, 24 g pro.

Start to Finish: 30 minutes
Makes: 6 servings

1½ **pounds fresh or frozen skinless red snapper or other fish fillets, ½ to ¾ inch thick**
⅛ **teaspoon salt**
⅛ **teaspoon black pepper**
1 **large onion, sliced and separated into rings**
2 **cloves garlic, minced**
1 **tablespoon cooking oil**
2 **large tomatoes, chopped (2 cups)**
¼ **cup sliced pimiento-stuffed green olives**
¼ **cup dry white wine or chicken broth**
2 **tablespoons capers, drained**
1 **to 2 fresh jalapeño or serrano chile peppers, seeded and chopped, or 1 to 2 canned jalapeño chile peppers, rinsed, drained, seeded, and chopped (see note, page 96)**
½ **teaspoon sugar**
1 **bay leaf**
    Snipped fresh parsley

Asian Glazed Salmon

This simple five-ingredient salmon fillet is fancy enough for company.

1 Thaw fish, if frozen. Rinse fish; pat dry with paper towels. If necessary, cut fish into 4 serving-size pieces. Set aside.

2 For glaze, in a small bowl combine brown sugar, soy, and mustard. Set aside 2 tablespoons of the mixture for sauce.

3 Preheat broiler. Place fish on the greased unheated rack of a broiler pan. Broil about 4 inches from the heat for 8 to 12 minutes or until fish flakes easily when tested with a fork, carefully turning once halfway through broiling and brushing with glaze the last 2 to 3 minutes of broiling.

4 For sauce, stir together rice vinegar and reserved brown sugar mixture until sugar is dissolved. Serve with salmon.

Nutrition Facts per serving: 214 cal., 4 g total fat (1 g sat. fat), 59 mg chol., 733 mg sodium, 19 g carbo., 0 g fiber, 24 g pro.

Prep: 15 minutes
Broil: 8 minutes
Makes: 4 servings

1 pound fresh or frozen skinless salmon fillets, 1 inch thick
⅓ cup packed brown sugar
2 tablespoons reduced-sodium soy sauce
1 tablespoon Dijon-style mustard
3 tablespoons rice vinegar

Ginger Scallion Fish

The lively combination of scallions, lemon juice, jalapeño pepper, ginger, and fish sauce turns ordinary fish into an Asian extravaganza.

1 Thaw fish, if frozen. Rinse fish; pat dry with paper towels. In a small bowl stir together scallions, 2 teaspoons of the lemon juice, the ginger, and garlic.

2 Arrange fish fillets in a single layer in a microwave-safe shallow baking dish, tucking under any thin edges. Spoon scallion mixture over fish. Cover dish with vented plastic wrap. Microwave on 100-percent power (high) for 3 to 5 minutes or until fish flakes easily when tested with a fork, giving the dish a half-turn halfway through cooking.

3 Using a slotted spatula, transfer fish to dinner plates. Stir together fish sauce, jalapeño pepper, and the remaining 2 teaspoons lemon juice; drizzle over fish.

Nutrition Facts per serving: 121 cal., 2 g total fat (1 g sat. fat), 46 mg chol., 312 mg sodium, 3 g carbo., 1 g fiber, 22 g pro.

Start to Finish: 15 minutes
Makes: 4 servings

- 4 4-ounce fresh or frozen skinless sea bass or other firm-fleshed white fish fillets, ¾ to 1 inch thick
- ⅔ cup thinly sliced scallions or green onions
- 4 teaspoons lemon juice or dry sherry
- 2 teaspoons grated fresh ginger
- 2 cloves garlic, minced
- 2 teaspoons bottled fish sauce or reduced-sodium soy sauce
- 1 small fresh jalapeño pepper, seeded and finely chopped (see note, page 96)

Easy Citrus Salmon Steaks

Remember this full-flavor salmon recipe when you're looking for a quick-to-fix dish for a weeknight dinner. It's ready in less than 20 minutes.

1 Thaw fish, if frozen. Rinse fish; pat dry with paper towels. In a small bowl stir together lemon peel, lemon juice, pepper, and garlic.

2 Preheat broiler. Place fish on the greased unheated rack of a broiler pan. Brush with half of the lemon juice mixture. Broil 4 inches from the heat for 5 minutes. Using a wide spatula, carefully turn fish. Brush with the remaining lemon juice mixture. Broil for 3 to 7 minutes more or until fish flakes easily when tested with a fork.

3 Cut the fish into 2 portions. Sprinkle with the green onion and serve with orange slices.

Nutrition Facts per serving: 226 cal., 10 g total fat (2 g sat. fat), 70 mg chol., 54 mg sodium, 9 g carbo., 2 g fiber, 25 g pro.

Prep: 10 minutes
Broil: 8 minutes
Makes: 2 servings

1   8-ounce fresh or frozen salmon fillet, cut 1 inch thick
1   teaspoon finely shredded lemon peel or orange peel
1   tablespoon lemon juice or orange juice
⅛ teaspoon black pepper
1   clove garlic, minced
1   tablespoon sliced green onion
1   medium orange, peeled and sliced crosswise

Lemon-Herb Swordfish Steaks

Thick dense fish, such as swordfish, tuna, and shark, grill swimmingly. They stand up to direct grilling without sticking or drying out, turn easily with tongs or a spatula without falling apart, and mate with a range of seasonings.

1 Thaw fish, if frozen. Rinse fish; pat dry with paper towels. Place fish in a resealable plastic bag set in a shallow dish. For marinade, in a small bowl combine parsley, chicken broth, lemon peel, lemon juice, rosemary, olive oil, shallot, tarragon, salt, and garlic. Pour marinade over fish; seal bag. Marinate at room temperature for 30 minutes, turning bag occasionally.

2 Drain fish, reserving marinade. Grill fish on the greased rack of an uncovered grill directly over medium coals for 5 minutes, brushing once with marinade. Turn fish and grill 3 to 7 minutes more or until fish flakes easily when tested with a fork. Discard any remaining marinade.

Nutrition Facts per serving: 248 cal., 10 g total fat (2 g sat. fat), 22 mg chol., 337 mg sodium, 2 g carbo., 0 g fiber, 34 g pro.

Prep: 10 minutes
Marinate: 30 minutes
Grill: 8 minutes
Makes: 4 to 6 servings

1½	pounds fresh or frozen swordfish, tuna, or shark steaks, cut 1 inch thick
¼	cup snipped fresh parsley
¼	cup reduced-sodium chicken broth
1	teaspoon finely shredded lemon peel
2	tablespoons fresh lemon juice
1	tablespoon snipped fresh rosemary
1	tablespoon olive oil
1	shallot, finely chopped
1½	teaspoons snipped fresh tarragon
¼	teaspoon salt
3	cloves garlic, minced

3 g
carb

Broiled Fish Steaks with Tarragon Cheese Sauce

The elegant three-ingredient sauce is equally delicious on salmon, swordfish, or tuna steaks.

1 Thaw fish, if frozen. Rinse fish; pat dry with paper towels. If necessary, cut fish into 4 serving-size pieces. For sauce, stir together yogurt, cheese, and tarragon. Set aside.

2 Preheat broiler. Place fish on the greased unheated rack of a broiler pan. Sprinkle fish with salt and black pepper. Broil about 4 inches from the heat for 6 to 9 minutes or until fish flakes easily when tested with a fork. Spoon sauce over fish steaks. Broil for 30 to 60 seconds more or until heated through and cheese starts to melt.

Nutrition Facts per serving: 188 cal., 8 g total fat (3 g sat. fat), 36 mg chol., 236 mg sodium, 3 g carbo., 0 g fiber, 25 g pro.

Prep: 10 minutes
Broil: 6½ minutes
Makes: 4 servings

1¼ pounds fresh or frozen salmon, swordfish, or tuna steaks, cut ¾ inch thick
½ cup plain yogurt or light dairy sour cream
½ cup shredded mozzarella or Monterey Jack cheese (2 ounces)
2 teaspoons snipped fresh tarragon or ½ teaspoon dried tarragon, crushed

Fish Fillets with Spinach, Red Pepper, and Onion

Sweet and spicy at the same time, this dish may win over those who think they don't like fish.

1 Place baby spinach in a large bowl; set aside. In a large skillet cook onion in the 1 teaspoon oil over medium heat until tender and slightly golden, stirring occasionally. Stir in 1 tablespoon of the jalapeño jelly. Add sweet pepper; cook and stir for 1 minute more. Remove from heat. Stir onion mixture into spinach; cover and set aside. Wipe skillet clean.

2 Meanwhile, rinse fish; pat dry with paper towels. Cut fish into 4 serving-size pieces. Sprinkle fish with the salt and pepper. In the same large skillet heat the 2 tablespoons oil over medium-high heat. Add fish and cook for 2 minutes on each side to sear. Reduce heat to medium; cook about 5 minutes more or until fish flakes easily when tested with a fork. Transfer fish to a serving platter; cover and keep warm.

3 Add the remaining 3 tablespoons jalapeño jelly to skillet. Cook and stir until melted; spoon over fish. Toss spinach mixture with vinegar. Serve spinach mixture with fish.

Nutrition Facts per serving: 241 cal., 9 g total fat (1 g sat. fat), 83 mg chol., 275 mg sodium, 18 g carbo., 2 g fiber, 22 g pro.

Start to Finish: 35 minutes
Makes: 4 servings

- 4 cups chopped baby spinach
- 1 medium onion, cut into thin wedges
- 1 teaspoon olive oil or cooking oil
- ¼ cup red jalapeño pepper jelly
- 1 small red or yellow sweet pepper, cut into thin strips
- 1 pound fresh mahi mahi or cod fillets, ¾ to 1 inch thick
- ¼ teaspoon salt
- ¼ teaspoon black pepper
- 2 tablespoons olive oil or cooking oil
- 1 tablespoon balsamic vinegar

1 g
carb

Mustard-Glazed Halibut Steaks

Although basil is the herb suggested for this easy fish entrée, other herbs, such as oregano or tarragon, are also good choices.

1 Thaw fish, if frozen. Rinse fish; pat dry with paper towels. In a small saucepan heat butter, lemon juice, mustard, and basil over low heat until melted. Brush both sides of fish with some of the mustard mixture.

2 Grill fish on the greased rack of an uncovered grill directly over medium coals for 8 to 12 minutes or until fish flakes easily when tested with a fork, gently turning once halfway through grilling and brushing occasionally with the remaining mustard mixture.

Nutrition Facts per serving: 243 cal., 10 g total fat (2 g sat. fat), 55 mg chol., 254 mg sodium, 1 g carbo., 0 g fiber, 36 g pro.

Prep: 10 minutes
Grill: 8 minutes
Makes: 4 servings

4 **6-ounce fresh or frozen halibut steaks, cut 1 inch thick**
2 **tablespoons butter or margarine**
2 **tablespoons lemon juice**
1 **tablespoon Dijon-style mustard**
2 **teaspoons snipped fresh basil or**
   ½ teaspoon dried basil, crushed

Grilled Tuna with Peanut Sauce

Tuna steaks, depending on the variety of tuna, range in color. Albacore and yellow fin tuna have light meat; blue fin has darker flesh and a stronger flavor. All tuna meat is compact. Use the flake test to check for doneness.

1 For peanut sauce, in a blender container or food processor bowl combine the ½ cup peanuts, ¼ cup water, green onion pieces, sesame oil, soy sauce, vinegar, sugar, ginger, and garlic. Cover and blend or process until nearly smooth; pour into a small saucepan. Stir in 2 or 3 tablespoons water; set aside.

2 Combine teriyaki sauce and the 1 tablespoon water. Rinse fish; pat dry with paper towels. Brush both sides of fish with the teriyaki mixture.

3 Grill fish on the lightly greased rack of an uncovered grill directly over medium coals for 8 to 12 minutes or until fish flakes easily when tested with a fork, turning once halfway through grilling.

4 Slowly warm peanut sauce over medium-low heat. (Sauce will thicken slightly as it is heated. If desired, stir in additional water.) Spoon sauce over fish. If desired, garnish with chopped peanuts and sliced green onion.

Prep: 15 minutes
Grill: 8 minutes
Makes: 4 servings

½ cup lightly salted peanuts
1 green onion, cut into 1-inch pieces
2 tablespoons toasted sesame oil
1 tablespoon reduced-sodium soy sauce
1 tablespoon rice vinegar
1 teaspoon sugar
1 teaspoon grated fresh ginger
1 clove garlic, quartered
1 tablespoon teriyaki sauce
1 tablespoon water
4 4-ounce fresh tuna steaks or fillets
    (albacore or yellow fin), 1 inch
    thick
Chopped peanuts (optional)
Sliced green onion (optional)

Nutrition Facts per serving: 301 cal., 17 g total fat (2 g sat. fat), 51 mg chol., 524 mg sodium, 6 g carbo., 2 g fiber, 32 g pro.

12 g
carb

Mahi Mahi
with Vegetable Slaw

Lime and cilantro impart a wonderfully fresh flavor to this delightful combination.

1 Thaw fish, if frozen. Rinse fish; pat dry with paper towels. Place fish in a shallow dish. For dressing, in a small bowl combine lime juice, cilantro, oil, honey, jalapeño pepper, salt, and garlic; divide in half. Stir lime peel into one portion of dressing. Pour dressing with lime peel over fish; turn fish to coat. Cover and marinate at room temperature for 30 minutes.

2 For slaw, in a medium bowl combine cabbage mixture and jicama. Pour remaining dressing over slaw; toss to coat. Cover and chill until ready to serve.

3 Drain fish, discarding marinade. Measure thickness of fish. Place fish in a greased grill basket, tucking under any thin edges. Grill fish on the rack of an uncovered grill directly over medium coals for 4 to 6 minutes per ½-inch thickness of fish or until fish flakes easily when tested with a fork, turning basket once halfway through grilling. Serve the fish with slaw.

Nutrition Facts per serving: 276 cal., 10 g total fat (1 g sat. fat), 67 mg chol., 130 mg sodium, 12 g carbo., 1 g fiber, 34 g pro.

Prep: 15 minutes
Marinate: 30 minutes
Grill: 4 to 6 minutes
  per ½-inch thickness
Makes: 4 servings

4 5- to 6-ounce fresh or frozen mahi mahi or pike fillets, ½ to ¾ inch thick
1 teaspoon finely shredded lime peel (set aside)
¼ cup lime juice
¼ cup snipped fresh cilantro
3 tablespoons olive oil
1 tablespoon honey
1 fresh jalapeño chile pepper, seeded and finely chopped (see note, page 96)
⅛ teaspoon salt
3 cloves garlic, minced
1½ cups packaged shredded cabbage with carrot (coleslaw mix)
1 cup shredded peeled jicama

Lemon and Parmesan Fish

This recipe is so easy that you can whip it up on a busy weeknight. Better yet, the crunchy Parmesan crumb topping on the oven-baked fillets pleases kids and adults alike.

1 Thaw fish, if frozen. Rinse fish; pat dry with paper towels. Measure thickness of fish. Coat a 15×10×1-inch baking pan with cooking spray. Place fish in prepared pan, tucking under any thin edges.

2 In a small bowl combine cornflakes, Parmesan cheese, butter, lemon peel, and pepper. Sprinkle crumb mixture on top of fish. Bake in a 450° oven for 4 to 6 minutes per ½-inch thickness of fish or until fish flakes easily when tested with a fork and crumbs are brown. Serve with lemon wedges.

Nutrition Facts per serving: 158 cal., 5 g total fat (1 g sat. fat), 62 mg chol., 221 mg sodium, 5 g carbo., 0 g fiber, 22 g pro.

Prep: 15 minutes
Bake: 4 to 6 minutes
  per ½-inch thickness
Oven: 450°F
Makes: 4 servings

- 4   4-ounce fresh or frozen flounder, sole, or orange roughy fillets, ½ to 1 inch thick
  Nonstick cooking spray
- ½   cup crushed cornflakes
- 1   tablespoon grated Parmesan cheese
- 1   tablespoon butter or margarine, melted
- 1   teaspoon finely shredded lemon peel
- ¼   teaspoon black pepper
  Lemon wedges

Smoked Pepper Halibut

The spicy red pepper sauce serves as both the marinade and table sauce. Any firm-textured fish steaks can be grilled directly on a grill rack without falling apart.

1 Thaw fish, if frozen. Rinse fish; pat dry with paper towels. If necessary, cut fish into 4 serving-size pieces. For marinade, in a blender container combine chipotle peppers, adobo sauce, sweet pepper, lime juice, oregano, and garlic. Cover and blend until pureed. Transfer half of the marinade to a shallow dish; set aside remaining marinade.

2 Add fish to dish, spooning some of the marinade over fish. Cover and marinate at room temperature for 30 minutes.

3 Drain fish, discarding marinade. Sprinkle fish with salt. Grill fish on the greased rack of an uncovered grill directly over medium coals for 8 to 12 minutes or until fish flakes easily when tested with a fork, turning once halfway through grilling. Heat reserved marinade and serve as sauce with fish.

Nutrition Facts per serving: 199 cal., 4 g total fat (1 g sat. fat), 55 mg chol., 284 mg sodium, 3 g carbo., 0 g fiber, 36 g pro.

Prep: 15 minutes
Marinate: 30 minutes
Grill: 8 minutes
Makes: 4 servings

1½ pounds fresh or frozen halibut, swordfish, or shark steaks, cut 1 inch thick
2 canned chipotle chile peppers in adobo sauce
2 tablespoons adobo sauce
1 medium red sweet pepper, cut up
2 tablespoons lime juice
1 teaspoon dried oregano, crushed
2 cloves garlic, halved
¼ teaspoon salt

Tangy Thyme Fish

Bottled ranch-style salad dressing is the base for the creamy sauce that complements these fish fillets.

1 Thaw fish, if frozen. Rinse fish; pat dry with paper towels. Measure thickness of fish. Set aside.

2 In a 10-inch skillet combine broth, onion, pepper, and thyme. Bring to boiling. Place fish in skillet, tucking under any thin edges. Return to simmering. Simmer, covered, for 4 to 6 minutes per ½-inch thickness of fish or until fish flakes easily when tested with a fork. Remove fish to a warm serving platter; cover and keep warm.

3 Bring liquid in skillet to boiling; boil gently, uncovered, over medium-high heat for 3 to 5 minutes or until reduced to about ½ cup. Combine water and cornstarch; stir into liquid in skillet. Cook and stir until thickened and bubbly. Cook and stir for 2 minutes more. Stir in the salad dressing and parsley. Serve the sauce with fish.

Nutrition Facts per serving: 236 cal., 13 g total fat (2 g sat. fat), 50 mg chol., 417 mg sodium, 3 g carbo., 0 g fiber, 24 g pro.

Start to Finish: 25 minutes
Makes: 4 servings

- 1 pound fresh or frozen salmon, sole, flounder, cod, or orange roughy fillets
- 1 cup reduced-sodium chicken broth
- ¼ cup chopped onion
- ⅛ teaspoon black pepper
- ⅛ teaspoon dried thyme or marjoram, crushed
- 2 tablespoons cold water
- 1 teaspoon cornstarch
- ¼ cup bottled original-style buttermilk ranch salad dressing
- 2 tablespoons snipped fresh parsley

Salmon-Vegetable Packets

The packets will be very hot when they come out of the oven. Transfer them to dinner plates, then open slowly to allow steam to escape.

1 Thaw fish, if frozen. Rinse fish; pat dry with paper towels. Set fish aside. In a covered small saucepan cook carrots in a small amount of boiling water for 2 minutes. Drain and set aside. Tear off four 24×18-inch pieces of heavy foil. Fold each in half to make an 18×12-inch rectangle.

2 In a large bowl combine carrots, mushrooms, green onions, orange peel, oregano, salt, pepper, and garlic; toss gently to combine.

3 Divide vegetables among the 4 pieces of foil, placing in center. Place fish on top of vegetables. Drizzle fish with oil. Sprinkle lightly with additional salt and pepper; top with orange slices. For each packet, bring together 2 opposite edges of foil and seal with a double fold. Fold remaining ends to completely enclose food, allowing space for steam to build.

4 Place packets on a baking sheet. Bake in a 350° oven about 30 minutes or until carrots are tender and fish flakes easily when tested with a fork.

Prep: 30 minutes
Bake: 30 minutes
Oven: 350°F
Makes: 4 servings

- 4 4-ounce fresh or frozen skinless salmon fillets, ¾ inch thick
- 2 cups thinly bias-sliced carrots
- 2 cups sliced mushrooms
- 4 green onions, sliced
- 2 teaspoons finely shredded orange peel
- 2 teaspoons snipped fresh oregano or ½ teaspoon dried oregano, crushed
- ¼ teaspoon salt
- ¼ teaspoon black pepper
- 4 cloves garlic, halved
- 4 teaspoons olive oil
- 2 medium oranges, thinly sliced

Nutrition Facts per serving: 226 cal., 9 g total fat (1 g sat. fat), 20 mg chol., 288 mg sodium, 19 g carbo., 5 g fiber, 19 g pro.

Lime-Marinated Swordfish with Southwestern Pesto

Combine the marinade ingredients ahead of time, but marinate the fish for only 1 hour before grilling. The lime juice will infuse the fish with citrus flavor without softening its texture.

1 Thaw fish, if frozen. Rinse fish; pat dry with paper towels. Place fish in a resealable plastic bag set in a shallow dish. For marinade, in a small bowl combine lime peel, lime juice, cilantro, oil, pepper, salt, and garlic. Pour marinade over fish; seal bag. Marinate in the refrigerator for 1 hour, turning bag occasionally.

2 Drain fish, discarding marinade. Grill fish on the greased grill rack of an uncovered grill directly over medium coals for 6 to 9 minutes or until fish flakes easily when tested with a fork, turning once halfway through grilling. Serve with Southwestern Pesto.

Southwestern Pesto: In a blender container or food processor bowl place 2 ounces room temperature Mexican grating cheese (such as anejo enchilado), cut up; 1 fresh jalapeño chile pepper, seeded and cut into quarters (see note, page 96); and 2 cloves garlic, peeled. Cover and blend or process until finely grated. Add two 4½-ounce cans diced green chile peppers, drained; ¼ cup pine nuts or slivered almonds; ¼ cup lightly packed fresh parsley; and ¼ cup lightly packed fresh cilantro leaves. With machine running, gradually add 2 tablespoons olive oil. Blend until nearly smooth. Store any remaining pesto in the refrigerator for up to 3 days or in the freezer for up to 1 month.

Prep: 15 minutes
Marinate: 1 hour
Grill: 6 minutes
Makes: 6 servings

- 6 4-ounce fresh or frozen swordfish or tuna steaks, cut ¾ inch thick
- ½ teaspoon finely shredded lime peel
- ¼ cup lime juice
- 1 tablespoon snipped fresh cilantro
- 2 teaspoons cooking oil
- 1 teaspoon coarsely ground black pepper
- ¼ teaspoon salt
- 2 cloves garlic, minced
- 1 recipe Southwestern Pesto

Nutrition Facts per serving: 212 cal., 11 g total fat (3 g sat. fat), 49 mg chol., 306 mg sodium, 3 g carbo., 0 g fiber, 25 g pro.

Sole with Feta and Tomatoes

When baking or broiling fish fillets, fold under the thin ends so the fish is an even thickness. This prevents the ends from cooking too quickly and drying out before the rest of the fish is done.

1 Thaw fish, if frozen. Rinse fish; pat dry with paper towels. Cut into 4 serving-size pieces. Set aside.

2 For sauce, in a large skillet combine undrained tomatoes, green onions, lemon juice, Italian seasoning, and pepper. Bring to boiling; reduce heat. Simmer, uncovered, for 8 to 10 minutes or until nearly all the liquid has evaporated.

3 Coat a 2-quart square or rectangular baking dish with cooking spray. Arrange fish in prepared dish, tucking under any thin edges. Spoon the sauce over fish.

4 Cover and bake in a 350° oven for 20 to 25 minutes or until fish flakes easily when tested with a fork. Serve fish and sauce on top of fettuccine. Sprinkle with cheese.

Nutrition Facts per serving: 299 cal., 4 g total fat (2 g sat. fat), 74 mg chol., 220 mg sodium, 34 g carbo., 2 g fiber, 31 g pro.

Prep: 25 minutes
Bake: 20 minutes
Oven: 350°F
Makes: 4 servings

1¼ pounds fresh or frozen sole or other fish fillets, ½ to ¾ inch thick
1 14½-ounce can low-sodium tomatoes, undrained and cut up
8 green onions, thinly sliced
2 tablespoons lemon juice
1 teaspoon dried Italian seasoning, crushed
¼ teaspoon black pepper
Nonstick cooking spray
3 cups hot cooked spinach fettuccine
2 tablespoons crumbled feta cheese

Tuna-Vegetable Salad

For a great sandwich, spread the tuna mixture between slices of whole wheat bread and top with tomato and lettuce.

1 In a medium bowl combine celery, carrot, and green onion. Add mayonnaise dressing, dill, lemon peel, garlic powder, and pepper. Gently fold in tuna. Cover; chill for 1 to 4 hours.

2 To serve, divide sliced tomatoes among salad plates. Spoon tuna mixture over tomato slices.

Nutrition Facts per serving: 109 cal., 1 g total fat (0 g sat. fat), 15 mg chol., 314 mg sodium, 13 g carbo., 3 g fiber, 13 g pro.

Prep: 15 minutes
Chill: 1 to 4 hours
Makes: 4 servings

- 1 cup chopped celery and/or chopped seeded cucumber
- ½ cup shredded carrot
- 2 tablespoons sliced green onion
- ⅓ cup fat-free mayonnaise dressing or salad dressing
- 1½ teaspoons snipped fresh dill or ½ teaspoon dried dill
- ½ teaspoon finely shredded lemon peel
- ⅛ teaspoon garlic powder
- ⅛ teaspoon black pepper
- 1 6½-ounce can low-sodium chunk light or white tuna (water pack), drained and broken into chunks
- 4 medium tomatoes, sliced

Salmon Chowder

Rosy-pink salmon is a popular fish because of its great taste. It is also a rich source of omega-3 oils that help protect the cardiovascular system.

1 In a large saucepan heat oil over medium-high heat. Cook and stir carrots, onion, and celery in hot oil about 10 minutes or until vegetables are tender, stirring occasionally.

2 Stir broth, potatoes, water, corn, dill, and salt into vegetables in saucepan. Bring to boiling; reduce heat. Cook, covered, over medium-low heat about 15 minutes or until the potatoes are tender, stirring occasionally.

3 Stir together ½ cup of the milk and the cornstarch. Add milk mixture to saucepan. Stir in the remaining 1½ cups milk. Cook and stir over medium heat until mixture is thickened and bubbly. Cook and stir for 2 minutes more. Gently stir in salmon. Heat through.

Nutrition Facts per serving: 211 cal., 5 g total fat (1 g sat. fat), 11 mg chol., 487 mg sodium, 30 g carbo., 3 g fiber, 14 g pro.

Start to Finish: 45 minutes
Makes: 8 servings

- 1 tablespoon cooking oil
- 2 cups shredded carrots
- 1 cup finely chopped onion
- ½ cup thinly sliced celery
- 4 cups reduced-sodium chicken broth
- 2½ cups cubed red-skinned potatoes (3 medium)
- 1½ cups water
- 1 10-ounce package frozen whole kernel corn
- 1 teaspoon snipped fresh dill or ½ teaspoon dried dill
- ¼ teaspoon salt
- 2 cups milk
- 2 tablespoons cornstarch
- 1 15-ounce can salmon, rinsed, drained, flaked, and skin and bones removed

Spicy Seafood Stew

You'll think you've been transported to the bayou when you sample this Cajun-seasoned shrimp and fish sensation.

1 Thaw fish and shrimp, if frozen. Rinse fish and shrimp; pat dry with paper towels. Cut fish into 1-inch pieces. Cover and chill fish pieces and shrimp until needed.

2 In a large saucepan heat oil over medium-high heat. Cook and stir onion, carrot, sweet pepper, and garlic in hot oil until tender. Stir in undrained tomatoes, tomato sauce, chicken broth, wine, bay leaves, dried thyme (if using), Cajun seasoning, cumin, and, if desired, crushed red pepper. Bring to boiling; reduce heat. Simmer, covered, for 20 minutes.

3 Gently stir in fish pieces, shrimp, and, if using, fresh thyme. Simmer, covered, about 5 minutes more or until the fish flakes easily when tested with a fork and shrimp turn opaque. Discard bay leaves.

Nutrition Facts per serving: 199 cal., 5 g total fat (1 g sat. fat), 84 mg chol., 341 mg sodium, 15 g carbo., 3 g fiber, 22 g pro.

Prep: 15 minutes
Cook: 25 minutes
Makes: 4 servings

- 8 ounces fresh or frozen skinless fish fillets (such as halibut, orange roughy, or sea bass)
- 6 ounces fresh or frozen peeled and deveined shrimp
- 2 teaspoons olive oil
- ⅔ cup chopped onion
- ½ cup finely chopped carrot
- ½ cup chopped green or red sweet pepper
- 2 cloves garlic, minced
- 1 14½-ounce can low-sodium tomatoes, undrained and cut up
- 1 8-ounce can low-sodium tomato sauce
- 1 cup reduced-sodium chicken broth
- ¼ cup dry red wine or reduced-sodium chicken broth
- 2 bay leaves
- 1 tablespoon snipped fresh thyme or 1 teaspoon dried thyme, crushed
- ½ teaspoon Cajun seasoning
- ¼ teaspoon ground cumin
- ¼ teaspoon crushed red pepper (optional)

Thai-Spiced Scallops

Sea scallops, not to be confused with bay scallops, are the larger of the two varieties. Sea scallops measure about 1½ inches in diameter and bay scallops measure ½ inch in diameter.

1 Thaw scallops, if frozen. Rinse scallops; pat dry with paper towels. Halve any large scallops. On four 8- to 10-inch metal skewers, thread scallops. Cover and chill until ready to grill.

2 For sauce, in a small bowl combine sweet-and-sour sauce, basil, Thai seasoning, and garlic. Remove ¼ cup of the sauce for basting; reserve remaining sauce until ready to serve.

3 Fold a 36×18-inch piece of heavy foil in half to make an 18-inch square. Place squash and carrots in center of foil. Sprinkle lightly with salt and black pepper. Bring up 2 opposite edges of foil and seal with a double fold. Fold remaining ends to completely enclose vegetables, leaving space for steam to build.

4 Grill vegetable packets on the rack of an uncovered grill directly over medium coals for 10 minutes, turning packets occasionally.

5 Place scallop kabobs on grill rack. Grill for 5 to 8 minutes more or until scallops turn opaque and vegetables are crisp-tender, turning kabobs and vegetable packets once and brushing scallops occasionally with the reserved ¼ cup sauce the last 2 to 3 minutes of grilling. Serve scallops and vegetables with remaining sauce.

Prep: 20 minutes
Grill: 15 minutes
Makes: 4 servings

1 pound fresh or frozen sea scallops
⅔ cup bottled sweet-and-sour sauce
2 tablespoons snipped fresh basil
1 teaspoon Thai seasoning or
    five-spice powder
½ teaspoon bottled minced garlic
2 medium yellow summer squash
    and/or zucchini, quartered
    lengthwise and sliced ½ inch thick
1½ cups packaged peeled baby carrots

Nutrition Facts per serving: 168 cal., 1 g total fat (0 g sat. fat), 34 mg chol., 370 mg sodium, 25 g carbo., 3 g fiber, 16 g pro.

Fiery Southwestern Seafood Skewers

Succulent shrimp and scallops keep company with tender onion and zucchini in these spicy-hot kabobs. Keep plenty of sparkling water handy to cool your palate.

1 Thaw shrimp and scallops, if frozen. Rinse shrimp and scallops; pat dry with paper towels. On 4 long metal skewers, alternately thread shrimp, scallops, sweet pepper, onion, and zucchini, leaving about ¼ inch between pieces.

2 In a small bowl combine chipotle peppers, lime juice, oil, brown sugar, salt, cumin, and garlic. Brush kabobs with chipotle mixture.

3 Grill kabobs on the greased rack of an uncovered grill directly over medium coals for 5 to 8 minutes or until shrimp and scallops turn opaque and vegetables are crisp-tender, turning occasionally to cook evenly. (Or place kabobs on the greased unheated rack of a broiler pan. Broil about 4 inches from the heat for 5 to 8 minutes, turning occasionally to cook evenly.) Sprinkle kabobs with cilantro and serve with lime wedges.

Nutrition Facts per serving: 180 cal., 5 g total fat (1 g sat. fat), 105 mg chol., 506 mg sodium, 11 g carbo., 2 g fiber, 22 g pro.

Prep: 25 minutes
Grill: 5 minutes
Makes: 4 servings

- 8 ounces fresh or frozen medium shrimp in shells, peeled and deveined
- 8 ounces fresh or frozen sea scallops
- 1 medium red sweet pepper, cut into 1-inch pieces
- 1 medium onion, cut into wedges
- 1 medium zucchini or yellow summer squash, cut into ¾-inch slices
- 2 tablespoons canned chipotle chile peppers in adobo sauce, mashed (see note, page 96)
- 1 tablespoon lime juice
- 1 tablespoon cooking oil
- 2 teaspoons brown sugar
- ½ teaspoon salt
- ½ teaspoon ground cumin
- 2 cloves garlic, minced
- 2 tablespoons snipped fresh cilantro
  Lime wedges

Zucchini Crab Cakes

You'll need to purchase about 1¼ pounds of crab legs to get 8 ounces crabmeat. Be sure to clean crabmeat carefully, removing and discarding any small pieces of shell or cartilage.

1 In a large skillet heat 2 teaspoons of the cooking oil. Cook and stir zucchini and green onions in hot oil about 3 minutes or just until vegetables are tender and liquid is evaporated. Cool slightly.

2 In a large bowl combine egg, bread crumbs, mustard, lemon thyme, and, if desired, cayenne pepper. Add zucchini mixture and crabmeat; mix well. Using about ¼ cup mixture for each crab cake, shape into 8 patties, about 2½ inches in diameter. Brush both sides of the crab cakes lightly with the remaining 4 teaspoons oil.

3 Grill crab cakes on the lightly greased rack of an uncovered grill directly over medium-hot coals for 6 to 8 minutes or until golden brown, turning once.

4 To serve, arrange crab cakes and sliced tomatoes on salad plates. Serve with Tomato-Sour Cream Dipping Sauce.

Tomato-Sour Cream Dipping Sauce: In a small bowl stir together ½ cup dairy sour cream, 3 tablespoons minced yellow and red tomatoes, 1 to 2 tablespoons lemon juice or lime juice, and ⅛ teaspoon seasoned salt. Cover and chill.

Prep: 20 minutes
Grill: 6 minutes
Makes: 4 servings

- 6 teaspoons cooking oil
- 1 cup coarsely shredded zucchini
- ¼ cup thinly sliced green onions
- 1 beaten egg
- ½ cup seasoned fine dry bread crumbs
- 1 tablespoon Dijon-style mustard
- ½ teaspoon snipped fresh lemon thyme or snipped fresh thyme
- ⅛ to ¼ teaspoon cayenne pepper (optional)
- 8 ounces cooked fresh crabmeat, chopped (1½ cups)
- 2 large red and/or yellow tomatoes, cut into ¼-inch slices
- 1 recipe Tomato-Sour Cream Dipping Sauce

Nutrition Facts per serving: 277 cal., 16 g total fat (5 g sat. fat), 123 mg chol., 424 mg sodium, 16 g carbo., 2 g fiber, 17 g pro.

Side Dishes

Asparagus with Warm Vinaigrette	**208**
Beans and Hot Ham Dressing	**209**
Braised Fall Vegetables	**222**
Brown Rice Pilaf	**224**
Great Greek Green Beans	**210**
Lemon-Braised Baby Broccoli	**212**
Lemony Mixed Vegetables	**219**
Mexicali Stuffed Zucchini	**218**
Orzo-Broccoli Pilaf	**223**
Pan-Fried Baby Bok Choy	**211**
Prosciutto and Peas	**213**
Roasted Cheddar Potatoes	**214**
Roasted Garlic Mashed Potatoes	**215**
Roasted Summer Cherry Tomatoes	**217**
Seared Vegetable Medley	**220**
Spinach-Mushroom Sauté	**216**
Vegetables Primavera	**221**

Asparagus with Warm Vinaigrette

The combination of ginger and apricot nectar creates a noteworthy vinaigrette for fresh asparagus.

1 For fresh asparagus, snap off and discard the woody bases of asparagus. If desired, use a vegetable peeler to scrape off scales. Cook, covered, in a small amount of boiling water for 3 to 5 minutes or until crisp-tender. (Cook frozen asparagus according to package directions.) Drain.

2 Meanwhile, for vinaigrette, in a small saucepan combine the cornstarch, garlic powder, and ginger. Stir in apricot nectar. Cook and stir over medium heat until mixture is thickened and bubbly. Cook and stir for 2 minutes more. Remove saucepan from heat; stir in vinegar. Pour over cooked asparagus; toss gently to coat.

Nutrition Facts per serving: 34 cal., 0 g total fat (0 g sat. fat), 0 mg chol., 4 mg sodium, 7 g carbo., 2 g fiber, 2 g pro.

Start to Finish: 20 minutes
Makes: 4 servings

- 1 pound asparagus spears or one 10-ounce package frozen asparagus spears
- ¾ teaspoon cornstarch
  Dash garlic powder
  Dash ground ginger
- ⅓ cup apricot nectar (½ of a 5½-ounce can)
- 1 tablespoon white wine vinegar

Beans and Hot Ham Dressing

Use a combination of green and wax beans for extra color. Or if both varieties aren't available in your market, use all fresh green beans and top them with the chunky chickpea topping.

1 Trim tips off green beans. In a covered large saucepan cook green beans in a small amount of boiling salted water about 3 minutes or until crisp-tender. Drain well. Transfer to a serving bowl; keep warm.

2 Meanwhile, in a medium skillet cook ham in 1 tablespoon of the olive oil over medium heat for 3 minutes, stirring occasionally. Add garbanzo beans and shallots. Cook and stir for 2 to 3 minutes more or until ham is crisp and golden brown. Reduce heat to medium low. Push mixture to one side of skillet.

3 Carefully add vinegar to skillet. Heat just until bubbly, scraping up the browned bits in bottom of skillet. Stir in the remaining 1 tablespoon olive oil. Stir together ham mixture and the vinegar mixture. Pour over beans; toss gently to coat.

Start to Finish: 15 minutes
Makes: 6 to 8 servings

1   pound whole green and/or yellow wax beans
½ cup diced (or cubed) cooked smoked ham or Canadian-style bacon
2   tablespoons olive oil
1   cup cooked or canned garbanzo beans (chickpeas), rinsed and drained
2   tablespoons finely chopped shallots
3   tablespoons red wine vinegar

Nutrition Facts per serving: 120 cal., 6 g total fat (1 g sat. fat), 7 mg chol., 303 mg sodium, 11 g carbo., 4 g fiber, 7 g pro.

15 g
carb

Great Greek Green Beans

Tomatoes, olives, oregano, and feta cheese lend the Greek notes to this zesty side dish. Serve it with grilled or broiled chicken breasts or lamb chops.

1 In a large skillet cook onion and garlic in hot oil about 5 minutes or until tender. Add undrained tomatoes, olives, and oregano. Bring to boiling; reduce heat. Boil gently, uncovered, for 10 minutes. Add beans. Return to boiling. Boil gently, uncovered, about 8 minutes or until desired consistency and beans are tender.

2 Transfer to a serving bowl; sprinkle with feta cheese. If desired, serve with a slotted spoon.

Nutrition Facts per serving: 132 cal., 5 g total fat (2 g sat. fat), 8 mg chol., 419 mg sodium, 15 g carbo., 5 g fiber, 4 g pro.

Prep: 10 minutes
Cook: 20 minutes
Makes: 6 servings

- ½ cup chopped onion
- 1 clove garlic, minced
- 1 tablespoon olive oil
- 1 28-ounce can diced tomatoes
- ¼ cup sliced pitted ripe olives
- 1 teaspoon dried oregano, crushed
- 2 9-ounce packages or one 16-ounce package frozen French-cut green beans, thawed and drained
- ½ cup crumbled feta cheese (2 ounces)

Pan-Fried Baby Bok Choy

Baby bok choy—a mild vegetable with pale-green stalks and leaves—is becoming more available. Look for it in Asian specialty markets or larger supermarkets throughout the spring and summer.

1 Cut any large pieces of baby bok choy in half lengthwise. Rinse bok choy in cold running water. Shake gently to remove water. Drain well. Set aside.

2 In a large skillet heat oil. Cook bread crumbs in hot oil about 1 minute or just until beginning to brown. Add garlic. Cook and stir about 1 minute more or until crumbs are golden brown. Using a slotted spoon, remove crumb mixture from skillet. Set aside.

3 Add bok choy to hot skillet. Cook, uncovered, for 3 to 5 minutes or until stalks are just heated through and leaves are wilted, turning often. Transfer to a serving dish. Toss with crumbs; drizzle with soy sauce. Sprinkle with sesame seeds.

Nutrition Facts per serving: 96 cal., 8 g total fat (1 g sat. fat), 0 mg chol., 314 mg sodium, 4 g carbo., 1 g fiber, 3 g pro.

Prep: 5 minutes
Cook: 5 minutes
Makes: 4 servings

12 ounces baby bok choy (4 to 8 pieces) or 1 small bunch regular bok choy, quartered lengthwise
2 tablespoons peanut oil or cooking oil
½ cup coarse soft sourdough bread crumbs
1 clove garlic, minced
1 tablespoon reduced-sodium soy sauce
2 teaspoons sesame seeds, toasted

Lemon-Braised Baby Broccoli

Baby broccoli, called broccolini, is a cross between broccoli and Chinese kale. Because of its tender stem, it can be cooked quickly.

1 In a large skillet combine chicken broth, dill, preserved lemon, red pepper, and black pepper. Bring to boiling; reduce heat. Simmer, covered, for 15 minutes.

2 Add baby broccoli and butter to skillet. Cook, covered, over medium heat for 6 to 8 minutes or until the baby broccoli is tender. Drain, if desired; transfer to a serving bowl. If desired, garnish with fresh lemon halves.

Nutrition Facts per serving: 47 cal., 3 g total fat (2 g sat. fat), 8 mg chol., 489 mg sodium, 4 g carbo., 2 g fiber, 2 g pro.

*Note: Preserved lemon can be found in large supermarkets and specialty food stores. Or substitute 2 teaspoons finely shredded lemon peel, 1 teaspoon olive oil, and ½ teaspoon kosher salt for the preserved lemon.

Start to Finish: 30 minutes
Makes: 8 servings

- 1 cup reduced-sodium chicken broth
- 1 tablespoon snipped fresh dill
- 2 slices preserved lemon*
- ⅛ teaspoon crushed red pepper
- ⅛ teaspoon ground black pepper
- 1 pound baby broccoli or broccoli rabe
- 2 tablespoons butter or margarine
  Fresh lemon halves or slices (optional)

Prosciutto and Peas

Toss slivers of prosciutto and toasted pine nuts with frozen peas to makes this easy side dish.

1 Cut prosciutto into thin strips. In a medium saucepan cook onion in hot oil until tender. Stir in peas, water, bouillon granules, dried oregano (if using), and pepper.

2 Simmer, covered, for 4 to 5 minutes or just until peas are tender. Stir in fresh oregano (if using) and toasted pine nuts.

Nutrition Facts per serving: 84 cal., 3 g total fat (0 g sat. fat), 3 mg chol., 241 mg sodium, 11 g carbo., 4 g fiber, 5 g pro.

Start to Finish: 20 minutes
Makes: 4 servings

- 1 ounce thinly sliced prosciutto or cooked ham
- ¼ cup chopped onion
- 1 teaspoon olive oil or cooking oil
- 1 10-ounce package frozen peas
- ¼ cup water
- ½ teaspoon instant chicken bouillon granules
- ¼ teaspoon dried oregano, crushed, or ¾ teaspoon snipped fresh oregano
  Dash black pepper
- 2 tablespoons pine nuts or chopped pecans, toasted

Roasted Cheddar Potatoes

To have hot potatoes always available, divide the wedges into two batches and heat them one at a time. The second batch will be ready to eat just as guests finish up the first round.

1 Preheat oven according to package directions for potatoes. Place frozen potatoes in a large resealable plastic bag. Combine cooking oil, paprika, salt, and garlic. Drizzle over potato wedges. Seal bag and shake to coat potatoes.

2 Lightly coat a 15×10×1-inch baking pan with cooking spray. Spread potato wedges in a single layer in the prepared pan. Bake the potatoes according to package directions, turning once.

3 In a small bowl combine the cheese and croutons. Sprinkle over the potatoes the last 3 minutes of baking. Use a large spatula to transfer potato wedges to a platter or large plate (keep potatoes in a single layer). If desired, serve with sour cream.

Prep: 10 minutes
Bake: 25 minutes
Oven: per package directions
Makes: 8 **servings**

1 **24-ounce package frozen potato wedges (skins on)**
2 **tablespoons cooking oil**
1 **teaspoon smoked paprika or paprika**
¼ **teaspoon salt**
4 **cloves garlic, minced**
 Nonstick cooking spray
1 **cup shredded reduced-fat cheddar cheese (4 ounces)**
⅔ **cup crushed croutons (about 1 cup croutons)**
 Light dairy sour cream (optional)

Nutrition Facts per serving: 149 cal., 6 g total fat (2 g sat. fat), 10 mg chol., 234 mg sodium, 19 g carbo., 1 g fiber, 6 g pro.

Roasted Garlic Mashed Potatoes

Skip the gravy with these mashed potatoes—they won't need it. The roasted garlic, herb, and sour cream flavor them to delicious perfection.

1 In a covered large saucepan cook potatoes in a small amount of boiling water for 20 to 25 minutes or until tender. Drain in a colander; return to saucepan.

2 Add roasted garlic to potatoes. Mash with a potato masher or an electric mixer on low speed. Add sour cream, milk, rosemary, salt, and pepper. Beat until light and fluffy.

Nutrition Facts per serving: 122 cal., 1 g total fat (1 g sat. fat), 5 mg chol., 168 mg sodium, 24 g carbo., 2 g fiber, 4 g pro.

*Note: To roast your own garlic, for every 1 teaspoon of roasted garlic, wrap 3 unpeeled garlic cloves in foil. Bake in a 400°F oven for 25 to 35 minutes or until cloves feel soft when pressed. When cool enough to handle, squeeze garlic paste from cloves.

Start to Finish: 35 minutes
Makes: 4 servings

- 1½ pounds Yukon gold potatoes or other potatoes, quartered
- 2 teaspoons bottled minced roasted garlic*
- ¼ cup light dairy sour cream
- 2 to 4 tablespoons milk
- 2 teaspoons snipped fresh rosemary, thyme, or oregano
- ¼ teaspoon salt
- ⅛ teaspoon black pepper

8 g
carb

Spinach-Mushroom Sauté

Portobellos and leeks take a gentle tumble in the skillet before the spinach is tossed into the pan to create this barely wilted vegetable side dish.

1 Cut mushrooms in half and slice. In a 12-inch skillet cook mushrooms, leeks, and garlic in butter over medium-high heat about 4 minutes or until tender and most of liquid has evaporated, stirring occasionally.

2 Add spinach, bok choy, and lemon pepper to skillet. Cook, covered, about 1 minute or just until greens are wilted.

Nutrition Facts per serving: 64 cal., 3 g total fat (2 g sat. fat), 7 mg chol., 262 mg sodium, 8 g carbo., 4 g fiber, 3 g pro.

Start to Finish: 20 minutes
Makes: 6 servings

8 ounces fresh portobello mushrooms
2 medium leeks, cut into 1½-inch pieces
2 large cloves garlic, minced
4 teaspoons butter or margarine
6 cups prewashed fresh spinach
2 cups coarsely shredded bok choy or napa cabbage
1 teaspoon lemon-pepper seasoning

Roasted Summer Cherry Tomatoes

Although you can make this super simple side dish any time of the year, it's truly superb with cherry tomatoes just picked from the garden.

1 Line a 13×9×2-inch baking pan with foil. Wash tomatoes; remove and discard stems. Pat tomatoes dry with paper towels. Pour the olive oil into prepared pan. Roll tomatoes in oil to coat. Sprinkle with snipped basil, salt, pepper, and garlic.

2 Bake in a 425° oven about 5 minutes or just until skins begin to split, stirring once. If desired, sprinkle with additional snipped fresh basil and garnish with basil sprigs.

Nutrition Facts per serving: 87 cal., 7 g total fat (1 g sat. fat), 0 mg chol., 142 mg sodium, 6 g carbo., 1 g fiber, 1 g pro.

Prep: 20 minutes
Bake: 5 minutes
Oven: 425°F
Makes: 4 to 6 servings

12 ounces cherry and/or pear-shape tomatoes
2 tablespoons olive oil or cooking oil
¼ cup snipped fresh basil
¼ teaspoon salt
⅛ teaspoon black pepper
1 tablespoon minced garlic

9 g
carb

Mexicali Stuffed Zucchini

These savory stuffed zucchini "wheels" can be made a day ahead: Prepare them up to the baking step, then cover the dish with plastic wrap and refrigerate. About 25 minutes before serving, simply remove the wrap and bake.

1 Trim ends from zucchini. Cut the zucchini into 1½-inch slices. Scoop out pulp, leaving ¼- to ½-inch shells. Chop enough of the pulp to make ⅓ cup. In a medium skillet cook garlic in hot oil over medium-high heat for 1 minute. Add the reserved zucchini pulp, the sweet pepper, onions, 1 tablespoon of the cilantro, and the jalapeño pepper. Cook and stir about 2 minutes or until vegetables are crisp-tender.

2 Place zucchini shells in a lightly greased 2-quart rectangular baking dish. Fill each shell with pepper mixture. Bake, uncovered, in a 350° oven for 20 to 25 minutes or until zucchini is tender. Sprinkle with Monterey Jack cheese. Bake for 1 to 2 minutes more or until cheese melts.

3 Sprinkle zucchini with the remaining 1 tablespoon cilantro. Serve with the Cucumber Raita.

Cucumber Raita: In a small bowl stir together ½ cup plain low-fat yogurt, ¼ cup peeled and finely chopped cucumber, 1 tablespoon snipped fresh cilantro, and ⅛ teaspoon salt.

Nutrition Facts per serving: 108 cal., 6 g total fat (3 g sat. fat), 11 mg chol., 143 mg sodium, 9 g carbo., 3 g fiber, 6 g pro.

Prep: 25 minutes
Bake: 21 minutes
Oven: 350°F
Makes: 5 or 6 servings

- 3 **medium zucchini (about 1¾ pounds)**
- 2 **cloves garlic, minced**
- 2 **teaspoons cooking oil**
- 1 **medium red sweet pepper, chopped**
- 3 **green onions, thinly sliced**
- 2 **tablespoons snipped fresh cilantro**
- 1 **fresh or canned jalapeño chile pepper, seeded and finely chopped (see note, page 96)**
- ½ **cup shredded reduced-fat Monterey Jack cheese (2 ounces)**
- 1 **recipe Cucumber Raita**

Lemony Mixed Vegetables

Be creative with seasonings! The inspired combination of coriander, oregano, and lemon peel lends character to this simple vegetable side dish.

1 In a large saucepan combine the chicken broth, coriander, salt, and black pepper. Bring to boiling; add green beans. Return to boiling; reduce heat. Simmer, covered, for 10 minutes. Add carrots, cauliflower, and sweet pepper. Return to boiling; reduce heat. Simmer, covered, for 4 to 5 minutes more or until vegetables are crisp-tender.

2 Using a slotted spoon, transfer vegetables to a serving bowl, reserving broth mixture in saucepan. Cover vegetables; keep warm.

3 In a small bowl stir together oregano, water, cornstarch, and lemon peel; stir into broth mixture in saucepan. Cook and stir over medium heat until slightly thickened and bubbly. Cook and stir for 2 minutes more. Stir in lemon juice. Pour thickened broth mixture over vegetables. Toss lightly to coat.

Nutrition Facts per serving: 49 cal., 0 g total fat (0 g sat. fat), 0 mg chol., 184 mg sodium, 11 g carbo., 3 g fiber, 2 g pro.

Start to Finish: 35 minutes
Makes: 6 servings

- 1 cup reduced-sodium chicken broth
- ¼ teaspoon ground coriander
- ⅛ teaspoon salt
- ⅛ teaspoon black pepper
- 8 ounces green beans, cut into 2-inch lengths (about 2 cups)
- 2 cups thinly bias-sliced carrots
- 1 cup cauliflower florets
- ½ of a medium red sweet pepper, cut into 1-inch pieces
- 1 tablespoon snipped fresh oregano or 1 teaspoon dried oregano, crushed
- 1 tablespoon cold water
- 1½ teaspoons cornstarch
- ½ teaspoon finely shredded lemon peel
- 4 teaspoons lemon juice

Seared Vegetable Medley

Popular at roadside vegetable stands, Romano beans have pods that are wider and flatter than green beans. Don't pass them up if you spot them. They're a wonderful addition to this casserole or terrific solo. Cook them as you would any fresh green bean.

1 Preheat broiler. In the bottom of a broiler pan combine cauliflower, sweet peppers, beans, and onions. In a small bowl combine oil, salt, black pepper, and garlic; drizzle over vegetables, tossing to coat.

2 Broil 5 to 6 inches from heat for 20 to 25 minutes or just until vegetables are tender and browned, stirring every 5 minutes. Watch carefully the last 5 to 10 minutes of broiling and stir more frequently, if needed, to prevent burning. Remove pan from oven. Sprinkle vegetables with lemon peel and juice; toss gently to coat.

Nutrition Facts per serving: 121 cal., 7 g total fat (1 g sat. fat), 0 mg chol., 215 mg sodium, 14 g carbo., 4 g fiber, 3 g pro.

Prep: 25 minutes
Broil: 20 minutes
Makes: 6 to 8 servings

- 3 cups cauliflower florets
- 2 medium yellow and/or red sweet peppers, cut into strips
- 12 ounces Romano or green beans, trimmed and cut into 2-inch pieces
- 2 medium onions, cut into wedges or chunks
- 3 tablespoons olive oil or cooking oil
- ½ teaspoon salt
- ¼ teaspoon black pepper
- 4 cloves garlic, minced
- 2 teaspoons finely shredded lemon peel
- 2 teaspoons lemon juice

Vegetables Primavera

Squash, carrots, sweet pepper, and broccoli combine to create a festival of colors. Just four ingredients make up the sauce.

1 In a small bowl combine 1 tablespoon of the chicken broth, the mustard, olive oil, and vinegar. Set aside.

2 Coat a large nonstick skillet with cooking spray. Heat the skillet over medium heat. Add squash, carrots, and sweet pepper to hot skillet. Cook and stir about 5 minutes or until nearly tender. Add broccoli and the remaining 2 tablespoons chicken broth to squash mixture. Cook, covered, about 3 minutes or until broccoli is crisp-tender.

3 Stir in mustard mixture; heat through. To serve, transfer vegetable mixture to serving bowl; sprinkle with parsley.

Nutrition Facts per serving: 56 cal., 3 g total fat (0 g sat. fat), 0 mg chol., 114 mg sodium, 7 g carbo., 3 g fiber, 2 g pro.

Start to Finish: 20 minutes
Makes: 6 servings

- 3 tablespoons reduced-sodium chicken broth
- 1 tablespoon Dijon-style mustard
- 1 tablespoon olive oil
- 2 teaspoons white wine vinegar
   Nonstick cooking spray
- 1½ cups sliced yellow summer squash
- 1 cup packaged peeled baby carrots
- 1 cup chopped red sweet pepper
- 3 cups broccoli florets
- 2 tablespoons snipped fresh parsley

9 g
carb

Braised Fall Vegetables

A touch of cardamom adds a spicy-sweet taste to this flavorful autumn side dish that's cooked in a skillet.

1 In a large skillet melt butter. Add the cabbage wedges and carrots. Cook, covered, over medium heat for 3 minutes, stirring once or twice with a wooden spoon.

2 Gently stir in the cauliflower, onion, ¼ cup water, vinegar, salt, pepper, and cardamom. Bring to boiling; reduce heat. Simmer, covered, for 7 to 10 minutes or just until vegetables are crisp-tender.

Nutrition Facts per serving: 74 cal., 4 g total fat (2 g sat. fat), 5 mg chol., 168 mg sodium, 9 g carbo., 4 g fiber, 2 g pro.

Start to Finish: 30 minutes
Makes: 6 to 8 servings

- 1 tablespoons butter or margarine
- ½ of a medium head red or green cabbage, cut into 6 wedges (about 1 pound)
- 12 small whole carrots (about 8 ounces with tops) or 3 medium carrots, quartered lengthwise and halved crosswise
- 2 cups white and/or green cauliflower florets
- 1 medium red onion, cut in wedges
- 2 tablespoons vinegar
- ¼ teaspoon salt
- ¼ teaspoon black pepper
- ¼ teaspoon ground cardamom

Orzo-Broccoli Pilaf

Orzo is a tiny, rice-shape pasta, larger than a grain of rice and slightly smaller than a pine nut. It is a great substitute for rice in this vegetable-filled pilaf.

1 In a large saucepan heat olive oil over medium-high heat. Cook and stir the mushrooms and onion in hot oil until onion is tender. Stir in the orzo. Cook and stir about 2 minutes more or until orzo is lightly browned. Remove from heat.

2 Carefully stir in the chicken broth, carrot, marjoram, and pepper. Bring to boiling; reduce heat. Simmer, covered, about 15 minutes or until orzo is tender but still firm. Remove saucepan from heat; stir in broccoli. Let stand, covered, for 5 minutes.

Nutrition Facts per serving: 113 cal., 2 g total fat (0 g sat. fat), 0 mg chol., 209 mg sodium, 19 g carbo., 2 g fiber, 4 g pro.

Prep: 20 minutes
Cook: 15 minutes
Stand: 5 minutes
Makes: 6 servings

- 2 teaspoons olive oil
- 1 cup sliced fresh mushrooms
- ½ cup chopped onion
- ⅔ cup dried orzo pasta (rosamarina)
- 1 14-ounce can reduced-sodium chicken broth
- ½ cup shredded carrot
- 1 teaspoon dried marjoram, crushed
- ⅛ teaspoon black pepper
- 2 cups small broccoli florets

Brown Rice Pilaf

Instant brown rice takes a lot less time to cook than regular brown rice. The nutty flavor of the rice makes this pilaf a tasty side dish for grilled or broiled meats, fish, or poultry.

1 In a medium saucepan stir together water and bouillon granules. Bring to boiling. Stir in mushrooms, uncooked rice, carrot, marjoram, and black pepper. Return to boiling; reduce heat. Simmer, covered, for 12 minutes.

2 Remove from heat. Let stand, covered, for 5 minutes. Add the green onions and parsley; toss gently with a fork.

Nutrition Facts per serving: 60 cal., 1 g total fat (0 g sat. fat), 0 mg chol., 230 mg sodium, 13 g carbo., 2 g fiber, 2 g pro.

Prep: 10 minutes
Cook: 12 minutes
Stand: 5 minutes
Makes: 4 servings

1   cup water
1   teaspoon instant chicken bouillon
      granules
1   cup sliced fresh mushrooms
¾   cup instant brown rice
½   cup shredded carrot
¾   teaspoon snipped fresh marjoram or
      ¼ teaspoon dried marjoram,
      crushed
      Dash black pepper
¼   cup thinly sliced green onions
1   tablespoon snipped fresh parsley

Desserts & Sweets

Almond Cake with Fresh Fruit	**227**
Baked Coffee Custards	**239**
Baked Rice Pudding	**241**
Berry Cheesecake Dessert	**229**
Berry Clafouti	**242**
Chocolate Shortbread	**237**
Country Apricot Tart	**231**
Deep-Dish Apple Pie	**230**
Easy Ice Cream Sandwiches	**247**
Lemon-Pistachio Biscotti	**236**
Mango and Raspberry Tart	**232**
Mango Mousse	**245**
Marinated Strawberries with Frozen Yogurt	**243**
Mocha Cream Puffs	**240**
Mocha Soufflés	**238**
Peach-Filled Phyllo Bundles	**234**
Spring Berry Tarts	**233**
Strawberry Gelato	**246**
Strawberry-Topped Cheesecake	**228**
Summer Fruits with Ricotta Dip	**244**
Top Banana Bars	**235**
Walnut Cream Roll	**226**

Walnut Cream Roll

This jelly roll has a delicious nutty layer of cake spiraling around lots of light and airy whipped cream.

1 Grease and flour a 15×10×1-inch baking pan; set aside. In a medium mixing bowl beat egg yolks with an electric mixer on high speed about 4 minutes or until thick and lemon-colored. Wash beaters thoroughly. In a large mixing bowl combine egg whites, vanilla, and salt. Beat on high speed until soft peaks form (tips curl); gradually add the ½ cup granulated sugar, beating until stiff peaks form (tips stand straight). Fold egg yolks into egg whites; carefully fold in flour and nuts. Spread in prepared baking pan.

2 Bake in a 375° oven about 12 minutes or until the top springs back when lightly touched.

3 Immediately loosen edges of cake from pan and turn out onto towel sprinkled with powdered sugar. Starting at short side, roll up cake and towel together. Cool completely on a wire rack.

4 Meanwhile, beat whipping cream and the 2 tablespoons granulated sugar with an electric mixer on medium speed until soft peaks form. Unroll cake; remove towel. Spread whipped cream over cake to within 1 inch of edges. Roll up. Cover and chill for 1 to 2 hours. To serve, cut into ¾-inch slices.

Prep: 25 minutes
Bake: 12 minutes
Oven: 375°F
Cool: 1 hour
Chill: 1 to 2 hours
Makes: 10 servings

- 4 egg yolks
- 4 egg whites
- 1 teaspoon vanilla
- ½ teaspoon salt
- ½ cup granulated sugar
- ¼ cup all-purpose flour
- ½ cup finely chopped walnuts
  Powdered sugar
- 1 cup whipping cream
- 2 tablespoons granulated sugar

Nutrition Facts per serving: 214 cal., 15 g total fat (6 g sat. fat), 118 mg chol., 141 mg sodium, 17 g carbo., 0 g fiber, 4 g pro.

Almond Cake with Fresh Fruit

Simple cake wedges make a delicious foundation for dessert. Mate them with any pear you please: fresh, dried, or both.

1 Grease and lightly flour an 8×1½-inch round baking pan; set aside. In a large bowl stir together flour, baking powder, and orange peel; set aside.

2 In a blender container or food processor bowl combine eggs and sugar. Cover and blend or process until smooth. Add nuts. Cover and blend or process about 1 minute or until nearly smooth. Stir into flour mixture. Spread batter evenly in prepared pan.

3 Bake in a 350° oven about 20 minutes or until lightly browned. Cool cake in pan on a wire rack for 10 minutes. Remove cake from pan. Cool thoroughly on wire rack.

4 To serve, cut cake into wedges. Arrange fruit and cake in dessert bowls.

Prep: 10 minutes
Bake: 20 minutes
Oven: 350°F
Makes: 6 servings

1 tablespoon all-purpose flour
½ teaspoon baking powder
½ teaspoon finely shredded orange peel
2 eggs
⅓ cup sugar
6 ounces whole unblanched almonds
3 pears, peeled, cored, and halved, plus
   ½ cup chopped dried pears; or
   2 cups fresh and/or dried fruit

Nutrition Facts per serving: 272 cal., 17 g total fat (2 g sat. fat), 71 mg chol., 65 mg sodium, 26 g carbo., 4 g fiber, 8 g pro.

Strawberry-Topped Cheesecake

To test for a perfectly baked cheesecake, gently shake the pan after the minimum baking time. The center should appear nearly set. If it still jiggles, bake it 5 minutes longer and test again.

1 In a small bowl stir together graham cracker crumbs and melted butter. Press into the bottom of an 8-inch springform pan. Set aside.

2 In a large food processor bowl combine undrained cottage cheese and the ¼ cup milk. Cover and process until smooth. Add cream cheese, the ¾ cup sugar, flour, 1 teaspoon of the vanilla, and lemon peel. Cover and process until smooth. Add eggs; cover and process just until combined. Do not overprocess. Pour mixture into prepared pan. Place pan on a baking sheet.

3 Bake in a 375° oven for 35 to 40 minutes or until set. Cool for 15 minutes. Using a narrow metal spatula, loosen the side of the cheesecake from pan. Cool 30 minutes more; remove the side of pan. Cool completely. Cover and chill for 4 to 24 hours.

4 In a small bowl combine sour cream, the 2 teaspoons milk, the 1 teaspoon sugar, and remaining ¼ teaspoon vanilla. To serve, arrange berries on top of cheesecake; drizzle with sour cream mixture.

Prep: 20 minutes
Bake: 35 minutes
Oven: 375°F
Cool: 2 hours
Chill: 4 to 24 hours
Makes: 12 servings

½ cup graham cracker crumbs
4 teaspoons butter or margarine, melted
1 cup fat-free cottage cheese
¼ cup milk
2 8-ounce packages fat-free cream cheese, cut up
¾ cup sugar
2 tablespoons all-purpose flour
1¼ teaspoons vanilla
½ teaspoon shredded lemon peel
3 eggs or ¾ cup refrigerated or frozen egg product, thawed
¼ cup fat-free or light dairy sour cream
2 teaspoons milk
1 teaspoon sugar
1 cup sliced strawberries

Nutrition Facts per serving: 163 cal., 3 g total fat (1 g sat. fat), 62 mg chol., 92 mg sodium, 22 g carbo., 0 g fiber, 11 g pro.

Berry Cheesecake Dessert

Cream cheese and ricotta cheese give rich taste to this creamy topping. Serve it when fresh berries are in season as a tempting finale to a festive dinner.

1 In a blender container or food processor bowl combine cream cheese, ricotta cheese, powdered sweetener, orange peel, and orange juice. Cover and blend or process until smooth. Cover and chill for 4 to 24 hours.

2 To serve, divide fruit among dessert dishes. Top with cream cheese mixture and sprinkle with broken cookies.

Nutrition Facts per serving: 115 cal., 2 g total fat (1 g sat. fat), 9 mg chol., 61 mg sodium, 17 g carbo., 2 g fiber, 8 g pro.

Nutrition Facts per serving using sugar option: 152 cal. and 26 g carbo.

Prep: 20 minutes
Chill: 4 to 24 hours
Makes: 4 servings

½ of an 8-ounce tub (about ½ cup) fat-free cream cheese
½ cup low-fat ricotta cheese
  Low-calorie powdered sweetener equal to 3 tablespoons sugar, or 3 tablespoons sugar
½ teaspoon finely shredded orange peel or lemon peel
1 tablespoon orange juice
3 cups sliced strawberries, raspberries, and/or blueberries
4 gingersnaps or chocolate wafers, broken

Deep-Dish Apple Pie

Bite into this all-American dessert and you'll experience one of the finest traditional treats. Each forkful boasts a luscious cinnamon-apple filling and flaky pastry.

1 Place apples in a 2-quart square baking dish. In a small bowl combine sugar and cinnamon; set aside 1 teaspoon of the mixture. Stir cornstarch and salt into remaining sugar mixture; sprinkle evenly over apples in baking dish.

2 In a medium bowl stir together flours and nutmeg. Using a pastry blender, cut in butter until mixture resembles coarse crumbs. Sprinkle 1 tablespoon of the water over part of mixture; gently toss with a fork. Push moistened dough to side of bowl. Repeat, using 1 tablespoon water at a time, until all dough is moistened. Form into a ball.

3 On a lightly floured surface, flatten dough. Roll dough from center to edges into a 10-inch square. Cut decorative vents in pastry. Carefully place pastry over apples. Using the tines of a fork, press edges to sides of dish. Brush pastry with milk and sprinkle with reserved sugar mixture.

4 Bake in a 375° oven about 40 minutes or until apples are tender and crust is golden brown. Serve warm.

Prep: 30 minutes
Bake: 40 minutes
Oven: 375°F
Makes: 8 servings

6   cups thinly sliced, peeled cooking apples (about 2 pounds)
¼   cup sugar
1   teaspoon ground cinnamon
1   tablespoon cornstarch
⅛   teaspoon salt
½   cup all-purpose flour
¼   cup whole wheat flour
    Dash ground nutmeg
3   tablespoons butter or margarine
2   to 3 tablespoons cold water
    Milk

Nutrition Facts per serving: 171 cal., 5 g total fat (1 g sat. fat), 0 mg chol., 85 mg sodium, 33 g carbo., 2 g fiber, 1 g pro.

Country Apricot Tart

The flavor of this cornmeal crust is outstanding. It's great for those who haven't mastered the art of making beautifully crimped pie edges; you simply fold the crust over the filling.

1 Grease and lightly flour a large baking sheet. Prepare Cornmeal Crust. On the baking sheet, flatten dough. Roll from center to edges into a 12-inch circle. Set aside.

2 For filling, in a bowl stir together sugar, flour, and nutmeg. Stir in apricots and lemon juice. Mound filling in center of crust, leaving a 2-inch border. Fold border up over filling. Brush top and sides of crust with milk.

3 Bake in a 375° oven about 40 minutes or until crust is golden and filling is bubbly. To prevent overbrowning, cover the edge of crust with foil the last 10 to 15 minutes of baking. Cool tart on the baking sheet on a wire rack for 30 minutes.

Cornmeal Crust: In a bowl stir together ¾ cup flour, ⅓ cup cornmeal, 2 tablespoons sugar, 1 teaspoon baking powder, and ⅛ teaspoon salt. Using a pastry blender, cut in 3 tablespoons butter until the size of small peas. Sprinkle 1 tablespoon of cold milk over part of mixture; gently toss with a fork. Push moistened dough to side of bowl. Repeat with 3 to 4 tablespoons additional fat-free milk, adding 1 tablespoon at a time, until all dough is moistened (dough will be crumbly). Turn out onto a lightly floured surface and knead 7 to 8 times or just until dough clings together. Form into a ball.

Prep: 30 minutes
Bake: 40 minutes
Oven: 375°F
Cool: 30 minutes
Makes: 8 servings

- 1 recipe Cornmeal Crust
- ⅓ cup sugar
- 3 tablespoons all-purpose flour
- ¼ teaspoon ground nutmeg or ground cinnamon
- 3 cups sliced, pitted apricots or 3 cups frozen, unsweetened peach slices, thawed (do not drain)
- 1 tablespoon lemon juice
- 2 teaspoons milk

Nutrition Facts per serving: 190 cal., 5 g total fat (3 g sat. fat), 12 mg chol., 128 mg sodium, 35 g carbo., 2 g fiber, 3 g pro.

Mango and Raspberry Tart

Impressive and easy to make, this fruit-filled tart is a superb ending for any meal.

1 In a medium bowl stir together flour, the 1 tablespoon sugar, and salt. Using a pastry blender, cut in butter until pieces are pea-size. Sprinkle 1 tablespoon of the water over part of the mixture; gently toss with a fork. Push moistened dough to side of bowl. Repeat, using 1 tablespoon water at a time, until all dough is moistened. Form into a ball.

2 On a lightly floured surface, flatten dough. Roll dough from center to edges into a 12-inch circle. Ease into a 10-inch tart pan with a removable bottom, being careful not to stretch pastry. Press pastry up the side of pan. Trim pastry even with rim of pan. Prick the bottom well with a fork. Bake in a 450° oven for 12 to 15 minutes or until golden brown. Cool on a wire rack.

3 Meanwhile, in a medium mixing bowl combine cream cheese, the ¼ cup sugar, and vanilla. Beat with an electric mixer on medium speed until smooth. Spread over cooled pastry. Arrange mangoes in a 3-inch ring around the edge of the tart. Fill the center with fresh raspberries.

4 In a small saucepan heat apricot spread until melted; cut up any large pieces. Spoon melted spread over fruit. Chill for 2 to 3 hours. Before serving, remove sides of pan.

Prep: 40 minutes
Bake: 12 minutes
Oven: 450°F
Chill: 2 to 3 hours
Makes: 12 servings

- 1 cup all-purpose flour
- 1 tablespoon sugar
- ¼ teaspoon salt
- ¼ cup butter
- 3 to 4 tablespoons cold water
- 1 8-ounce package fat-free cream cheese, softened
- ¼ cup sugar
- 1 teaspoon vanilla
- 1 26-ounce jar refrigerated mango slices, drained and chopped, or 2 cups chopped, peeled mangoes (2 medium)
- 1 cup fresh raspberries
- ½ cup low-calorie apricot spread

Nutrition Facts per serving: 152 cal., 4 g total fat (3 g sat. fat), 14 mg chol., 90 mg sodium, 25 g carbo., 2 g fiber, 4 g pro.

Spring Berry Tarts

Crisp crust, satiny filling, and a selection of juicy berries—there's no more divine dessert than these tarts.

1 Lightly coat six 4-inch fluted individual tart pans with cooking spray; set aside.

2 In a medium bowl stir together all-purpose flour, whole wheat pastry flour, and salt. Using a pastry blender, cut in shortening until mixture resembles fine crumbs. Sprinkle 1 tablespoon of the water over part of the mixture; gently toss with a fork. Push moistened dough to the side of the bowl. Repeat, using 1 tablespoon water at a time, until all dough is moistened. Form dough into a ball.

3 Divide dough into six equal portions. On a lightly floured surface, roll each portion into a 5-inch circle; fit circles into tart pans, pressing firmly against sides. Trim excess crust even with rims of pans. Prick bottom and sides with a fork. Place tart pans on a baking sheet. Line tart shells with a double thickness of foil. Bake in a 450° oven for 8 minutes. Remove foil and bake 5 to 6 minutes more or until golden. Transfer to wire racks and let cool.

4 For filling, in a blender container or food processor bowl combine cream cheese, ricotta cheese, sugar, vanilla, and lemon peel. Cover and blend or process until smooth. Divide mixture among cooled tart shells. Top with berries.

Prep: 25 minutes
Bake: 13 minutes
Oven: 450°F
Makes: 6 servings

Nonstick cooking spray
⅔ cup all-purpose flour
⅓ cup whole wheat pastry flour
¼ teaspoon salt
3 tablespoons shortening
3 to 4 tablespoons cold water
1 8-ounce package reduced-fat cream cheese (Neufchâtel), softened
⅓ cup light ricotta cheese
⅓ cup sugar
1 teaspoon vanilla
½ teaspoon finely shredded lemon peel
1 cup raspberries, blueberries, blackberries, and/or quartered strawberries

Nutrition Facts per serving: 284 cal., 16 g total fat (7 g sat. fat), 32 mg chol., 259 mg sodium, 28 g carbo., 2 g fiber, 7 g pro.

Peach-Filled Phyllo Bundles

Phyllo dough creates a delicate shell for a fresh or frozen peach and chocolate filling.

1 For filling, in a medium bowl combine peaches, granulated sugar, chocolate pieces, flour, and lemon juice. Toss to combine; set aside.

2 Lightly coat four 6-ounce custard cups with cooking spray; set aside. Lightly coat 1 phyllo sheet with cooking spray. (Keep remaining phyllo sheets covered with a damp cloth to keep them from drying out.) Place another sheet of phyllo on top of the first sheet; lightly coat with cooking spray. Repeat with remaining phyllo. Cut stack in half lengthwise and in half crosswise, forming 4 rectangles.

3 Gently ease one stack of phyllo into bottom and up the sides of one custard cup (phyllo will hang over edge). Spoon about ½ cup of the filling into center. Bring phyllo up over filling, pinching together to form a ruffled edge. Lightly coat again with cooking spray. Repeat with remaining cups, phyllo, and filling. Place custard cups in a 15×10×1-inch baking pan.

4 Bake in a 375° oven for 20 minutes. Cool 5 minutes in custard cups; remove from cups. Serve warm or cool.

Prep: 20 minutes
Bake: 20 minutes
Oven: 375°F
Makes: 4 servings

3 medium peaches, peeled, pitted, and coarsely chopped, or 2¼ cups frozen unsweetened peach slices, thawed and coarsely chopped
2 tablespoons granulated sugar
4 teaspoons miniature semisweet chocolate pieces
1 tablespoon all-purpose flour
1 teaspoon lemon juice
   Nonstick cooking spray
4 sheets frozen phyllo dough (17×12-inch rectangles), thawed

Nutrition Facts per serving: 137 cal., 2 g total fat (0 g sat. fat), 0 mg chol., 92 mg sodium, 28 g carbo., 1 g fiber, 2 g pro.

Tip: If using frozen peaches, blot well with paper towels after thawing to remove excess moisture.

Top Banana Bars

Everyone in the family will find something to love about these scrumptious bar cookies packed with ripe banana, mixed dried fruit, and a touch of nutty wheat germ.

1 Grease an 11×7×1½-inch baking pan; set aside. In a bowl combine all-purpose flour, whole wheat flour, wheat germ, baking powder, cinnamon, and salt; set aside.

2 In another bowl stir together egg, sugar, milk, oil, and vanilla. Stir in banana and fruit bits. Add banana mixture to flour mixture, stirring to combine. Spread batter evenly in prepared pan.

3 Bake in a 350° oven for 20 to 25 minutes or until a wooden toothpick inserted near center comes out clean. Cool in pan on a wire rack. Cut into bars.

Nutrition Facts per bar: 91 cal., 3 g total fat (1 g sat. fat), 11 mg chol., 27 mg sodium, 15 g carbo., 1 g fiber, 1 g pro.

Prep: 15 minutes
Bake: 20 minutes
Oven: 350°F
Makes: 20 bars

½ cup all-purpose flour
½ cup whole wheat flour
 1 tablespoon toasted wheat germ
 1 teaspoon baking powder
½ teaspoon ground cinnamon
⅛ teaspoon salt
 1 beaten egg
½ cup packed brown sugar
⅓ cup milk
¼ cup cooking oil
½ teaspoon vanilla
 1 ripe medium banana, mashed
⅓ cup mixed dried fruit bits

Lemon-Pistachio Biscotti

If you are passionate about pistachios—and it's hard not to be—this pretty cookie is the perfect vehicle for that sublime nut.

1 Lightly grease 2 cookie sheets; set aside. In a large mixing bowl beat butter with an electric mixer on medium to high speed for 30 seconds. Add sugar, baking powder, and salt. Beat until combined, scraping sides of bowl occasionally. Beat in eggs and vanilla until combined. Beat in as much of the flour as you can with the mixer. Stir in any remaining flour and lemon peel. Stir in pistachio nuts.

2 Divide dough into 3 equal portions. Shape each portion into an 8-inch roll. Place rolls at least 3 inches apart on prepared cookie sheets; flatten slightly until about 2½ inches wide.

3 Bake in a 375° oven for 20 to 25 minutes or until golden brown and tops are cracked (loaves will spread slightly). Cool on cookie sheet for 30 minutes.

4 Use a serrated knife to cut each roll diagonally into ½-inch slices. Place slices, cut sides down, on ungreased cookie sheets. Bake in a 325° oven for 8 minutes. Turn slices over and bake for 8 to 10 minutes more or until dry and crisp (do not overbake). Transfer to a wire rack and let cool.

Prep: 35 minutes
Bake: 36 minutes
Oven: 375°F; 325°F
Cool: 30 minutes
Makes: about 36 cookies

- ⅓ cup butter, softened
- ⅔ cup sugar
- 2 teaspoons baking powder
- ½ teaspoon salt
- 2 eggs
- 1 teaspoon vanilla
- 2 cups all-purpose flour
- 4 teaspoons finely shredded lemon peel
- 1¼ cups pistachio nuts

Nutrition Facts per cookie: 84 cal., 4 g total fat (1 g sat. fat), 17 mg chol., 76 mg sodium, 10 g carbo., 1 g fiber, 2 g pro.

Chocolate Shortbread

In the minds of true chocolate-lovers, there's only one way to improve upon classic, pure butter shortbread. This one's for them.

1 Lightly grease a 9-inch fluted tart pan with removable bottom or a cookie sheet; set aside.

2 In a medium bowl stir together flour and cocoa powder; set aside. In a large mixing bowl beat butter with an electric mixer on medium to high speed for 30 seconds. Add powdered sugar, vanilla, almond extract, and salt. Beat until combined, scraping sides of bowl occasionally. Add flour mixture and beat until mixture resembles fine crumbs and starts to cling. Form mixture into a ball and knead until smooth.

3 Pat dough evenly into prepared pan or pat into a 9-inch circle on the prepared cookie sheet. If desired, use your fingers to scallop the edge. Score into 12 wedges and prick each wedge 3 times with fork tines, making sure to go all the way through the dough. Press an almond slice into each wedge about ½ inch from the edge.

4 Bake in a 325° oven about 30 minutes or until top looks dry. Cool in pan on a wire rack for 5 minutes. If using, remove sides of tart pan. Cool completely on wire rack. Cut into wedges.

Prep: 15 minutes
Bake: 30 minutes
Oven: 325°F
Makes: 12 wedges

1½ **cups all-purpose flour**
⅓ **cup unsweetened cocoa powder**
¾ **cup butter, softened**
¾ **cup sifted powdered sugar**
½ **teaspoon vanilla**
½ **teaspoon almond extract**
⅛ **teaspoon salt**
12 **almond slices**

Nutrition Facts per wedge: 196 cal., 13 g total fat (7 g sat. fat), 31 mg chol., 24 mg sodium, 19 g carbo., 1 g fiber, 2 g pro.

Mocha Soufflés

A classic combination—cocoa powder and coffee crystals—flavors these light-as-air soufflés.

1 Allow egg whites to stand at room temperature for 30 minutes.

2 Meanwhile, in a small saucepan combine sugar, cocoa powder, cornstarch, and coffee crystals. Stir in milk all at once. Cook and stir over medium heat until bubbly. Remove from heat. Stir in vanilla. Pour into a medium bowl. Cover surface of mixture with plastic wrap. Set aside.

3 In a medium mixing bowl beat egg whites and cream of tartar with an electric mixer on medium speed until stiff peaks form (tips stand straight). Fold about one-fourth of the beaten egg whites into chocolate mixture to lighten. Fold in remaining beaten egg whites. Gently pour into 4 ungreased 1-cup soufflé dishes. Place soufflé dishes in a shallow baking pan.

4 Bake in a 375° oven for 15 to 20 minutes or until a knife inserted near the centers comes out clean. Serve immediately.

Prep: 45 minutes
Bake: 15 minutes
Oven: 375°F
Makes: 4 servings

- 4 egg whites
- 3 tablespoons sugar
- 2 tablespoons unsweetened cocoa powder
- 4 teaspoons cornstarch
- 1 teaspoon instant coffee crystals
- ⅔ cup canned evaporated milk
- 2 teaspoons vanilla
- ¼ teaspoon cream of tartar

Nutrition Facts per serving: 136 cal., 4 g total fat (2 g sat. fat), 12 mg chol., 100 mg sodium, 18 g carbo., 0 g fiber, 7 g pro.

Baked Coffee Custards

Silky custards with a mild coffee flavor offer just the right finish to a special meal. The best part is that you can cover and chill these up to 4 hours before serving.

1 In a medium bowl combine eggs, milk, sugar, and vanilla. Dissolve coffee crystals in hot water. Add coffee mixture to egg mixture. Beat until combined but not foamy.

2 Place four 6-ounce custard cups in a 2-quart square baking dish. Divide egg mixture evenly among custard cups. Place baking dish on an oven rack. Pour boiling water into the baking dish around custard cups to a depth of 1 inch. Bake in a 325° oven for 25 to 35 minutes or until a knife inserted near the centers comes out clean.

3 Remove custard cups from water. To serve warm, cool slightly on a wire rack. To serve chilled, cool completely in custard cups; cover and chill until ready to serve. To unmold custards, loosen edges with a knife, slipping its point between the custard and cup to let in air. Invert a dessert plate over each custard; turn custard cup and plate over together. Remove custard cup.

Prep: 15 minutes
Bake: 25 minutes
Oven: 325°F
Makes: 4 servings

  4 beaten eggs
1½ cups milk
  ¼ cup sugar
  1 teaspoon vanilla
  2 teaspoons instant coffee crystals
  1 tablespoon hot water

Nutrition Facts per serving: 172 cal., 7 g total fat (3 g sat. fat), 219 mg chol., 109 mg sodium, 17 g carbo., 0 g fiber, 9 g pro.

14 g
carb

Mocha Cream Puffs

This dazzling dessert blends the airy lightness of cream puffs with coffee-spiked pudding and fresh berries.

1 Grease a baking sheet; set aside. In a small saucepan combine water and butter. Bring to boiling. Add flour all at once, stirring vigorously. Cook and stir until mixture forms a ball that doesn't separate. Remove from heat. Cool for 5 minutes. Add eggs, one at a time, beating after each addition until mixture is shiny and smooth. Drop mixture in 8 mounds, 3 inches apart, on the prepared baking sheet.

2 Bake in a 400° oven for 25 to 30 minutes or until golden brown. Remove from oven. Split puffs and remove any soft dough from inside. Cool completely on wire rack.

3 Meanwhile, for filling, prepare pudding mix according to package directions, using the 2 cups milk and adding espresso powder. Cover surface with plastic wrap. Chill thoroughly.

4 To serve, spoon about ⅓ cup of the filling into the bottom half of each cream puff. Top with strawberries. Replace cream puff tops.

Prep: 20 minutes
Bake: 25 minutes
Oven: 400°F
Chill: 5 hours
Makes: 8 servings

- ½ cup water
- 2 tablespoons butter or margarine
- ½ cup all-purpose flour
- 2 eggs
- 1 4-serving-size package fat-free instant chocolate pudding mix or reduced-calorie regular chocolate pudding mix
- 2 cups milk
- 2 teaspoons espresso powder or 1 tablespoon instant coffee crystals
- 1 cup sliced fresh strawberries

Nutrition Facts per serving: 116 cal., 4 g total fat (1 g sat. fat), 54 mg chol., 246 mg sodium, 14 g carbo., 1 g fiber, 5 g pro.

Baked Rice Pudding

This pleasantly sweet, Indian-style rice pudding is smooth and custardy with a hint of cardamom.

1 In a medium bowl combine egg whites, egg, milk, sugar, and vanilla. Beat until combined but not foamy. Stir in rice, apricots, cardamom, and orange peel.

2 Place five 6-ounce custard cups or soufflé dishes in a 3-quart rectangular baking dish. Divide rice mixture among cups. Place baking dish on an oven rack. Pour boiling water into baking dish around custard cups to a depth of 1 inch.

3 Bake in a 325° oven about 40 minutes or just until set, stirring after 20 minutes. Serve warm or chilled.

Nutrition Facts per serving: 126 cal., 1 g total fat (0 g sat. fat), 44 mg chol., 84 mg sodium, 22 g carbo., 0 g fiber, 7 g pro.

Prep: 15 minutes
Bake: 40 minutes
Oven: 325°F
Makes: 5 servings

3	egg whites
1	egg
1½	cups milk
¼	cup sugar
1	teaspoon vanilla
⅔	cup cooked rice
2	tablespoons snipped dried apricots and/or golden raisins
¼	teaspoon ground cardamom
¼	teaspoon finely shredded orange peel

Berry Clafouti

A French dessert, clafouti (kla-foo-TEE) is simply fruit that is topped with a batter and baked. Cherries are the classic fruit choice but are by no means the only option. Use berries, as we did, or chopped peaches, plums, or pears.

1 In a large mixing bowl combine egg whites, whole egg, granulated sugar, honey, liqueur, vanilla, and salt. Beat with a wire whisk or an electric mixer on low speed until light and frothy. Stir in yogurt until mixture is smooth. Add flour; beat until mixture is smooth.

2 Grease six 6-ounce individual quiche dishes. Arrange berries in the bottoms of dishes. Spoon batter over berries. (Batter will not cover berries completely.) Bake in a 375° oven for 20 to 25 minutes or until centers appear set when shaken. Cool on a wire rack for 30 minutes.

3 Just before serving, if desired, sprinkle desserts with powdered sugar.

Nutrition Facts per serving: 141 cal., 1 g total fat (0 g sat. fat), 36 mg chol., 76 mg sodium, 27 g carbo., 3 g fiber, 6 g pro.

Prep: 15 minutes
Bake: 20 minutes
Oven: 375°F
Cool: 30 minutes
Makes: 6 servings

2 slightly beaten egg whites
1 slightly beaten egg
3 tablespoons granulated sugar
1 tablespoon honey
1 tablespoon fruit-flavored liqueur (such as orange or raspberry liqueur), or ½ teaspoon rum extract plus 2 tablespoons orange juice
½ teaspoon vanilla
  Dash salt
¾ cup plain fat-free yogurt
½ cup all-purpose flour
3 cups raspberries, blueberries, and/or sliced strawberries
2 teaspoons sifted powdered sugar (optional)

Marinated Strawberries with Frozen Yogurt

You'll be delightfully surprised by the hint of balsamic vinegar that enhances the flavor of the ripe, red strawberries.

1 Remove stems from strawberries; halve or quarter berries lengthwise. In a medium bowl combine strawberries, sugar, balsamic vinegar, mint, and lemon juice. Cover and chill for 20 minutes to 4 hours.

2 To serve, spoon strawberry mixture over scoops of frozen yogurt.

Nutrition Facts per serving: 157 cal., 3 g total fat (2 g sat. fat), 15 mg chol., 86 mg sodium, 30 g carbo., 2 g fiber, 5 g pro.

Prep: 15 minutes
Chill: 20 minutes to 4 hours
Makes: 6 servings

- 4 cups (2 pints) strawberries
- 2 tablespoons sugar
- 2 tablespoons balsamic vinegar
- 2 tablespoons finely shredded fresh mint
- 1 tablespoon lemon juice
- 3 cups low-fat or fat-free vanilla frozen yogurt

Summer Fruits with Ricotta Dip

Be creative and substitute different flavored yogurts, such as strawberry or peach, for the vanilla yogurt.

1 For dip, in a blender container or food processor bowl combine ricotta cheese, sugar, orange peel, and orange juice. Cover and blend or process until smooth. Stir cheese mixture into yogurt.

2 If desired, cover and chill up to 24 hours. Serve with assorted fresh fruit.

Nutrition Facts per serving: 88 cal., 2 g total fat (1 g sat. fat), 6 mg chol., 34 mg sodium, 16 g carbo., 1 g fiber, 3 g pro.

Start to Finish: 10 minutes
Makes: 4 servings

- ⅓ cup low-fat ricotta cheese
- 1 tablespoon sugar
- 1 teaspoon finely shredded orange peel
- 1 tablespoon orange juice
- ⅓ cup low-fat vanilla yogurt
- 2 cups sliced nectarines, cubed cantaloupe, cubed honeydew melon, cut-up kiwifruit, and/or fresh pineapple chunks

Mango Mousse

How do you tell if a mango is ripe? Look for fruit that has a colorful green or gold skin with a blush of red or purple. Mangoes are ready to eat when they are soft enough to yield to gentle pressure.

1 Place mangoes in a food processor bowl or blender container. Cover and process or blend until smooth. Add enough water to make 2 cups total. Transfer mango mixture to a medium saucepan. Bring to boiling.

Prep: 20 minutes
Freeze: 45 minutes
Chill: 2 hours
Makes: 6 servings

2 ripe mangoes, peeled, seeded, and chopped
2 tablespoons sugar
1 envelope unflavored gelatin
2 teaspoons lemon juice
1 8-ounce container frozen light whipped dessert topping, thawed

2 Meanwhile, in a large bowl stir together sugar and gelatin. Pour mango mixture over gelatin mixture; stir until gelatin dissolves. Stir in lemon juice. Cover and freeze for 45 to 60 minutes or until mixture mounds, stirring occasionally. Beat mango mixture with an electric mixer for 2 to 3 minutes or until thick and light. Fold in whipped topping.

3 Spoon or pipe mango mixture into dessert dishes or parfait glasses. Cover and chill about 2 hours or until set.

Nutrition Facts per serving: 149 cal., 5 g total fat (0 g sat. fat), 1 mg chol., 31 mg sodium, 25 g carbo., 2 g fiber, 1 g pro.

Tip: Removing the large seed of a mango takes a little cutting know-how. Place the fruit on its blossom end and align a sharp knife slightly off-center of the stemmed end of the fruit. Slice down through the peel and flesh, next to the pit. Repeat on other side. Cut off the remaining flesh around the seed. Cut off the peel; cut the mango into pieces as directed.

Strawberry Gelato

Who can resist this creamy, sweet Italian ice cream-like dessert? It's especially good when made with fresh summer strawberries.

1 In a medium saucepan combine milk, egg product, and sugar. Cook and stir over medium heat about 10 minutes or until mixture is thickened. Do not boil. Remove saucepan from heat.

2 Place saucepan in a sink or bowl of ice water for 1 to 2 minutes, stirring constantly. Pour custard mixture into a bowl; set aside.

3 Place strawberries in a blender container or food processor bowl. Cover and blend or process until nearly smooth. Stir strawberries and lemon juice into custard mixture. Cover the surface of custard with plastic wrap. Chill for several hours or overnight until thoroughly chilled. (Or to chill quickly, place bowl in a sink of ice water.)

4 Freeze the mixture in a 2- or 3-quart ice cream freezer according to the manufacturer's directions.

Prep: 25 minutes
Chill: several hours or overnight
Freeze: per manufacturer's directions
Makes: 14 servings

- 2 cups milk
- 1 cup refrigerated or frozen egg product, thawed
- ½ cup sugar
- 4 cups strawberries
- 1 teaspoon lemon juice

Nutrition Facts per serving: 65 cal., 1 g total fat (0 g sat. fat), 3 mg chol., 41 mg sodium, 12 g carbo., 1 g fiber, 3 g pro.

Easy Ice Cream Sandwiches

Cookies and ice cream rank highly as kids' favorite snacks. Both favorites together in this frosty treat get high marks from youngsters—and from those grown-ups lucky enough to get a taste.

1 In a large mixing bowl beat butter with an electric mixer on medium to high speed for 30 seconds. Add granulated sugar, brown sugar, unsweetened cocoa powder, and baking powder. Beat until combined, scraping sides of bowl occasionally. Beat in egg and vanilla until combined. Stir in melted chocolate. Beat in as much of the flour as you can with the mixer. Stir in any remaining flour.

2 Drop dough by slightly rounded teaspoons 2 inches apart onto an ungreased cookie sheet. Spread each dough portion to about 2 inches in diameter.

3 Bake in a 350° oven for 7 to 8 minutes or until edges are firm. Immediately (while still warm) top half of the cookies with the candies. Transfer cookies to a wire rack and cool thoroughly.

4 To assemble, let ice cream stand at room temperature for 10 minutes to soften slightly. Place about 2 tablespoons ice cream on the flat side of each cookie without the candy topping. Carefully place the candy-topped cookies on top of the ice cream, candy sides up. Press each cookie gently in the center to slightly flatten sandwich.

5 Wrap each sandwich in plastic wrap; freeze at least 2 hours. To serve, let stand at room temperature for 5 minutes. Store in the freezer up to 1 month.

Prep: 30 minutes
Bake: 7 minutes per batch
Oven: 350°F
Freeze: 2 hours to 1 month
Stand: 5 minutes
Makes: 18 sandwiches

- ½   cup butter, softened
- ⅓   cup granulated sugar
- ¼   cup packed dark brown sugar
- 1½ teaspoons unsweetened cocoa powder
- ¼   teaspoon baking powder
- 1   egg
- ½   teaspoon vanilla
- 1½ ounces unsweetened chocolate, melted and slightly cooled
- 1   cup plus 2 tablespoons all-purpose flour
      Assorted miniature candies
- 1   pint vanilla or other flavor ice cream

Nutrition Facts per sandwich: 149 cal., 8 g total fat (5 g sat. fat), 32 mg chol., 74 mg sodium, 18 g carbo., 0 g fiber, 2 g pro.

Index

A - B

Almond Cake with Fresh Fruit, 227
Appetizers. *See also* Snacks
Artichoke-Feta Tortilla Wraps, 46
Chile Chicken Appeteasers, 47
Deviled Eggs with Spicy Crab, 48
Greek Salad Bites, 49
Prosciutto-Arugula Roll-Ups, 50
Soy-Glazed Squash, 53
Tortellini, Olive, and Cheese
Kabobs, 51
Apples
Apple-Glazed Chicken with
Spinach, 153
Deep-Dish Apple Pie, 230
Sage Pork Roast with Apple, 141
Sweet and Spicy Turkey
Skillet, 172
Apricots, Country Apricot Tart, 231
Artichokes
Artichoke and Orange Salad, 70
Artichoke-Feta Tortilla Wraps, 46
Hot Artichoke Dip, 57
Italian Bean and Artichoke
Salad, 86
Mediterranean Chicken and
Pasta, 161
Arugula
Arugula and Pea Salad, 73
Pasta with Arugula and
Sausage, 178
Prosciutto-Arugula Roll-Ups, 50
Asian Beef and Noodle Bowl, 128
Asian Glazed Salmon, 186
Asian Pea Pod Salad, 81
Asian Vinaigrette, 74

Asparagus
Asparagus and Carrots with Asian
Vinaigrette, 74
Asparagus Finger Salad, 77
Asparagus with Warm
Vinaigrette, 208
Spring Asparagus Slaw, 79
Turkey and Asparagus
Stir-Fry, 175
Turkey Breast with Roasted
Asparagus, 167
Autumn Frittata, 100
Bacon, Weekend Scramble, 94
Baked Brie Strata, 108
Baked Coffee Custards, 239
Baked Rice Pudding, 241
Banana, Top Banana Bars, 235
Basil Halibut Steaks, 184
Beans
Black Bean Salad, 87
Braised Chicken with Beans and
Squash, 156
cooking dried beans, 87
Southwestern Breakfast
Bake, 102
Beans, green
Beans and Hot Ham
Dressing, 209
French Beef Stew, 126
Great Greek Green Beans, 210
Italian Bean and Artichoke
Salad, 86
Seared Vegetable Medley, 220
Beef. *See also* Veal
Asian Beef and Noodle
Bowl, 128
Beef Roast with Vegetables, 123

Beef Tenderloin Fillets with
Horseradish Chili, 115
Beef-Vegetable Ragout, 127
Braised Short Ribs with
Beets, 125
Filet Mignon with Portobello
Sauce, 114
French Beef Stew, 126
Grilled Vegetables and Beef
Kabobs, 120
Herbed Beef Tenderloin, 124
Italian Steak Sandwiches, 122
Italian Wedding Soup, 129
Lemony Flank Steak, 119
Pizza-Topped Meat Loaf, 130
Spicy Steak Tortillas, 121
Spinach-Stuffed Flank Steak, 118
Steak with Roasted Garlic and
Herbs, 117
Top Sirloin with Smoky Pepper
Sauce, 116
Beer-Brined Turkey, 166
Beets
Braised Short Ribs with
Beets, 125
Orange-Beet Salad, 89
Berries. *See also* specific berries
Berry Cheesecake Dessert, 229
Berry Clafouti, 242
Spring Berry Tarts, 233
Beverages
Fruit Juice Cooler, 64
Hit-the-Spot Lemon Water, 68
Make-Believe Champagne, 67
Peppy Tomato Sipper, 66
Really Hot Iced Coffee, 65
Summertime Quencher, 63

Big Green Salad with Two-Pepper
  Dressing, 83
Biscuits, 162
Black Bean Salad, 87
Bok choy
  Pan-Fried Baby Bok Choy, 211
  Spinach-Mushroom Sauté, 216
Braised Chicken with Beans and
  Squash, 156
Braised Fall Vegetables, 222
Braised Short Ribs with Beets, 125
Bread, drying bread cubes, 107
Breakfast and Brunch
  Autumn Frittata, 100
  Baked Brie Strata, 108
  Breakfast Casserole, 106
  Farmer's Breakfast, 95
  Grecian Quiche, 109
  Salmon and Eggs Benedict, 103
  Southwestern Breakfast
    Bake, 102
  Spinach and Cheese Omelet, 98
  Weekend Scramble, 94
Broccoli
  Broccoli Omelet Provençale, 99
  Chicken and Broccoli
    Stir-Fry, 159
  Lemon-Braised Baby
    Broccoli, 212
  Orzo-Broccoli Pilaf, 223
  Summer Rice Salad, 91
Broiled Fish Steaks with Tarragon
  Cheese Sauce, 190
Brown Rice Pilaf, 224
Butternut Squash Salad, 80

C - D

Cabbage
  Cranberry-Walnut Cabbage
    Slaw, 78
  Spring Asparagus Slaw, 79

Cabbage, Chinese
  Gingered Pork and Cabbage
    Soup, 142
Cakes
  Almond Cake with Fresh
    Fruit, 227
  Walnut Cream Roll, 226
Cantaloupe and Tomato Salad, 84
Carrots
  Asparagus and Carrots with Asian
    Vinaigrette, 74
  Asparagus Finger Salad, 77
  Braised Fall Vegetables, 222
  Roasted Carrot Stick Snack, 54
  Vegetables Primavera, 221
Cauliflower
  Braised Fall Vegetables, 222
  Seared Vegetable Medley, 220
Celery, Stuffed Celery Bites, 52
Cheese, cheddar/Monterey Jack
  Corn and Tomato Bread
    Pudding, 107
  Roasted Cheddar Potatoes, 214
  Scrambled Egg Fajitas, 96
  Southwestern Breakfast
    Bake, 102
  Spinach and Cheese Omelet, 98
  Tortellini, Olive, and Cheese
    Kabobs, 51
Cheese, Brie
  Baked Brie Strata, 108
  Weekend Scramble, 94
Cheese, cottage
  Spinach and Ham Lasagna, 144
  Yogurt-Herb Dip, 55
Cheese, feta
  Artichoke-Feta Tortilla Wraps, 46
  Grecian Quiche, 109
  Greek Salad Bites, 49
  Sole with Feta and Tomatoes, 200
Cheese, goat (chèvre)
  Cantaloupe and Tomato Salad, 84
  Prosciutto-Arugula Roll-Ups, 50

Cheese, Gorgonzola/blue
  Tomato and Sweet Pepper
    Salad, 71
Cheese, Gouda
  Cheese-Stuffed Pecans, 61
Cheese, Italian blend
  Stuffed Celery Bites, 52
  Pizza-Topped Meat Loaf, 130
Cheese, mozzarella
  Broiled Fish Steaks with Tarragon
    Cheese Sauce, 190
  Popover Pizza Casserole, 177
Cheese, Parmesan
  Hot Artichoke Dip, 57
  Italian Wedding Soup, 129
  Lemon and Parmesan Fish, 195
  Lemony Caesar Salad, 88
  Poached Eggs on Polenta, 111
  Spinach Cheese Puff, 101
  Zucchini and Swiss Pie, 110
Cheese, provolone
  Vegetable Pasta Salad, 92
Cheese, Swiss
  Breakfast Casserole, 106
  Spinach Cheese Puff, 101
  Zucchini and Swiss Pie, 110
Cheesecakes
  Berry Cheesecake Dessert, 229
  Strawberry-Topped
    Cheesecake, 228
Cheese-Stuffed Pecans, 61
Cherries
  Cherry Sauce, 138
Chicken
  Apple-Glazed Chicken with
    Spinach, 153
  Braised Chicken with Beans and
    Squash, 156
  Chicken and Broccoli
    Stir-Fry, 159
  Chicken and Dumplings, 162
  Chicken with Chipotle Barbecue
    Sauce, 154
  Chile Chicken Appeteasers, 47

Grilled Citrus Chicken, 155
Grilled Curried Lime Chicken
  Kabobs, 157
Grilled Fiery Chicken and Potato
  Fingers, 160
Kale, Lentil, and Chicken
  Soup, 165
Maple-Mustard-Glazed Chicken
  and Winter Squash, 149
Mediterranean Chicken and
  Pasta, 161
Roasted Italian Chicken, 148
Roasted Tarragon Chicken, 150
Smoked Chicken-Egg Bake, 104
Spanish-Style Chicken, 151
Summer Chicken and Mushroom
  Pasta, 158
Tandoori Chicken Burgers, 163
Vegetable-Stuffed Chicken, 152
Wild Rice Chicken Soup, 164
Chile Chicken Appeteasers, 47
Chipotle Barbecue Sauce, 154
Chocolate Shortbread, 237
Citrus-Spice Marinade, 155
Coffee
  Baked Coffee Custards, 239
  Really Hot Iced Coffee, 65
Confetti Summer Salad, 85
Cookies and bars
  Lemon-Pistachio Biscotti, 236
  Top Banana Bars, 235
Corn and Tomato Bread
  Pudding, 107
Cornmeal Crust, 231
Country Apricot Tart, 231
Couscous, Curried Turkey and
  Couscous Pie, 174
Crabmeat
  Deviled Eggs with Spicy Crab, 48
  Zucchini Crab Cakes, 206
Cranberries
  Cranberry Sauce, 168
    Cranberry-Walnut Cabbage
    Slaw, 78

Crepes
  Moo Shu Vegetable and Egg
    Crepes, 97
Cucumbers
  Cucumber Raita, 218
  Greek Salad Bites, 49
  Minty Cucumbers, 163
Curry
  Curried Turkey and Couscous
    Pie, 174
  Grilled Curried Lime Chicken
    Kabobs, 157
Custards, Baked Coffee
  Custards, 239
Deep-Dish Apple Pie, 230
Desserts. *See also* Cakes; Cookies;
  Ice cream; Pies and Tarts
  Berry Clafouti, 242
  Mango Mousse, 245
  Mocha Cream Puffs, 240
  Mocha Soufflés, 238
  Peach-Filled Phyllo Bundles, 234
Deviled Eggs with Spicy Crab, 48
Dips
  Fennel and Onion Dip, 58
  Fresh Fruit Dip, 59
  Hot Artichoke Dip, 57
  Summer Fruits with Ricotta
    Dip, 244
  Thai Spinach Dip, 56
  Yogurt-Herb Dip, 55
Dough, tip for rolling dough, 109

E - G

Easy Citrus Salmon Steaks, 188
Easy Ice Cream Sandwiches, 247
Egg and Vegetable Salad Wraps, 112
Egg Cakes with Sweet-and-Sour
  Plum Sauce, 105
Eggs
  Autumn Frittata, 100
  Baked Brie Strata, 108
  Breakfast Casserole, 106

  Broccoli Omelet Provençale, 99
  Corn and Tomato Bread
    Pudding, 107
  Deviled Eggs with Spicy Crab, 48
  Egg and Vegetable Salad
    Wraps, 112
  Egg Cakes with Sweet-and-Sour
    Plum Sauce, 105
  Farmer's Breakfast, 95
  Grecian Quiche, 109
  Lemony Caesar Salad, 88
  Moo Shu Vegetable and Egg
    Crepes, 97
  Poached Eggs on Polenta, 111
  Salmon and Eggs Benedict, 103
  Scrambled Egg Fajitas, 96
  Smoked Chicken-Egg Bake, 104
  Southwestern Breakfast
    Bake, 102
  Spinach and Cheese Omelet, 98
  Spinach Cheese Puff, 101
  Weekend Scramble, 94
  Zucchini and Swiss Pie, 110
Enchiladas, Turkey, 179
Farmer's Breakfast, 95
Fennel and Onion Dip, 58
Fiery Southwestern Seafood
  Skewers, 205
Filet Mignon with Portobello
  Sauce, 114
Fish. *See also* Crabmeat; Salmon;
  Scallops; Shrimp; Tuna
  Basil Halibut Steaks, 184
  Broiled Fish Steaks with Tarragon
    Cheese Sauce, 190
  Fish Fillets with Roasted Red
    Pepper Sauce, 183
  Fish Fillets with Spinach, Red
    Pepper, and Onion, 191
  Ginger Scallion Fish, 187
  Lemon and Parmesan Fish, 195
  Lemon-Herb Swordfish
    Steaks, 189

Lime-Marinated Swordfish with Southwestern Pesto, 199
Mahi Mahi with Vegetable Slaw, 194
Mustard-Glazed Halibut Steaks, 192
Pecan-Crusted Fish with Vegetables, 182
Smoked Pepper Halibut, 196
Snapper Veracruz, 185
Sole with Feta and Tomatoes, 200
Spicy Seafood Stew, 203
Tangy Thyme Fish, 197
French Beef Stew, 126
Fruit
Almond Cake with Fresh Fruit, 227
Fresh Fruit Dip, 59
Fruit Juice Cooler, 64
Summer Fruits with Ricotta Dip, 244
Summertime Quencher, 63
Garlic
Roasted Garlic Mashed Potatoes, 215
roasting, 215
Steak with Roasted Garlic and Herbs, 117
Gingered Pork and Cabbage Soup, 142
Ginger Scallion Fish, 187
Great Greek Green Beans, 210
Grecian Quiche, 108
Greek Salad Bites, 49
Grilled Citrus Chicken, 155
Grilled Curried Lime Chicken Kabobs, 157
Grilled Fiery Chicken and Potato Fingers, 160
Grilled Mango-Berry "Chalsa" with Pork, 140
Grilled Mustard-Glazed Pork Tenderloin, 139

Grilled Pork Chops with Mushroom Stuffing, 133
Grilled Tuna with Peanut Sauce, 193
Grilled Turkey Steaks with Sweet Pepper-Citrus Salsa, 170
Grilled Turkey with Pepper Sauce, 169
Grilled Veal Chops with Pesto Mushrooms, 131
Grilled Vegetables and Beef Kabobs, 120

H - J
Ham
Beans and Hot Ham Dressing, 208
Breakfast Casserole, 106
Egg Cakes with Sweet-and-Sour Plum Sauce, 105
Farmer's Breakfast, 95
Spinach and Ham Lasagna, 144
Herbs
Herb Crust, 109
Herbed Beef Tenderloin, 124
Herbed Soy Nuts and Seeds, 60
Lemon-Herb Swordfish Steaks, 189
Roasted Italian Chicken, 148
Steak with Roasted Garlic and Herbs, 117
Yogurt-Herb Dip, 55
Hit-the-Spot Lemon Water, 68
Hot Artichoke Dip, 57
Ice cream
Easy Ice Cream Sandwiches, 247
Strawberry Gelato, 246
Indian Spiced Popcorn, 62
Italian Bean and Artichoke Salad, 86
Italian Steak Sandwiches, 122
Italian Wedding Soup, 129
Jicama-Berry Salad, 75

Juice
Fruit Juice Cooler, 64
Peppy Tomato Sipper, 66

K - M
Kale, Lentil, and Chicken Soup, 165
Lamb
Lamb Chops and Peppers, 145
Moroccan Lamb Roast, 146
Lasagna, Spinach and Ham Lasagna, 144
Leek, Hot Artichoke Dip, 57
Lemons and lemon juice
Hit-the-Spot Lemon Water, 68
Lemon and Parmesan Fish, 195
Lemon-Braised Baby Broccoli, 212
Lemon-Herb Swordfish Steaks, 189
Lemon-Pistachio Biscotti, 236
Lemony Caesar Salad, 88
Lemony Flank Steak, 119
Lemony Mixed Vegetables, 219
Lentil, Kale, and Chicken Soup, 165
Lettuce
Asian Pea Pod Salad, 81
Big Green Salad with Two-Pepper Dressing, 83
Italian Bean and Artichoke Salad, 86
Lemony Caesar Salad, 88
Lime-Marinated Swordfish with Southwestern Pesto, 199
Mahi Mahi with Vegetable Slaw, 194
Make-Believe Champagne, 67
Mangoes
Grilled Mango-Berry "Chalsa" with Pork, 140
Mango and Raspberry Tart, 232
Mango Mousse, 245
Pork and Mango Picadillo, 143
Seeding, 245

Maple-Mustard-Glazed Chicken and
  Winter Squash, 149
Marinades
  Citrus-Spice Marinade, 155
  Marinated Strawberries with
    Frozen Yogurt, 243
  Pineapple-Rum Turkey
    Kabobs, 173
Mediterranean Chicken and
  Pasta, 161
Mesclun with Oranges and
  Olives, 76
Mexicali Stuffed Zucchini, 218
Mexican-Style Turkey Soup, 180
Mocha
  Mocha Cream Puffs, 240
  Mocha Soufflés, 238
Moo Shu Vegetable and Egg
  Crepes, 97
Moroccan Lamb Roast, 146
Mushrooms
  Filet Mignon with Portobello
    Sauce, 114
  Grecian Quiche, 109
  Grilled Pork Chops with
    Mushroom Stuffing, 133
  Grilled Veal Chops with Pesto
    Mushrooms, 131
  Pork Chops in Creamy Vegetable
    Sauce, 136
  Savory Turkey-Mushroom
    Burgers, 176
  Skillet Veal Scalloppine with
    Marsala, 132
  Smoked Chicken-Egg Bake, 104
  Spinach-Mushroom Sauté, 216
  Summer Chicken and Mushroom
    Pasta, 158
  Turkey Mushrooms Marsala, 171
  Vegetable-Stuffed Chicken, 152
  Weekend Scramble, 94
Mustard-Glazed Halibut Steaks, 192

N - P

Nectarines, Chile Chicken
  Appeteasers, 47
Noodles, Asian Beef and Noodle
  Bowl, 128
Nuts. *See also* Almonds; Pecans
  toasting, 86
Nuts, Soy
  Herbed Soy Nuts and Seeds, 60
Olives
  Mesclun with Oranges and
    Olives, 76
  Sweet Pepper and Olive
    Pork, 137
  Tortellini, Olive, and Cheese
    Kabobs, 51
Onions
  Fennel and Onion Dip, 58
  Fish Fillets with Spinach, Red
    Pepper, and Onion, 191
Oranges
  Artichoke and Orange Salad, 70
  Mesclun with Oranges and
    Olives, 76
  Orange-Beet Salad, 89
Orzo-Broccoli Pilaf, 213
Pan-Fried Baby Bok-Choy, 211
Pasta. *See also* Couscous; Noodles;
  Tortellini
  Mediterranean Chicken and
    Pasta, 161
  Orzo-Broccoli Pilaf, 223
Pasta with Arugula and
    Sausage, 178
  Summer Chicken and Mushroom
    Pasta, 158
  Vegetable Pasta Salad, 92
Peaches
  Chile Chicken Appeteasers, 47
  Peach-Filled Phyllo Bundles, 234
  tip for using frozen peaches, 234
Peanut Sauce, 193
Pears, Pork and Pear au Jus, 134

Peas
  Arugula and Pea Salad, 73
  Asian Pea Pod Salad, 81
  Prosciutto and Peas, 213
  snow, 127
  sugar snap, 127
Pecans
  Cheese-Stuffed Pecans, 61
  Pecan-Crusted Fish with
    Vegetables, 182
Peppers, chile
  Black Bean Salad, 87
  Chicken with Chipotle Barbecue
    Sauce, 154
  Grilled Mango Berry "Chalsa" with
    Pork, 140
  handling, 96
  Scrambled Egg Fajitas, 96
  Smoked Pepper Halibut, 196
  Southwestern Breakfast Bake, 102
  Spicy Steak Tortillas, 121
  Top Sirloin with Smoky Pepper
    Sauce, 116
  Two-Pepper Dressing, 83
Peppers, sweet
  Black Bean Salad, 87
  Confetti Summer Salad, 84
  Fish Fillets with Roasted Red
    Pepper Sauce,e 183
  Fish Fillets with Spinach, Red
    Pepper, and Onion, 191
  Grilled Citrus Steaks with Sweet
    Pepper Citrus Salsa, 170
  Grilled Turkey with Pepper
    Sauce, 169
  Lamb Chops and Peppers, 145
  Red Pepper Relish, 98
  Seared Vegetable Medley, 221
  Southwestern Breakfast
    Bake, 102
  Sweet and Spicy Turkey
    Skillet, 172
  Sweet Pepper and Olive
    Pork, 137

Tomato and Sweet Pepper
Salad, 71
Two-Pepper Dressing, 83
Peppy Tomato Sipper, 66
Pesto
Grilled Veal Chops with Pesto
Mushrooms, 131
Lime-Marinated Swordfish with
Southwestern Pesto, 199
Southwestern Pesto, 199
Tortellini, Olive, and Cheese
Kabobs, 51
Phyllo dough
Curried Turkey and Couscous
Pie, 174
Peach-Filled Phyllo Bundles, 234
Pies and Tarts
Country Apricot Tart, 231
Deep-Dish Apple Pie, 230
Mango and Raspberry Tart, 232
Spring Berry Tarts, 233
Pineapple-Rum Turkey Kabobs, 173
Pizza-Topped Meat Loaf, 130
Plums
Egg Cakes with Sweet-and-Sour
Plum Sauce, 105
Sweet-and-Sour Plum Sauce, 105
Poached Eggs on Polenta, 111
Polenta, Poached Eggs on
Polenta, 111
Popcorn
Indian Spiced Popcorn, 62
Spiced Popcorn, 62
Popover Pizza Casserole, 177
Pork. *See also* Ham
Gingered Pork and Cabbage
Soup, 142
Grilled Mango-Berry "Chalsa"
with Pork, 140
Grilled Mustard-Glazed Pork
Tenderloin, 139
Grilled Pork Chops with
Mushroom Stuffing, 133
Pork and Mango Picadillo, 143

Pork and Pear au Jus, 134
Pork Chops in Creamy Vegetable
Sauce, 136
Pork Medallions with Cherry
Sauce, 138
Sage Pork Roast with Apple, 141
Spice-Rubbed Pork Chops, 135
Sweet Pepper and Olive
Pork, 137
Potatoes
Breakfast Casserole, 106
Farmer's Breakfast, 95
Grilled Fiery Chicken and Potato
Fingers, 160
Roasted Cheddar Potatoes, 214
Roasted Garlic Mashed
Potatoes, 215
Skillet-Roasted Potato Salad, 90
Spanish-Style Chicken, 151
Zucchini and Swiss Pie, 110
Prosciutto
Prosciutto and Peas, 213
Prosciutto Arugula Roll-Ups, 50
Puddings
Baked Rice Pudding, 241
Corn and Tomato Bread
Pudding, 107

R - T

Raspberries
Grilled Mango-Berry "Chalsa"
with Pork, 140
Mango and Raspberry Tart, 232
Really Hot Iced Coffee, 65
Relishes, Red Pepper Relish, 98
Rice
Baked Rice Pudding, 241
Brown Rice Pilaf, 224
Summer Rice Salad, 91
Wild Rice Chicken Soup, 164
Roasted Carrot Stick Snack, 54
Roasted Cheddar Potatoes, 214

Roasted Garlic Mashed
Potatoes, 215
Roasted Italian Chicken, 148
Roasted Summer Cherry
Tomatoes, 217
Roasted Tarragon Chicken, 150
Sage Pork Roast with Apple, 141
Salad Dressings, 87
Asian Vinaigrette, 74
Beans and Hot Ham
Dressing, 209
Sage Vinaigrette, 80
Sparkling Vinaigrette, 82
Strawberry Vinegar, 73
Two-Pepper Dressing, 83
Warm Vinaigrette, 208
Salads
Artichoke and Orange Salad, 70
Arugula and Pea Salad, 73
Asian Pea Pod Salad, 81
Asparagus and Carrots with Asian
Vinaigrette, 74
Asparagus Finger Salad, 77
Big Green Salad with Two-
Pepper Dressing, 83
Black Bean Salad, 87
Butternut Squash Salad, 80
Cantaloupe and Tomato Salad, 84
Confetti Summer Salad, 85
Cranberry-Walnut Cabbage
Slaw, 78
Italian Bean and Artichoke
Salad, 86
Jicama-Berry Salad, 75
Lemony Caesar Salad, 88
Mesclun with Oranges and
Olives, 76
Orange-Beet Salad, 89
Skillet-Roasted Potato Salad, 90
Sparkling Kumquat Salad, 82
Spring Asparagus Slaw, 79
Stacked Tomato Salad, 72
Summer Rice Salad, 91

Tomato and Sweet Pepper
  Salad, 71
Tuna-Vegetable Salad, 201
Vegetable Pasta Salad, 92
Salmon
  Asian Glazed Salmon, 186
  Easy Citrus Salmon Steaks, 188
  Salmon and Eggs Benedict, 103
  Salmon Chowder, 202
  Salmon-Vegetable Packets, 198
Salsa, Sweet Pepper-Citrus
  Salsa, 170
Sandwiches
  Egg and Vegetable Salad
    Wraps, 112
  Italian Steak Sandwiches, 122
Sauces. *See also* Salsa
  Cranberry Sauce, 168
  Peanut Sauce, 193
  Portobello Sauce, 114
  Roasted Red Pepper Sauce, 183
  Spicy Apple and Sweet Pepper
    Sauce, 172
  Sweet-and-Sour Plum Sauce, 105
  Tarragon Cheese Sauce, 190
  Thai-Spiced Scallops, 204
  Tomato-Sour Cream Dipping
    Sauce, 206
  Turkey Enchiladas, 179
  Vegetable Sauce, 136
  Yogurt-Chive Sauce, 46
Sausage, Pasta with Arugula and
  Sausage, 178
Savory Turkey-Mushroom
  Burgers, 176
Scallops
  Fiery Southwestern Seafood
    Skewers, 205
  Thai-Spiced Scallops, 204
Scrambled Eggs Fajitas, 96
Seared Vegetable Medley, 220
Seeds, pumpkin
  Herbed Soy Nuts and Seeds, 60

Seeds, sesame
  toasting, 81
Shortbread, Chocolate Shortbread,
  237
Shrimp
  Fiery Southwestern Seafood
    Skewers, 205
  Spicy Seafood Stew, 203
  Stacked Tomato Salad, 72
Skillet-Roasted Potato Salad, 90
Skillet Veal Scaloppine with
  Marsala, 132
Smoked Chicken-Egg Bake, 104
Smoked Pepper Halibut, 196
Snacks. *See also* Appetizers
  Cheese-Stuffed Pecans, 61
  Herbed Soy Nuts and Seeds, 60
  Roasted Carrot Stick Snack, 54
  Spiced Popcorn, 62
  Stuffed Celery Bites, 52
Snapper Veracruz, 185
Sole with Feta and Tomatoes, 200
Soups and Stews
  French Beef Stew, 126
  Gingered Pork and Cabbage
    Soup, 142
  Italian Wedding Soup, 129
  Kale, Lentil, and Chicken
    Soup, 165
  Mexican-Style Turkey Soup, 180
  Spicy Seafood Stew, 203
  Wild Rice Chicken Soup, 164
Southwestern Breakfast Bake, 102
Southwestern Pesto, 199
Soy-Glazed Squash, 53
Spanish-Style Chicken, 151
Sparkling Kumquat Salad, 82
Sparkling Vinaigrette, 82
Spiced Popcorn, 62
Spice-Rubbed Pork Chops, 135
Spicy Seafood Stew, 203
Spicy Steak Tortillas, 121

Spinach
  Apple-Glazed Chicken with
    Spinach, 153
  Fish Fillets with Spinach, red
    Pepper, and Onion, 191
  Italian Wedding Soup, 128
  Spinach and Cheese Omelet, 98
  Spinach and Ham Lasagna, 144
  Spinach Cheese Puff, 101
  Spinach-Mushroom Sauté, 216
  Spinach-Stuffed Flank Steak, 118
  steaming, 94
  Thai Spinach Dip, 56
  Weekend Scramble, 94
Spring Asparagus Slaw, 79
Spring Berry Tarts, 233
Stacked Tomato Salad, 72
Steak with Roasted Garlic and
  Herbs, 117
Stews. See Soups and Stews
Strawberries
  Jicama-Berry Salad, 75
  Marinated Strawberries with
    Frozen Yogurt, 243
  Strawberry Gelato, 246
  Strawberry-Topped
    Cheesecake, 228
  Strawberry Vinegar, 73
Stuffed Celery Bites, 52
Summer Chicken and Mushroom
  Pasta, 158
Summer Fruits with Ricotta
  Dip, 244
Summer Rice Salad, 91
Summertime Quencher, 63
Sweet-and-Sour Plum Sauce, 105
Sweet and Spicy Turkey Skillet, 172
Sweet Pepper and Olive Pork, 137
Sweet potatoes
  Autumn Frittata, 100
  cooking, 100
Tandoori Chicken Burgers, 163
Tangy Thyme Fish, 197
Tarts. See Pies and Tarts

Thai-Spiced Scallops, 204
Thai Spinach Dip, 56
Tomatoes
  Baked Brie Strata, 108
  Cantaloupe and Tomato Salad, 84
  Corn and Tomato Bread
    Pudding, 107
  Great Greek Green Beans, 210
  Peppy Tomato Sipper, 66
  Roasted Summer Cherry
    Tomatoes, 217
  Sole with Feta and Tomatoes, 200
  Spanish-Style Chicken, 151
  Stacked Tomato Salad, 72
  Tomato and Sweet Pepper
    Salad, 71
  Tomato-Sour Cream Dipping
    Sauce, 206
Top Banana Bars, 235
Top Sirloin with Smoky Pepper
  Sauce, 116
Tortellini, Olive, and Cheese
  Kabobs, 51
Tortillas
  Artichoke-Feta Tortilla Wraps, 46
  Egg and Vegetable Salad
    Wraps, 112
  Scrambled Egg Fajitas, 96
  Spicy Steak Tortillas, 121
  Turkey Enchiladas, 179
Tuna
  Grilled Tuna with Peanut
    Sauce, 193
  Tuna-Vegetable Salad, 201
Turkey
  Beer-Brined Turkey, 166
  Curried Turkey and Couscous
    Pie, 174
  Grilled Turkey Steaks with Sweet
    Pepper-Citrus Salsa, 170
  Grilled Turkey with Pepper
    Sauce, 169
  Mexican-Style Turkey Soup, 180

Pasta with Arugula and
  Sausage, 178
Pineapple-Rum Turkey
  Kabobs, 173
Popover Pizza Casserole, 177
Savory Turkey-Mushroom
  Burgers, 176
Sweet and Spicy Turkey
  Skillet, 172
Turkey and Asparagus
  Stir-Fry, 175
Turkey Breast with Roasted
  Asparagus, 167
Turkey Enchiladas, 179
Turkey Mushroom Marsala, 171
Turkey with Cranberry
  Sauce, 168
Two-Pepper Dressing, 83

V - W

Veal
  Grilled Veal Chops with Pesto
    Mushrooms, 131
  Skillet Veal Scaloppine with
    Marsala, 132
Vegetables. *See also* Specific
  vegetables
  Beef Roast with Vegetables, 123
  Beef-Vegetable Ragout, 127
  Braised Fall Vegetables, 222
  Confetti Summer Salad, 85
  Egg and Vegetable Salad
    Wraps, 112
  Grilled Citrus Chicken, 155
  Grilled Vegetables and Beef
    Kabobs, 120
  Lemony Mixed Vegetables, 219
  Mahi Mahi with Vegetable
    Slaw, 194
  Mexican-Style Turkey Soup, 180
  Moo Shu Vegetable and Egg
    Crepes, 97

Pecan-Crusted Fish with
  Vegetables, 182
Salmon-Vegetable Packets, 198
Seared Vegetable Medley, 220
Spicy Seafood Stew, 203
  Tuna-Vegetable Salad, 201
  Vegetable Pasta Salad, 92
  Vegetable Sauce, 136
  Vegetables Primavera, 221
  Vegetable-Stuffed Chicken, 152
Vinegar, Strawberry, 73
Walnuts
  Cranberry-Walnut Cabbage
    Slaw, 78
  Walnut Cream Roll, 226
Watercress
  Cantaloupe and Tomato Salad, 84
Weekend Scramble, 94
Wild Rice Chicken Soup, 164
Wraps, Egg and Vegetable Salad
  Wraps, 112

Y - Z

Yogurt-Chive Sauce, 46
Yogurt-Herb Dip, 55
Zucchini
  Fiery Southwestern Seafood
    Skewers, 205
  Grilled Citrus Chicken, 155
  Mexicali Stuffed Zucchini, 217
  Zucchini and Swiss Pie, 110
  Zucchini Crab Cakes, 206

Metric Information

The charts on this page provide a guide for converting measurements from the U.S. customary system, which is used throughout this book, to the metric system.

Product Differences

Most of the ingredients called for in the recipes in this book are available in most countries. However, some are known by different names. Here are some common American ingredients and their possible counterparts:

- Sugar (white) is granulated, fine granulated, or castor sugar.
- Powdered sugar is icing sugar.
- All-purpose flour is enriched, bleached or unbleached white household flour. When self-rising flour is used in place of all-purpose flour in a recipe that calls for leavening, omit the leavening agent (baking soda or baking powder) and salt.
- Light-colored corn syrup is golden syrup.
- Cornstarch is cornflour.
- Baking soda is bicarbonate of soda.
- Vanilla or vanilla extract is vanilla essence.
- Green, red, or yellow sweet peppers are capsicums or bell peppers.
- Golden raisins are sultanas.

Volume and Weight

The United States traditionally uses cup measures for liquid and solid ingredients. The chart below shows the approximate imperial and metric equivalents. If you are accustomed to weighing solid ingredients, the following approximate equivalents will be helpful.

- 1 cup butter, castor sugar, or rice = 8 ounces = ½ pound = 250 grams
- 1 cup flour = 4 ounces = ¼ pound = 125 grams
- 1 cup icing sugar = 5 ounces = 150 grams

Canadian and U.S. volume for a cup measure is 8 fluid ounces (237 ml), but the standard metric equivalent is 250 ml.

1 British imperial cup is 10 fluid ounces.

In Australia, 1 tablespoon equals 20 ml, and there are 4 teaspoons in the Australian tablespoon.

Spoon measures are used for smaller amounts of ingredients. Although the size of the tablespoon varies slightly in different countries, for practical purposes and for recipes in this book, a straight substitution is all that's necessary. Measurements made using cups or spoons always should be level unless stated otherwise.

Common Weight Range Replacements

Imperial / U.S.	Metric
½ ounce	15 g
1 ounce	25 g or 30 g
4 ounces (¼ pound)	115 g or 125 g
8 ounces (½ pound)	225 g or 250 g
16 ounces (1 pound)	450 g or 500 g
1¼ pounds	625 g
1½ pounds	750 g
2 pounds or 2¼ pounds	1,000 g or 1 Kg

Oven Temperature Equivalents

Fahrenheit Setting	Celsius Setting*	Gas Setting
300°F	150°C	Gas Mark 2 (very low)
325°F	160°C	Gas Mark 3 (low)
350°F	180°C	Gas Mark 4 (moderate)
375°F	190°C	Gas Mark 5 (moderate)
400°F	200°C	Gas Mark 6 (hot)
425°F	220°C	Gas Mark 7 (hot)
450°F	230°C	Gas Mark 8 (very hot)
475°F	240°C	Gas Mark 9 (very hot)
500°F	260°C	Gas Mark 10 (extremely hot)
Broil	Broil	Grill

*Electric and gas ovens may be calibrated using celsius. However, for an electric oven, increase celsius setting 10 to 20 degrees when cooking above 160°C. For convection or forced air ovens (gas or electric) lower the temperature setting 25°F/10°C when cooking at all heat levels.

Baking Pan Sizes

Imperial / U.S.	Metric
9×1½-inch round cake pan	22- or 23×4-cm (1.5 L)
9×1½-inch pie plate	22- or 23×4-cm (1 L)
8×8×2-inch square cake pan	20×5-cm (2 L)
9×9×2-inch square cake pan	22- or 23×4.5-cm (2.5 L)
11×7×1½-inch baking pan	28×17×4-cm (2 L)
2-quart rectangular baking pan	30×19×4.5-cm (3 L)
13×9×2-inch baking pan	34×22×4.5-cm (3.5 L)
15×10×1-inch jelly roll pan	40×25×2-cm
9×5×3-inch loaf pan	23×13×8-cm (2 L)
2-quart casserole	2 L

U.S. / Standard Metric Equivalents

⅛ teaspoon	= 0.5 ml
¼ teaspoon	= 1 ml
½ teaspoon	= 2 ml
1 teaspoon	= 5 ml
1 tablespoon	= 15 ml
2 tablespoons	= 25 ml
¼ cup = 2 fluid ounces	= 50 ml
⅓ cup = 3 fluid ounces	= 75 ml
½ cup = 4 fluid ounces	= 125 ml
⅔ cup = 5 fluid ounces	= 150 ml
¾ cup = 6 fluid ounces	= 175 ml
1 cup = 8 fluid ounces	= 250 ml
2 cups = 1 pint	= 500 ml
1 quart	= 1 litre